HOW PRODUCTIVITY RAISES ECONOMIC GROWTH

JOHN LOK

Made with ♥ on the Notion Press Platform
www.notionpress.com

Contents

Foreword

As my view explores in my work, applying behavioral principles can lead to significant social and economic benefits by aligning individual incentives with broader productivity goals. Productivity, in an economic sense, is often measured as the ratio of output to input. Whether productivity of improvement can bring economic growth in possible?

Preface

I am an author with a background in behavioral economics, applies behavioral economic theory to explain how productivity influences economic growth, particularly in my book "HOW PRODUCTIVITY RAISES ECONOMIC GROWTH." His work integrates insights from psychology with traditional economic theories to offer a comprehensive understanding of human behavior in economic contexts].

My approach to explaining productivity and economic growth through behavioral economics can be broken down into several logical steps:

1. Identifying Key Drivers of Human Development

My book emphasizes that continued development and economic growth are not uniform across countries and require tailored approaches .My view identifies key areas of focus for human development, which directly impact productivity:

Training and Education: These are fundamental for enhancing human capital, leading to a more skilled and productive workforce . For instance, he suggests England needs to enhance its education system .

Economy: A robust economic framework supports innovation, investment, and efficient resource allocation, all of which are crucial for productivity .

Medical Capacity Development: Improved health outcomes lead to a healthier, more active, and productive population. Lok specifically points out India's need to advance its medical technology .

Technology Development: Advancements in technology can significantly boost productivity by automating tasks, improving efficiency, and creating new industries. Japan, for example, is highlighted as needing to improve technology development .

Culture: Societal culture can influence work ethic, innovation, and adaptability, all of which are critical for sustained economic growth. My view suggests America needs to improve its culture .

2. Applying the Human Brain Creative Ability Method

My view utilizes what he terms the "human brain creative ability method" to explain how these diverse factors influence global human development . This method likely draws from behavioral economics by acknowledging that human decision-making, often influenced by cognitive biases and emotional factors, plays a significant role in how these drivers are implemented and how effectively they contribute to productivity and growth]. For example, a country's cultural norms (a behavioral aspect) can either foster or hinder technological adoption and educational attainment, thereby impacting productivity .

3. Bridging Traditional and Behavioral Economic Theories

My work aims to bridge the gap between traditional economic theories, which often assume rational actors, and behavioral economic theory, which recognizes the influence of psychological factors on economic decision-making . My challenges the traditional assumption that individuals are always self-interested and make purely rational decisions . Instead, he suggests that human behavior often leads to economically irrational decisions, which can impact productivity at both individual and national levels . For instance, cognitive biases like overconfidence or loss aversion can affect investment decisions, labor market participation, and policy implementations, all of which have direct implications for productivity .

4. Analyzing the Impact of Technology and Societal Factors

My view investigates how technology, including AI and robotics, influences human talent, creativity, and organizational performance . While technology can improve economic development and reduce costs, he also addresses broader societal issues, such as the potential negative impacts of robots on future societies and the influence of environmental pollution on economic development . These considerations are crucial for a holistic understanding of productivity, as they highlight how external factors and human responses to them can either enhance or detract from overall economic output].

5. Informing Policy and Practice

By analyzing cognitive biases, market behavior, and the interplay of psychological factors with economic outcomes, My work contributes to policy recommendations. My view suggests ways policymakers can utilize behavioral insights to design more effective interventions aimed at improving economic outcomes For example, understanding how framing or heuristics influence public perception of education or healthcare initiatives can lead to more successful policy implementation, ultimately boosting productivity .

In essence, my view applies behavioral economic theory to explain productivity and economic growth by demonstrating that these are not merely outcomes of resource allocation or technological advancement, but are deeply intertwined with human behavior, decision-making processes, and societal factors. He argues that by understanding and addressing these behavioral elements, countries can more effectively foster the conditions necessary for sustained economic development .

Prologue

Table Of Contents

CHAPTER ONE

Economic growth relationship influences human development

I believe that economic growth must have relationship to influence human development. But it must not lead positive human development. Otherwise, when one country is experiencing stable economic growth in long term. It is possible to lead negative human development. I shall indicate as below:

To explain whether economy growth can influence human development. We need to research whether economy growth has relationship to influence human development. What is economic growth meaning? Economists explain it means an increase in gross national product (GNP) if all products and services that an economy produces during a specified time period. So, it brings one interesting question concerns economic growth: IS it a quantity based concept, not quality based concept? If economic growth is an only relationship to economic development Otherwise, if it also has quality based concepts, then it has relationship to influence or lead human development. When economy growth is a direct measure of changes in the size of the economy. Whether it is a measure of welfare to human development or sustainable development.

Why do we need to concern economic growth? Because political importance means domestic and international trading income and the country's people earning income measurement as well as humanitarian importance means an indicator of welfare, an indicator of human development and an indicator of sustainable development measurement. However, if seems GNP or GDP measures that value of products and services produces within an economy (economic income) in a given year, but it can also measure of welfare development, sustainable anything. Otherwise, human development includes welfare, which measures quality of life and human development, which means quality based concept as well as sustainable income, which means how much we can spend without running down capital stocks, we can maintain same level of spending in perpetuity. Hence, human development concerns our quality of life or standard of living. So, human welfare separation of means from a direct measure of well-being as well as economic welfare separation of means GNP or GDP corrected for expenditures on various necessities. So, it brings this question: Can GDP (economic growth measurement) be an indicator of human development or human welfare? I shall indicate cases to attempt to explain as below:

For GDP per capita and happiness case example, I assume that the country , US increases rapidly up to capita US $4,000 per capita in this year and small returns after that. What does this mean? What influences US people feel happy or happiness feeling causes? For another changing in GDP correlate to changes in environment quality case. Environmental KC (Kuznets Curve) showed the graphical representation of Kuznets theory from the 1940 year that economic inequality increases over time, then at a critical point begins to decrease. Environmental KC (EKC) shows a hypothesized relationship between various indicators of environmental degradation and income per capita.

The EKC (environment Kuznets Curve), shows that in the early stages of economic growth degradation and pollution increase, when beyond some level of income per capita , which varies for different indicators. The trend reverses , so that at high-income levels economic growth leads to environment improvement. This implies that the environment impact is an inverted u-sharped function of income per capita. Thus, EKC implies that economic growth has relationship to influence or lead environmental pollution causing, due to many factories are manufacturing any products during economic growth period. All air or water pollution will increase, due to factories manufacturers manufacture lot of products. The scale effort brings that economic growth increases environmental pollution if there is no change in other factors. The other factors include that change in output mix, change in input mix, state of technology, production efficiency and demand for " improved environment". Hence, when these factors have no change and factories need to use many resources to manufacture lot of products in the manufacturing process. It will bring serious pollution, due to these factories have not improved its technology, production efficiency to avoid to pollute environment to cause local pollutants, deforestation, biodiversity, river low quality, carbon and air low quality, waste increases with increased income. Hence, it is an evidence to explain economic growth will have possible to cause pollution indirectly as well as poor quality of life (standard of living) to influence our life. IT is a good evidence to explain how economic growth can lead human's quality of life (standard of living) to be poor. SO, it brings these questions as below:

Should we always aim to increase GDP? Should we choose to either gain ultimate happiness or either increasing GDP? Is it an indicator of wealth to depend on what GDP really measures? Should we need to concern environment degradation cost or our nervous stress from environmental pollution causing?

In conclusion, it implies that economic growth can lead positive human development , such as economic welfare influence, but it can also lead negative human welfare of long term air or water pollution influence and this challenge can not be solved to any countries in our life if any countries do not attempt to keep balance between achieving economic growth and clean environment in order to not influence our quality of life to be poor. The important evidence , it explain it has relationship between economic growth and human development and they have cause and effect relationship.

● Economic growth leads human employment growth

I believe that when one developed cuntry is experiencing stable economic growth, it can lead human employment growth in high technologic job market, but it can also bring unemployment to low knowledge or skill job, such as cleaning, laboring job market, due to artificial intelligence technology will replace many low skillful job in the future. I shall explain as below:

I assume that it has positive relationship between the accumulation of human capital relation to total employment and GDP growth. It means that a positive relationship between economic growth and the demand for qualified labor are consistent with the hypotheses of the form in the industrial export sector positively influenced by the accumulation of human capital. I shall explain the reason why economic growth can lead positive human employment growth as below:

Namik, (1965) explained that economic growth theories reflect on the continuous increases in the gross national product, because of interaction that occurs in a given environment; in a certain time period, including various changes in the presentation of productive factors in society labor, capital and nature resources to lead these radical changes to increase successive demand on commodities and hence an increase in national income.

Hence, society labor knowledge or skillful development will be one important factor to influence any country's economic growth. If the country has many good educational and skillful labor, then the country will have more possible to raise economic growth for long term, due to they can apply their expertise skills and knowledge to attribute to their country's different kinds of high skillful or knowledge jobs or occupations to do in order to raise themselves country's productivities efficiently. Hence, economic growth has more effort to raise human (labor) these knowledge or skillful development in possible. Considering how economic growth leads labor's skillful and knowledge development positively, I shall indicate these factors as below:

Firstly, on manufacturing industry labors development factor hand, I assume that China's industrial export sector has been positively influenced by the accumulation of human capital , due to many China young people who had graduated any different kinds of degrees, e.g. engineering, education, law, accounting, business, management, chemical , medical , architectural , biology, medicine, computer science, earth science, space science, ocean science, environmental science etc. different kinds of subjects from overseas universities or local universities. Them they apply their expertise knowledge to attribute their skills to do any kinds of professional jobs in China's society. Due to China's sudden economic growth , so it reflects on the continuous increase in the good gross national product, because it occurs in a given good economic environment in a certain time period, due to the global different kinds of China's product number need is increasing as well as many China product manufacturers need many high educational and skillful labors to attribute their effort to help them to develop their businesses in China during the good economic growth period. Hence, China's economic growth leads China's any kinds of product manufacturers who need to employ any kinds of high educational and skillful employees (labors) to do their different kinds of jobs , due to global any kinds of China product consumers' needs are increasing suddenly. Then, it causes the effort to China employees who prefer to spend expenditure to train any young graduated people to be qualified high educational skillful labors with the good conditions of production; which leads to competitive sectors to attract these lacking working experiences of young graduated people t to be the availability of qualified labors in China in order to raise enough employment supply number to satisfy China's manufacturers' labor needs. So, it is a reason to explain that China's high educational and skillful labors development aims to attract foreign investment at a time. The overseas countries seek to provide investment environment through international laws and regulated that only provide qualified labor able to deal with modern technology to China's manufacturing industry development. So, China's economic growth will lead China's knowledge and skillful labors development in possible.

Secondly, on human capital education accumulation factor hand, economic growth will lead human capital educational level to be raised. I shall explain that why economic growth can lead human capital education accumulation positive reason as below:

I shall suppose that the negative impacts in the economic growth rate, it will bring the poor qualified human capital education level. I believe that it has direct relationship between education and the economic growth rate. I shall also suppose that the principle variable of interest determining GDP per capita is the level of labor supply which accounts for all the different educational level, (i.e. primary education, secondary education and university education).

Human capital accumulation can be explained to contribute to utility maximization. In general, it is a direct contribution in the utility function, this is because the more human capital each individual can accumulate in terms of knowledge and skills, the more happiness will be obtained for each one. Hence, it brings this question: Why can economic growth lead human capital accumulation educational level to be raised? The reason is because that when one country has good economic growth, then any primary, secondary and university schools have enough effort or resource to raise teacher individual teaching skills in order to teach many high knowledge and skillful level of students and satisfy their learning needs. Hence, the factors of these primary, secondary and university schools' educational inputs will also be raised, such as the teacher individual characteristics, their educational quality and educational experiences and qualities of their educational services provided and the interest of the country in accumulating educational high level of human capital need. For example, when the country encounters a high economic growth rate, it is able to demand new technology ,as a result of its well-educated society , such as China is one developing country, it needs a well-educated society to educate or train its high educational or skillful labors when it is experiencing in one good economic growth period. So, China's firms encouraged to adopt the advanced technologies developed in high income countries , when global economic growth is coming. It will cause the country, such as China will need to educate many high educational and skillful level labors to do any kinds of high technological jobs in itself country. So, China is a developing country because it needs to develop high technological manufacturing industry, it explains how its economic growth leads high educational and skillful labors development.

Consequently, such as these two cases indicate that one country's economic growth will be possible to lead high educational and skillful labors development in order to raise its competitive ability in different kinds of industries. In specially, high technological development industry , it needs significant high number of educational and skillful labors to satisfy the country's labor market when it is experiencing good economic growth period because many country's high technological product industry is their main income source. So, when the these countries are experiencing good economic growth period, it will lead the human employment growth positive effect for this kind of industry in possible.

- Economic growth leads income inequality

I believe that when one country is experiencing stable economic growth, it will bring serious negative influence to raise income inequality bewteen high education and low education people's income. I shall explain the reasons as below:

Why does the country's economic growth lead negative income inequality influence? Does either the country's high economic growth lead high income inequality or its low economic growth lead low income inequality in appropriate rate? I shall explain that what reasons to lead income inequality, when the country has high or low economic growth influence as below:

Many economists believed that the relationship of reverse causation from inequality to growth. It has a negative relationship between high economic growth and income inequality. I assume that the gross domestic products per capita to the level of inequality in income distribution. The unequal distribution of income seems similarity to the economic development process.

In fact, the first time , the economic development tends to increase inequality, but the trend is reversed, inequality stabilizes, the decrease until it reaches the lowest level that can be seen in the industrialized economies. So, when the country is encountering farming or agricultural economies or this farming industry won't be easier to lead income inequality. Such as Africa is a farming industry African Income level won't have significant income inequality, due to it lacks high technological economic development in itself country and its main jobs are most relate to farming, low technological and low educational need of different kinds of farming jobs. So, the high income and low income people's salaries are not significant difference too much. Otherwise, industrialized economic country, such as China, many Chinese workers are working in different kinds of industrialized jobs in China. However, although, the industrial industry brings economic growth in China society. But, China's high and low income of industrialized workers' wages, they have large significant difference. For example, the computer programmers and computer inventor salaries and the computer manufacturing workers' salaries, they have large significant difference, for another example, the vehicle designer and vehicle inventor salaries and vehicle manufacturing workers' salaries, they have large significant difference. Due to computer programmer or computer inventor needs have high technical knowledge, but computer manufacturing needs have low technical knowledge as well as vehicle designer or vehicle inventor needs have high vehicle components knowledge to invent any kinds of new styles of vehicles, so their salaries must have high income significant difference to compare the vehicle or computer manufacturing worker. Hence, due to their educational and skillful level is significant difference, so it causes their income will have much

significant difference in industrialized industry.
Hence, although China is encountering economic growth, but it also leads high income inequality to China's labors, due to it is one industrialized country. For Africa farming country example, its main industry is agricultural sector, designed as the traditional low-productivity sector in the Africa economy and it can not be replaced easily by the industrial sector. In this traditional farming industry, Africa can not develop its economy to grow up easily. So, it leads its labors' salaries level , which has less or low income inequality causes. Otherwise, such as China is a industrialized industry country, it has different kinds of industrialized development of this sector, such as the computer manufacturing or computer program sector and the vehicle manufacturing and vehicle design invention sector, which produces a movement of labor form low-productivity to high productivity sector, e.g. the vehicle sector is one low number productivity sector and computer sector is one high number productivity sector. This is reflected by an increase in income inequality in China's industrialized society.

Hence, such as above cases, Africa is one farming country, so it causes economic growth is slow and African income level is less inequality. Otherwise, China is one industrialized country, so it causes economic growth is fact and Chinese's income level is more inequality. It can conclude that fast economic growth country will lead high income inequality. Otherwise, slow economic growth country will lead low income inequality.

Banerjee and Newman (1993) indicated a relationship between the choice of occupation and the development process with the presence of an imperfect credit market. In this context, the occupation requiring a high level of investment is undoubtedly devoted to the wealthiest of the population. So, they believed that and industrialized countries will have more occupation choice to let themselves country's people to choose the best salary level of jobs to work. Due to industrialized development causes their economic growth is fact. So, it causes many occupations are created to let themselves country's workers to choose to work, then fast economic growth causes many occupations creating and it leads high income inequality. Otherwise , the farming countries, they have slow economic growth. So, it causes less occupations choice to let themselves people to choose to work and the slow economic growth countries will lead low income inequality.

Consequently, it explains that it has relationship between whether the country is industrialized economy or farming economy or technological economy as well as high economic growth or low economic growth . Then, it has also relationship between high or low economic growth and more or less occupation choices. In final, it has relationship between more or less occupation choices and high and low income inequality. In sum up, high or low economic growth will lead high or low income inequality in possible.

CHAPTER TWO

Economic growth leads healthier

I beleive that when one country is experiencing stable economic growth, it will lead more healthier, I shall indicate reasons as below:

How can economic growth lead healthier to poor people? Can economic growth influence medical service quality and doctors and nurses medical service performance of hospitals? Can economic growth influence quality of medicine to let patients to eat in order to raise more healthier? Has economic growth and medical health service (production of medicine quality) direct or indirect relationship to lead patients more healthier? What are health impact income?

I assume that life expectancy will be better, if the country has better economic growth or it improves its economic growth. I shall indicate the reasons include as below:

Firstly on relationship hand , I believe that it has relationship between income and health or life expectancy hand, due to the country can develop or grow up or grow its economy to remain long term good economic development. So, its citizen can have more jobs supply to do to treat any sickness. So, they will have effort to buy different kinds of medicine to eat in order to raise more healthier. It seems that some economists support long term good economic growth will bring the country's medical development, e.g. many hospitals can have more effort money to spend to research any new kinds of medicines to let patients to choose the most health medicines to eat, when patietns have different kinds of medicines to choose to eat in order to choose to eat th enough nutrition improvement of different kinds of medicines. Then, the country's patients will have more chance to treat their sickness to be improved health.

Hencc, it seems that hospitals will have enough money to research ,when the country has long term better economic growth condition. When the country can remain long term better environment growth improvement, it can lead many jobs to be supplied to people to work and they will have more income to save to buy any expensive medicines, if they are facing serious sickenss, e.g. cancer. Then, they can buy this cancer medicines to eat to treat cancer disease

(non common sickness) in order to be more healthier.
Thus, economic growth can lead medical industry has enough money to carry on researching any new kinds of medicines to attempt to treat any serious diseases in order to provide different kinds of new medicines to human to eat to treat any serious diseases more healthier. For example, U.S., U.K. these both developed countries can remain long term good economic groth. So, these both countries have enough money to assist domestic hospitals to carry on researching any new kinds of medicines to let patients to choose the most effective or more healthier medicines to let patients eat to attempt to treat their serious diseases more successfully. So, U.S., U.K. serious diseases of patients whose death ratio is decreasing in these two countries as well as their death ratio, due to serious diseases causing is the least to compare to other countries.

Secondly, I shall indicate on the improvement in health and economic growth hand, how any why it has relationship between improvement of human health and economic health. I shall focuse in particular on the question of how much of the improvement in health can be attributed. The improvements in the health can include that human's living of standard, better nutrition, changes in the public health environment, it includes sanitation and supply of clean water. Finally an improvement in medical technology, for example, both sanitation improvements and treatment with antibiotics will reduce mortality from infectious diseases.

However, we can explain why economic growth and improvements of human's health , which has relationship. It can be measured by mortality, it can be linked to specific changes in both ages at which people, i.e. an increase age of the number of patients to disease, such as U.S. , U.K. these both countries, the number of old age people who have serious diseases of the total population ratio is less than the developing countries, e.g. China, Africa. It is possible to explain because these both countries have stable long term better economic growth to compare these both developing countries.

Thirdly, I shall indicate on the better nutrition of food supply and economic growth relationship hand. It seems that better economic growth in the country , it will encourage the country people have more consumption effort, then they have enough food to earn more better nutrition to live. So, their diseases will be reduced, due to they have enough food to supply to them to eat to earn more nutrition from different kinds of foods every day, e.g. beef, pork meat, vegetable , fruit etc. food. Hence, economic growth can encourage any food consumers have effort to spend too much expenditure to buy any kinds of fresh and good taste and better nutrition of food to eat. So, it implies the long term stable economic growth will encourage human to buy any kinds of better nutriction of food to eat every day. It can lead human has better healthier, due to human can hace more money to buy better nutriction of food to eat. It includes the special poor people who have effort to buy better nutriction of food to eat.

To sum up, the better nutrition of food is mainly to be consumed by the more effort of the country' poor people when the country have good economic growth environment. So, economic growth can lead any countries' hospitals to research more different kinds of medicines to be attempted to provide to any serious diseases patients to eat. The country's poor people can be raised more healthier to live in the stable economic growth countries.

- Economic growth can become knowledge-based economic society

I believe that when one country is experiencing stable economic growth, it can raise knowledge -based economic society, I shall indicate reasons as below:

I shall explain why and how economic growth can raise the country to become one knowledge-based economic society. Knowledge investment means that knowledge distribution is through formal and informal networks, which is essential to economic performance, knowledge -based economies which are directly based on the production, distribution and use of knowledge and information. Knowledge is increasingly being codified and transmitted through computer an communications networks in the information societ. For example, the developed countries, e.g. U.S., U.K. . They have long term stable economic growth for may years. So, they had been experiencing the knowledge-based economic developed social coutries. Their knowledge-based economic societies will provide them the enabling organizational change at the U.S., U.K. firm level to maximize the benefits to them in both manufacturing and service technology for producing sectors.

The effect of "knowledge"-based economy, which will led a fuller recognition of the role of knowledge and technology in economic growth (human technologial capital) growth to assist or encourage human development. For example, the exports of high technology industries had grown fastly for these knowledge of economic growth developed countries, e.g. Canada, U.S. , U.K. , Australia, Japan, New Zealand, Europe etc. developed countries.

Knowledge-based economic development can also lead more intangible investments in research and development, training of the labor force, computer software and technical expertise to those above countries. So, knowledge-based economic development can lead human's talent development to create new talent human's knowledge to different technological development aspects, e.g. internet invention, 3 D printer invention, advanced medical equipment invention, space boats, nuclear energy invention, prior speed railway transportation tool invention etc. technological products. So, any one of high technological products invention which must need have good economic growth to the country, then when the country has good economic growth condition,it will have effort to train or educate talent human to attribute to knowledge -based societies to encourage or give these chance to talent human or inventors to invent any kinds of high technological products for human to use. Hence, when one country can have effort to be developed to one knowledge-based economic developed country. Then, it can have possible to provide high technological resources to educate or train " talent" humans or scientific inventors to invent any new kinds of high technological products to provide to human to use. So, in the future, oue standard of living will be improved in possible, due to economic growth causes any kinds of high technological products to be invented to provide human to use.

However, I bring this question: Can economic growth bring knowledge-based economic society to lead talent human development really? I shall indicate reasons to explain whether they have relationship to lead talent human development as below:

When the country has good economic growth , employers need skilled labor number will increase in the highest demand. Although, the manufacturing sector is losing jobs, but employment is growing in high-technology, science-based sectors ranging from computers to pharmaceuticals, high knowledge-based jobs. These jobs are more highly skilled and pay higher wages than those in low technology sectors, e.g. textiles and food processing. Moreover, knowledge-based jobs in service sectors are also growing strongly. Indeed, non-production or knowledge-based job in service sectors engage in the output of physical products are the employees in most demand in a wide range of activities from computer technicians, through physical therapists to marketing specialists. The use of new technologies, which are the engine of long -term gains in productivity and employment. Generally improve the " skills base" of the labor force in both manufacturing and services. And it is largely balance of technology that employers now pay more for knowledge than for manual work. So, it seems that economic growth will have possible to cause knowledge-based economic society to any countries.

Then, I shall explain the question: Can knowledge-based economic society lead talent human development? In fact, it is not a new idea that knowledg plays an important role in the economy . Also economists are now developing new growth theories to explain the forces which drive long-term economic growth. In new growth theory, knowledge can raise the returns on invetment, which can contribute to the accumulation of knowledge. It is done by stimulating more efficient methods of production organization as well as new and improved products and services. Knowledge can also spill over from one firm or industry to another with new ideas used repeatedly at little extra cost. Such spillovers can ease the constraints placed on growth by scarcity of capital.

Hence, it seems knowledge-based economic society will encourage employers to train talent human to contribute their any new kinds of knowledge to do any kinds of new creating jobs. Moreover, knowledge-based economy can also encourage employers to create more different kinds of new knowledge jobs to lead talent human development. The talent human development includes these complex-areas of knowledge in order to fulfil their jobs as below:

For example, practitioners of law and medicine belong to know-who , it refers to knowledge about " facts ". This knowledge is close to what is normally called information. Know-why refers to scientific knowledge of the principles and laws of nature. It means technological development and product and process advances in most industries, e.g. research laboratories and universities organizations. So, firms need to interact with these organizations either through recruiting scientifically -trained labor or directly through contracts and joint activities. Know-how refers to skills or the capability to do something. A new product or a personnel manger neede to select and train staff have to use their know-how.

One of the most important reasons for the formation of industrial networks is the need for firms to be able to share and combine elements of know-how. Finally, this is why know-who because increasingly important. Know-who involves information about who knows what and who knows how to do what. It is possible that any talent human expects he.she knows how to use whose knowledge efficiently. The know-who kind of knowledge is internal to the organization to a higher degree than any other kind of knowledges. It is significant in economics, skills are widely disposed because of a highly developed division of labor among organization and experts. For example, for a modern manager who must need to own this kind of knowledge to manage whose organization efficiently and effectively in order to achieve the most maximum beneficial to productivities and raising employee individual working performance.

In conclusion, it seems that it explains why the knowledge-based economic country's employers need to spend expenditure to train talent humans in order to raise their different aspects of knowledge development, when the country is experiencing " knowledge-based economic society".

CHAPTER THREE

Economic growth leads urban environmental planning development need

I beleive that when one country is experiencing stable economic growth, it must lead urban environmental planning development need, I shall indicate reasons as below:

Can one country's long term stable economic growth lead urban environmental planning development to itself country? Do they have direct or indirect cause and effect relationship between them? I shall indicate some causes to explain whether they have cause and effect relationship between of them existed.
Mexico city is one good example to explain whether itself economic growth has relationship to lead itseld urban environmental planning development recently. Nowadays, Mexico city's economic growth is stable, so it has effort to develop a more livable interlinkage of economic social, and good environmental city to provide to Mexico people to live. It has been developing more livable city by building an efficient intra-urban bus system, expanding urban green space, and meeting the basic needs of the urban poor. Hence, it implies that when one country has long term stable economic growth effort, it is possible that it will plan to develop it's urban environment in order to let its people to live more comfortable, such as Mexico city recent urban environmental planning development core example. So, it explain that why economic growth will bring human's living needs to gain satisfaction in possible.

However, I bring one question: Does it has possible to develop the urban environmental development to achieve the most effective and beneficial to the country's cities , when it had been experiencing the long term stable economic growth period? I shall indiate some evidences to explain this issue whether it can be possible to occur as below:

Every country has thousands of possible sustainable cities, for each city has unique historical , cultural, political and environmental circumstances. Such as U.S. , U.K. these both countries, which have many cities, e.g. Washington, New York, London etc. cities. Every city has unique cultural, historical , political and environmental circumstances backgrounds. So, their urban environmental planning needed to be adapt from approaches formulated in cities and regions, where problems of infrastructure, social equity, and urbanization of the environment have been creatively addresses. They need to know how to design every city's urban to impact on the environment more adapt to make cities more livable for human.

In fact, in economic view point, due to our earth has limited natural resources will continue to provide life support for humanity's lives. So, every country needs to know how to use our earth's limited natural to use our earth's limited natural resources to develop every city's urban environment to let every city's people to live more comfortable to avoid the lacking enough earth's natural resources to be supplied to them to design urban environmental function for every city use in the future one day. Because every country's cities; human population tends to grow, but every country's cities' lands area supply is limited. So, it will cause every city's natural resource is not enough to supply to human to use, when the city's human population growing number has exceeded the city' land area supply to suppot the city's human normal population to live. Hence, it is a value considering question: How to use our earth's natural resource effectively and efficiently and organizing, e.g. land area. It can avoid future natural resource, such as land supply shortage causes human can not satisfy comfortable living environmental need in every cities.

Traditionally, economists have been concerned with the efficiency of resource use. They have been slow in developing economic models that adequately account for resource scarcity and pollution. Only rarely have economists worried that some resources may be short supply, such as clean land and soil , clean water, clear air and theat if these resources are used indiscriminately, they may become exhausted for every city population growth need for which, the city's urban environmental is needed to plan and develop. So, human expected to have comfortable lifestyles.

We need to know how to choose to do our behaviors to avoid environmental pollution, e.g. land, air, water qualities dirty pollution, when the country has long term stable economic growth, it can not neglect how to avoid environmental pollution to every city as the same time. So, when one country has long term stable economic growth. It also needs to plan how to reduce land, air, water natural resources are used by human's wrong attitudes or behaviors to use our earth's natural resources. So, it implies that when one country has long term stable economic growth, it also needs to consider how to plan to develop its urban environment efficiently and effectively and organizing in order to satisfy every city's people's comfortable living needs.

Hence, I bring this question: How to keep stable economic growth and enough natural resources supply to urban environmental development to different countries' cities? I recommend that when every country government needs to encourage businessmen consider environment protection issue when they choose to do and kinds of businesses in themselves countries.

Keating, (1993) explained that how to utilize local materials and are energy-efficient, non-polluting and labor intensive as well as every country government needs to achieve action progress of energy conservation and renewable energy, such as wind, solar, hydro-electric renewable energy, and biomass. For transport policies that favor public, bicycle, and food transport over automobiles municipal development designed to reduce commuting and land use that contains urban sprawl and prevents it from encroaching upon agriculturall land and environmentally sensitive areas are enunciated.

To sum up, in human development history, our earth was relatively empt of human beings and our belongings are only include (man-made capital) and relatively full of other species and our habitats (natural capital). In ago human development history, because human had no any business economic activites. So, human does not need to expand much natural resources to do any business economic activities. Hence, human had enough natural resource to be supplied to use. Till to nowadays, years of economic growth have changed that basic owning enough natural resource supply pattern. As a result, the limiting factor on future encouraging growth has changes. If man-made and natural capital were good substitutes for one another, then natural capital could be totally replaced.

How the two are complementary or however , which means that the short supply of one imposes limits. I shall indicate fishing boats catching fishes to sale business example to explain the economic growth and natural resource shortage relationship issue. If one day, the country's ocean had enough fishing boats to catch fished to sell, but it has without enough population of fishes to be caught to let the fishing boats to catch to sell in the ocean. Once the number of fish sold at market was primarily limited by the number of boats that could be built and manned, not limited by the number of fish in the sea. This suitation is better, due to the natural resources of fishes supply number is enough in the sea. It is only the fish catching boats number is not built enough factor. This cas is similiar to urban environmental development to cities case. When the country had developed long term stable economic growth ,it needs to consider whether human's standard of living is raising up or falling down as the same time. Such as this fishing boats catching fishes business case. If human only consider whether the fishes catching number is increasing every day . But human neglect to consider that one ocean will be polluted and fished will be killed by pollutants. Then, the shortage of different kinds of good taste fishes number challange will cause. Although, human has enough woods or steels resources to build any kinds of fishing boats, but it can't solve fishes shortage challenge. Then, it will lead fishes supply number shortge and it can lead human's living of standard to b fallen down, due to human has no enough fishes to be supplied to eat because many fishes are killed by pollutants in sea. It is similiar to human's urban environmental planning development case. When, human only consider how to remain long term stable economic growth, e.g. building many houses in the limited land area cities, it will damage the city's land green plant and tree growth natural environment as well as the city product manufacturers neglect to avoid to pollute river, air and ocean in their factories manufacturing process. Then , in long term time, when our natural environment is polluted. Any cities will have only polluted dirty air to human to breathe and dirty water to provide to human to drink and any cities lack enough green and clean soil to grow trees and plants to let human to live comfortable in different cities. Then, human's standard of living or quality of life will be fallen down. So, human ought consider economic growth will lead natural resources number to be decreased as well as environmental pollution challenge causes, due to human's economic action lead this challenge causes.

Consequently, economic growth has possible to lead urban environment planning development needs, due to human had polluted our natural environment and consume the exceed number of natural resource to cause any vegetable and fish and food supply number to be reduced in long term stable economic growth period to every country's economic development. To avoid human needs to reorganize cities and urban environmental development need. Huaman must need to find solutions to avoid to cause serious pollution to our land, sea and river and air in our long term stable economic growth period.

In conclusion, when one country is experiencing stable economic growth , it can perform better economic development. But, it can not absolute perform better human development. Due to human only considers how to do any business behavior to damage our natural environment and misuse our natural resource. Otherwise, when one country is not experiencing stable economic growth, it is possible to lead human development. Due to it's economic development stage is not reach the maximum period. So, the country won't do business behavior to damage its natural environment and misuse natural resource to cause itself people's standard of living to be worse.

Reference

Banerjee, A. Newman, A. (1993). Occupational choice and the process of development . Journal of political economy, 101 (2). 274-298.

Keating, M. (1993). The earth summit's agenda for change. Geneva: centre for our common future, viii, x, 12-13. 63-67.

Namik, S.D. (1965). The theories of economic growth, Cario: Knowledge House.

CHAPTER FOUR

The relationship between productivity and economy

Can productivity influence economic growth?

Economists define four factors of production: land, labor, capital and entrepreneurship. These can be considered the building blocks of an economy. However, production is a concept in economics that is defined as the process of taking various inputs and combining them using labor to create an output that has a benefit. If labour productivity increases, firms will demand more labour at each wage rate and the firm's demand for labour itself will increase. This would shift the labour demand curve outwards. In addition, productivity growth can increase the demand for goods and services, raising the demand for workers. Firms with higher productivity can expand and lower prices, increasing their sales and labor demand.

Causes of Economic Problem:

(i) Unlimited Wants. Human wants are unlimited in numbers. ...

(ii) Limited Resources: In economics, scarcity means that commodities and resources to produce goods and services are less in relation to their demand. ...

(iii) Alternative Uses of Resources:

What is productivity, and why is it important? Productivity is key to a company's profitability and long-term success. It measures how much output a company can produce from resources such as labor, capital or raw materials. If a company improves its productivity, it can generate more output from its resources.

Increasing productivity over time allows businesses to produce more goods and services per unit of input. This ultimately enables higher wages, aids economic growth, increases profitability, and boosts tax revenues. Productivity can affect profitability when, for example: you don't produce as many goods as projected. the cost of raw material exceeds your cost budget. the cost of labour is higher than expected. Poor management is one of the major causes of low productivity. According to studies, almost 80% of workers have encountered poor management, which demotivates them from giving their all to the organization for which they work. There are still a lot of managers in organizations who like to micromanage their employees. It's possible to have high productivity even when efficiency is low. This is definitely at the expense of good quality production. In such cases, it becomes about having the numbers, even if it means lowering standards.

Economic growth often is driven by consumer spending and business investment. Tax cuts and rebates are used to return money to consumers and boost spending. Deregulation relaxes the rules imposed on businesses and has been credited with creating growth but can lead to excessive risk-taking. But in capitalism, money is the main source of motivation, whether of the worker, the manager or the owner. One way an owner can get more money is via capital investment, which can increase worker productivity and generate greater profits.

Deflation can be caused by an increase in productivity, a decrease in overall demand, or a decrease in the volume of credit in the economy. Most of the time, deflation is unambiguously a positive trend for the economy, but it can also under certain conditions occur along with a contraction in the economy. Low productivity creates a cascade of problems. When there are issues with workflow, poor decision-making or scope creep, it can cause low morale within your entire team. Employees don't want to feel like they're wasting their time. If a project's moving at a snail's pace, they often disengage.

With growth in productivity, an economy is able to produce—and consume—increasingly more goods and services for the same amount of work. Productivity is important to individuals (workers and consumers), business leaders, and analysts (such as policymakers and government statisticians). For example, by reducing unit labor cost increases, productivity growth reduces inflationary pressure on prices. Hourly wages can rise faster than prices, increasing buying power for workers and consumers. So, any increase in production leads to economic growth as measured by GDP. This metric merely represents the total production of all goods and services in an economy.

Otherwise, a decline in productivity stunts the GDP or the economic output in comparison to the number of people. Low productivity indicates that resources are not utilizing their skills and competencies to their maximum potential which increases company's resourcing costs. Improved economic growth raises the standard of living by lowering costs and raising wages. Moreover, increased productivity is also associated with a market economy. In any economy, people need money to purchase goods and services. In a market economy, this need leads to increased motivation because workers want to earn more money to supply their needs and to live comfortably.

However, a key mechanism through which economic growth is understood to lead to higher living standards is productivity growth. Economic growth can also be the result of increased employment or investment, but these processes do not necessarily lead to rising wages or incomes.

An economy grows when it has the capacity to produce more. Production is based on how much capital, labor, natural resources, and technology it has to produce. Policies that encourage the accumulation of any of these leads to economic growth. Although we have mastered the technology of producing as much of any particular good as we may want, we cannot at the same time produce an infinite quantity of everything. The economic problem of production is one of producing goods and services in their proper proportions.

When a workforce is more productive it produces more goods and services, and at a lower cost per unit. This means there is a greater supply of these things, which puts downward pressure on prices and is therefore associated with lower inflation. How do we raise productivity?Production is the process of combining various inputs, both material (such as metal, wood, glass, or plastics) and immaterial (such as plans, or knowledge) in order to create output. Ideally this output will be a good or service which has value and contributes to the utility of individuals. For example, data from the Bureau of Labor Statistics indicate that in the most recent recession, which started in December 2007 and ended in June 2009, the percent decline in aggregate hours worked was larger than the decline in output, suggesting an increase in overall labor productivity. It follows that the more goods that are produced, the lower the prices of goods. This connection between the level of production and the level of prices also holds for the rate of change of production (that is, the rate of economic growth) and the rate of change of prices (that is, the inflation rate).

Sustained long-term economic growth comes from increases in worker productivity, which essentially means how well we do things. In other words, how efficiently does a nation use its workers and other resources? Like capital growth, the rate of technical growth is highly dependent on the rate of savings and investment, as they are necessary to engage in research and development. The four factors of production are land and natural resources, labor, capital equipment, and entrepreneurship.

At their most effective, strategies include analyzing the local economic context; identifying economic opportunities and resources; and collaborating with industry, government, academic, and community stakeholders.

CHAPTER FIVE

Can technological productivity bring economic growth

Technology invention can bring what change to our future societies. However, when technology may bring positive or negative impact to ourselves societies in the same time.

Would technology also impact to ourselves as human behavioral change ? I shall attempt to apply behavioral economic view to indicate cases and explain this question as below:

I assume that technology and human behavior which have close relationship (e.g. working behavior , living behavior), For robot case example, if robots can influence human behavioral change, and future human working environment will need to cooperate with robots or human living environment will depend on robots' helping. How human behavior will be influenced to change in order to adapt to accept robots invention when human needs to live or work with robots together in the same time.

In organizational working environment, staffs will need to accept digital, data and robot technology in our industries or implementing a business strategy , why organizations need to be made decision making by robots. However, staffs have possible to depend on robots to help them to make decision, e.g. staffs behavior on analysis or judgement which can be controlled or managed by robots in possible. CEO, or manager leaders , their managing ability will be supervised or managed by robots in any organizations . So, it seems that robots may be any organizational top leader, if they can manage CEO or manager or supervisor in any organizations.

Business organizational leader individual managing behavior must be controlled by robots. Robots (supervised learning) is the most popular type of machine learning and robots can learn any new kinds of knowledge to compare human easily and rapidly. So, any organizational business decision or strategy decision may be made or influenced by supervising robots in organizations in possible. CEO, manager, supervisor their managing ability or managing skill may be influenced to reduce by supervising learning supervising or leading robots cooperation.

However, we can follow these aspects to explain how robots may influence our behavior change. Robots may be applied to participate in sales and marketing , HR, finance, customer service, education, legal and government organizations. Robots will be superintelligence to impact human lives in due time, In future, robots has insight , such as perceives, learns, understands, comprehends. It is one deep learning machines. It can make right or wrong , true or wrong judgement or answer and make good or bad predictions.

Hence, if robots can be applied to work in our future societies in popular, they may be social leader to replace human leader, e.g. government leader, organizational leader, CEO, manager, supervisor. Robots can not only human's worker role, e.g. home servants, shopping center cleaner, kitchen cooker. If robots can be organizational leaders, they may supervise worker individual working attitude or working performance whether his/her performance is satisfactory or perfect or to be needed to improve.

In organization, robots won't be only workers role. They may be supervisor role to supervise, manage or dominate or control all organizational top, middle , low level staffs their behavior and make judgement whether whom staffs can either stay to work or leave the organization.

However, some behavioral economists feel robots are Unfair to make judgement on staff individual working behavior. But on behavioral economic view, robots may help business owners to make judgement whether whom staffs ought stay the firm to work or leave the firm. They can help the organization to bring long term economic benefit. Hence, robots may be right to be future any organizational leader, such as CEO, manager, supervisor role more than worker role. If robots can be supervisor role in any organizations, I believe that they can help the organizations to bring much long term economic benefits to compare human CEO, manager, or supervisor for future global business economic development environment because robots may help any organizations to improve efficiency , or raise productivity to compare human staff decision making abilities.

Ought robots be leader role? In any organizations robots can bring this economic benefits to customer service aspect. For example, in order to reduce mind-numbing repetition for human workers, some economists recommend that future organizations seriously consider use of robots to field calls and process requests at a basic level. Such robots could be used to authenticate users for basic access to the organization in order for staffs to obtain the least risky information that they need. As customer need rise is complexity and business risk failure to satisfy that customer's need and to cause the customer chooses to buy another product or use another service. The work of ticket creation and case routing can be enhanced by robots, but a human should oversee it according to business risk assessment.

Hence, robot analytics can help to any organizations to predict those cases most likely headed for escalation in real time, all the date of the chatbot need to be presented to the human , so that the poor, annoyed customer does not have to start all over again with self-identification and description of the problem.

So, future robots can be perfect customer service leader, they can help satisfy your customers and retain them. Robots can know whether what the customer's real need , how to let the customer feels satisfactory more compare human customer service staffs. They can be customer service leader, service recommendation professionals. They can help organizations to retain old customers , even increase new customers easily to compare human customer service staffs. Hence, robots ought participate to marketing, customer service teams to help staffs how to do right customer service decision with human customer service staffs together. Hence, customer service staffs need to follow up customer service robots' ideas how to help them to solve any customer complain or enquiry in order to improve customer service performance. Consequently, the organization will increase new customer number and retain old customers easily if robots can be applied to participate on marketing, customer service departments.

How be robots in business? They may include three main areas: More intelligence products, services and business process. The first perspective is external. AI enhanced product and service means what you need to deliver to your customers. Both product and service -based business, which means they're all about making customers' lives easier, understanding and anticipating their needs, and solving their problems.

The second perspective is internal, making business processes more intelligent means looking at your business from the inside, assessing every aspect of your operations. To see how to make the business more efficient and enhance from manufacturing to the supply chain.

The third perspective is creating more intelligent products. How robots influence human living behavior? The internet of things means a whole host of everyday products are getting smart. Smart devices like smart phones, smart TV, smart watches on the market, smart office buildings, smart houses, they can influence staffs work or households live whom feel more comfortable.

On AI products aspect,. Intelligent smart running shoes products are like a fitness tracker, but provide more specialist information for runners. A smart AI chip that and how monitors movement (including gait and how feet strike the ground), the shoes provide feed- that helps runners improve their form and reduce the risk of injury. SO, AI smart shoes can influence runners feel comfortable and safe when runners run long time on gardens and they will predict or know whether the running places are dangerous or safe as well as smart running shoes can help runners to collect data on their running style , and the accompanying app provides real -time analysis of the runners' performance and running technique.

Smart running shoes can be runner coach on how to run better and avoid running injuries. It's not only running shoes that are being fitted with sensors to gather data and provide feedback.

The " wearable" technology sector is booming due to AI technology development to influence human needs to pursue more comfortable lives. Hence, AI smart products may help human to build health lives daily. Human begins to attempt to learn how to live more health by robots (AI) products.

When robots can be applied to human ourselves living environment , e.g. working, home, social , transport (non manual driving public transport tools service) , leisure environment. How behavioral economists feel they can bring positive or negative economic influence to our future societies?

Robots will bring human to experience economic anxiety. Wy? After centuries of development, basic science, applied science and technology had been rapidly developing. Material science, additive manufacturing , nanotechnology, bio-tech , new batteries, smart phones, non human driving public transport or non public transport tools invention. All of these new technological products include robots may help human to create new technological economic social development and technology also impacts human behavioral change.

Consequently, this leads us to the Fourth industrial revolution" or Klaus Schwab for the world economic forum in his 2015 article and 2016 book, he indicated

The first industrial revolution used water and stream power to mechanize production . The second used electric power to create production. The third used electronic and information technology to automate production. How a Fourth industrial revolution is building on the third, the digital revolution that has been occurring since the middle of the last century. It is characterized by a fusion of technology that is developed by scientists between the physical, digital and biological science.

Ref: Excerpts from the fourth industrial revolution.

Consequently, human have expanded capabilities to communicate, to connect, to work without actual physical environment. Human behavior may be influenced alone or live lonely because robots can help organizations to reduce many workers to work together and working hours. When robots can replace human workers to do their tasks. Moreover, human will have driverless vehicles and drones, which help in more than moving people and goods. They assist us in farming, in pollution control, human have machine-aided surgery, and human have smart cities, smart contract, smart product to use. So, any kinds of new invention of technological tools will be needed to use in any organizations in order to improve performance. Even our homes also need (AI) tools to help us to live more comfortable.

Technological invention have changed our lives to be Better, continuing a trend in previous experiencing of Industrial revolutions, smartphones, connected with Computing power, change the many we decide on Travelling, entertaining purchasing or connecting with Friends. Our day-to-day behavior and decisions are seriously affected by and dependent on the digital network technology.

In fact, machines are more than substitute for people In routine jobs, they can even take over some jobs, that require cognitive functions. Consequently, it may bring unemployment ratio rises or jobs need reduce in our societies. Machine-search changes the life of lawyers, accountants, engineers, even doctors when (AI) tools help them to deal every tasks. So, many professionals will have chance to lose jobs if robots can do their most tasks.

On conclusion, the fast process in machine-human – capital substitution means that experts need to seek new competitive advantages, this time against intelligence machines . So, technology may change human behavior to bring positive and negative both impact in our societies, such as the usefulness in -skill sets as capital labor substitution has become capital -human capital substitution. All of these will raise economic anxiety, because companies will have a reduced staffs number and increase robots number sense of security. Also, workers need to spend time to learn new skills in order to adapt to work with robots together in any organizations. So, technology can not influence workers become lazy. Otherwise, they influence workers become hard because they need to spend time to learn how to work with machine together in organizations. But, technology can also influence human pursue more comfortable to live.

Can technology influence consumers reduce spending on visiting shopping

Why may knowledge influence economic growth? Have they close relationship between knowledge and economic growth or recession in behavioral economy view? I shall attempt to indicate evidences to explain these two questions as below:

IN fact, human development had been experiencing from agricultural stage to industrial manufacturing stage, till to nowadays, service section stage,e.g. hotel tourism leisure development, and technological development stage, e.g. computer and robot development. All of these stages, which are created by ourselves knowledge, it means that how we decide choice, what social development direction will be caused. It it is true, it seems that global human knowledge may influence how our social future continue development. Our social economic growth or recession will be brought to influence from knowledge

indirectly.

It is focus on " behavioral economic concept" Economists define scarcity as the condition of wanting more than we can get with available resources. Scarcity is a fact of

life. So, human can arrange ourselves resources in a lot of different ways, such as watching TV, buying a book, a car or traveling, but at any given time, ourselves have a fixed range of possibilities. SO, scarcity also describes the world on a collective level. As a society, we can produce only so many things, and we have to decide how those things are divided among many people. But, when social development, knowledge is very important to cause human (scientists) choose how to decide to invent any new things in order to

satisfy human not limited need and using desire. So, the total quantity of available knowledge does not diminish as more and more people acquire it. So, ourselves every behavioral decision in life involves weighing the trade off between costs and benefits . We look at our options and decide whether it is worth giving up in order to get the other.

Economists explain this time cost of choice the " opportunity cost", opportunity cost is the value you could gained by choosing your next best alternative, the opportunity you have to pass up in order to take your first choice. Why may ourselves behavior have relationship between opportunity cost and economic growth? For computer invention example, when scientists feel compute products will be future human needs daily, for student learning using need, office tasks needs, watching movie, listening music leisure need,even playing game need. So, scientists had chose to spend time and resource and labor to invent computer products , they forgave to spend time and resource

and labor to invent other products. They computer invention is their opportunity cost, includes time, money, resource, labour, knowledge, mind on computer scientists , they had forgiven to spend these resources to research how to invent other kinds of new products.

However, when computer new products had been invented in success, e.g. desktop, laptop, can be popular to be accept to provide to global computer users to use. This kind of computer

invention , its users number had been increasing, manufacturing computer number will be influenced to grow, due to computer invention will help developing and developed countries GDP

growth rapidly since 1980 year , the early first stage of computer invention had been experiencing during our global technological development history.

So, it implies that computer scientists had been confirmed to do right choice decision to forgive to spend resources, time, money and labour and knowledge to research how to invent any kinds of new products. They make right decision to research how to invent new computer products,even improve desktop to laptop and smart phone , hand carrying smart phone and computer both functions new products to satisfy computer users daily using needs. It is true opportunity cost to computer scientists case. Also, when past, our scientists do right choice to invent this kind of computer product, this kind of computer products can bring global economic benefits, such as government can increase profit tax form computer sellers, offices can use computers to reduce employees number, when computers can help offices to save much document, clerical employees number may be influenced to reduce, tasks can be simple from complex tasks, spending tasks time may be influenced to reduce by computerization of office, factories can apply computers or robots to replace workers to manufacture any kinds of products, such as cars, washing machine, rice cookers, radios, fans ,television etc. different kinds of electrical products.

So workers number may be influenced to reduce and wage expenditure must be reduce.

Hence, new knowledge may help global societies to bring economic growth, such as past scientists had decided to forgive to spend time, resource, money, labor, skill, knowledge to research how to invent any kinds of new products, it is possible that they have some different kinds of new products concept choices, computer concept is only one kinds of choice among these new different kinds of new products invention concepts. However, they need to choose only one kind of new product invention among of these different kinds of new product concept choices, because they have not enough resource to provide to them to invent in the past. Finally, they evaluate the weigh and cost between computer invention concept and other new products invention concepts. In fact, computer is one kind of "the bringing much economic benefits" new concept invention product choice.

I believe that if computer will be continue improved in order to bring more economic growth in possible. SO, scientists need to spend more time, resource, money, labor, skill, knowledge to research how to continue to improve traditional computers to bring more using functions, in order to help global different industries to reduce resource, time, labour , money aim to bring reducing cost spending expenditure benefits to global industries , due to societies had been experiencing " knowledge social stage". If societies need to apply computer technology to assist our societies can continue develop, when our societies‘ different industries, such as service, manufacturing, even agricultrial sectors, e.g. robots may help farmers to predict when it is right time to grow vegetable, or replace farmers to grow vegetable, fruit in farms to provide human have enough food to eat, or robots can help hotel to clean rooms, serve clients, robots can help cinemas to sell tickets, robots can help manufacturers to product new products in factories. So, technological products may help any kinds of industries to reduce employees number, improve efficiencies and productivities and reduce wages expenditure economic cost benefits.

Production possibilites economic concept knowledge indicates about who produces which goods and why. The fact that millions of people and firms around the global coordinate their activities to provide consumers with the right combination of goods and services seem like magic.

In fact, coordination doe snot happen by chance, nor does super-planner tells every one where to go and what to do. Instead, the global production time is a natural outcome of people every acting in their own self interest to improve their own lives. Economists call this coordination mechanism the " invisible hand", an idea that was first suggested by economic thinker Adam Smith.

To get some insight into the who and why of production, such as shirt production case, most shirts are made in China, and other countries when factory wages are low. Have American workers become worse at making shirts over the last two countries? Definitely not, In fact, as are better than American workers at making shirts. Instead , each good tends to be produced by that country, company, or person with the lowest opportunity cost of producing that shirt kind of product, such as scientists make cooperation decision to invent computer products together, they can earn high invention royalty income, computer sale and manufacturing number increases, governments can earn more profit tax, different kinds of service, manufacturing industries can reduce workers number, wage expenditure, improving performance economic benefits . So, countries and firms and persons need a specialize in making goods for which they have the lowest opportunity cost. They than trade with one another to get the coordination of goods. They want to consume, such as computer manufacturing , if IBM and Microsoft both companies can cooperate to research how to improve themselves traditional model of laptops and desktops to create new improved and more using functions laptops and desktops, e.g. small size, more new using functions, clear colour and easier visible screen, or small book cover design, new computer model. I believe that the resulting, gains from themselves computer trade can be shared much that every computer buyers ends up better offer, global computer users will choose to buy and use these both IBM and Microsoft future new computer invention products to compare other kinds of computer manufacturers.

In production possibilities frontier economic concept, it explains why IBM and Microsoft ought cooperate to manufacturer computers, their cooperation can bring more economic benefits to themselves and global computer users, e.g. more computer functions, reducing sale price, reduce computer workers manufacturing wages, and computer manufacturing workers number, increasing computer manufacturing and demand number, increasing profit to themselves and government profit tax income, increasing buyers number, offices can improve efficiencies and employees performance, reducing manufacturing cost expenditure, improving student learning ability, etc. different kinds of global economic benefits. Hence, in production possibilities frontier economic concept, IBM and Microsoft ought make cooperation decision in order to bring global economic benefits.

In fact, computer manufacturing industry is one competitive market, it is one in which truly informed, prices taking buyers and seller easily trade a standardized good or service. IBM and Microsoft need to cooperate in order to win their computer manufacturing competitors , if they hope to earn in global computer manufacturing top leader position. Otherwise, if IBM and Microsoft do not choose to cooperate to invent new kind of computer products, their traditional computer products will be not popular to be accept to use to compare their computer manufacturing competitors. Because, future computer trends to cheap, more using functions, small size, light weight , clear visible and touch feeling screen. in order to attract computer buyers choices more easily.

On conclusion, it is possible that scientists invention knowledge may bring economic growth indirectly. Their invention choice or invention decision may assist our future economy development rapidly or slowly. Hence, knowledge is one invisible hand to influence global economy either it can bring growth or recession in possible.

Knowledge how influences global online shopping times increase

Why may knowledge influence economic growth? Have they close relationship between knowledge and economic growth or recession in behavioral economy view? I shall attempt to indicate evidences to explain these two questions as below:

IN fact, human development had been experiencing from agricultural stage to industrial manufacturing stage, till to nowadays, service section stage,e.g. hotel tourism leisure development, and technological development stage, e.g. computer and robot development. All of these stages, which are created by ourselves knowledge, it means that how we decide choice, what social development direction will be caused. It it is true, it seems that global human knowledge may influence how our social future continue development. Our social economic growth or recession will be brought to influence from knowledge

indirectly.

It is focus on " behavioral economic concept" Economists define scarcity as the condition of wanting more than we can get with available resources. Scarcity is a fact of life. So, human can arrange ourselves resources in a lot of different ways, such as watching TV, buying a book, a car or traveling, but at any given time, ourselves have a fixed range of possibilities. SO, scarcity also describes the world on a collective level. As a society, we can produce only so many things, and we have to decide how those things are divided among many people. But, when social development, knowledge is very important to cause human (scientists) choose how to decide to invent any new things in order to satisfy human not limited need and using desire. So, the total quantity of available knowledge does not diminish as more and more people acquire it. So, ourselves every behavioral decision in life involves weighing the trade off between costs and benefits . We look at our options and decide whether it is worth giving up in order to get the other.

Economists explain this time cost of choice the " opportunity cost", opportunity cost is the value you could gained by choosing your next best alternative, the opportunity you have to pass up in order to take your first choice. Why may ourselves behavior have relationship between opportunity cost and economic growth? For computer invention example, when scientists feel compute products will be future human needs daily, for student learning using need, office tasks needs, watching movie, listening music leisure need,even playing game need. So, scientists had chose to spend time and resource and labor to invent computer products , they forgave to spend time and resource

and labor to invent other products. They computer invention is their opportunity cost, includes time, money, resource, labour, knowledge, mind on computer scientists , they had forgiven to spend these resources to research how to invent other kinds of new products.

However, when computer new products had been invented in success, e.g. desktop, laptop, can be popular to be accept to provide to global computer users to use. This kind of computer invention , its users number had been increasing, manufacturing computer number will be influenced to grow, due to computer invention will help developing and developed countries GDP growth rapidly since 1980 year , the earily first stage of computer invention had been experiencing during our global technological development history.

So, it implies that computer scientists had been confirmed to do right choice decision to forgive to spend resources, time, money and labour and knowledge to research how to invent any kinds of new products. They make right decision to research how to invent new computer products,even improve desktop to laptop and smart phone , hand carrying smart phone and computer both functions new products to satisfy computer users daily using needs. It is true opportunity cost to computer scientists case. Also, when past, our scientists do right choice to invent this kind of computer product, this kind of computer products can bring global economic benefits, such as government can increase profit tax form computer sellers, offices can use computers to reduce employees number, when computers can help offices to save much document, clerical employees number may be influenced to reduce, tasks can be simple from complex tasks, spending tasks time may be influenced to reduce by computerization of office, factories can apply computers or robots to replace workers to manufacture any kinds of products, such as cars, washing machine, rice cookers, radios, fans ,television etc. different kinds of electrical products. So workers number may be influenced to reduce and wage expenditure must be reduce.

Hence, new knowledge may help global societies to bring economic growth, such as past scientists had decided to forgive to spend time, resource, money, labor, skill, knowledge to research how to invent any kinds of new products, it is possible that they have some different kinds of new products concept choices, computer concept is only one kinds of choice among these new different kinds of new products invention concepts. However, they need to choose only one kind of new product invention among of these different kinds of new product concept choices, because they have not enough resource to provide to them to invent in the past. Finally, they evaluate the weigh and cost between computer invention concept and other new products invention concepts. In fact, computer is one kind of "the bringing much economic benefits" new concept invention product choice.

I believe that if computer will be continue improved in order to bring more economic growth in possible. SO, scientists need to spend more time, resource, money, labor, skill, knowledge to research how to continue to improve traditional computers to bring more using functions, in order to help global different industries to reduce resource, time, labour , money aim to bring reducing cost spending expenditure benefits to global industries , due to societies had been experiencing " knowledge social stage". If societies need to apply computer technology to assist our societies can continue develop, when our societies' different industries, such as service, manufacturing, even agricultrial sectors, e.g. robots may help farmers to predict when it is right time to grow vegetable, or replace farmers to grow vegetable, fruit in farms to provide human have enough food to eat, or robots can help hotel to clean rooms, serve clients, robots can help cinemas to sell tickets, robots can help manufacturers to product new products in factories. So, technological products may help any kinds of industries to reduce employees number, improve efficiencies and productivities and reduce wages expenditure economic cost benefits.

Production possibilities economic concept knowledge indicates about who produces which goods and why. The fact that millions of people and firms around the global coordinate their activities to provide consumers with the right combination of goods and services seem like magic.

In fact, coordination doe snot happen by chance, nor does super-planner tells every one where to go and what to do. Instead, the global production time is a natural outcome of people every acting in their own self interest to improve their own lives. Economists call this coordination mechanism the " invisible hand", an idea that was first suggested by economic thinker Adam Smith.

In production possibilities frontier economic concept, it explains why IBM and Microsoft ought cooperate to manufacturer computers, their cooperation can bring more economic benefits to themselves and global computer users, e.g. more computer functions, reducing sale price, reduce computer workers manufacturing wages, and computer manufacturing workers number, increasing computer manufacturing and demand number, increasing profit to themselves and government profit tax income, increasing buyers number, offices can improve efficiencies and employees performance, reducing manufacturing cost expenditure, improving student learning ability, etc. different kinds of global economic benefits. Hence, in production possibilities frontier economic concept, IBM and Microsoft ought make cooperation decision in order to bring global economic benefits.

In fact, computer manufaturing industry is one competitive market, it is one in which truly informed, prices taking buyers and seller easily trade a standardized good or service. IBM and Microsoft need to cooperate in order to win their computer manufacturing competitors , if they hope to earn in global computer manufacturing top leader position. Otherwise, if IBM and Microsoft do not choose to cooperate to invent new kind of computer products, their traditional computer products will be not popular to be accept to use to compare their computer manufacturing competitors. Because, future computer trends to cheap, more using functions, small size, light weight , clear visible and touch feeling screen. in order to attract computer buyers choices more easily.

On conclusion, it is possible that scientists invention knowledge may bring eocnomic growth indirectly. Their invention choice or invention decision may assist our future economy development rapidly or slowly. Hence, knowledge is one invisible hand to influence global economy either it can bring growth or recession in possible.

Technology how influences consumer behavioral change

Can human behavior may help economic growth? Why human behavior and economic growth have close relationship? I believe that productivity growth in different industries, how the shares of

wages and profits, how taxation affects growth, how inventions which can bring global economic growth, create working chance, sale income chance, consumption chance, productivity chance,

wealth chance. These factors may bring global short term or long term economic growth. All of these factors hace close relationship between human invention and economic growth. I shall

explain as below:

For any kinds of things inventions example, are best regarded as a form of investments, and their volume depends in like manner, on their expected profitability. Investments opportunities are recreated by inventions investment. However, inventions may not be economig growth factor, but there is a high profitability that prior circumstances will bring them about, so learning from human past prior experience is important not just in scientific or engineering matters, but in other fields, such as business and social organization. So, research and development, such as human invention behavior which has chance to bring long term or short term economic growth.

I mean that human invention may be one kind of investment opportunity to bring global economic growth in possibility, because human new knowledge learning behavior may attribute to global new business invention chance to bring unlimited economic growth chance in nowadays society.

Hence, human can not neglect to create ourselves " invention mind or invention behavior" in order to help global economic growth more easily. SO, human invention may be one kind helping global economic growth new investment opportunity, which is created from " human learning behavior". IN fact, an improvement in investment opportunity method may be created by human " any kinds of new inventions behavior". SO, nowadays society, any kinds of new inventions of product, which ought help global societies to bring economic growth chance.

The theory of economic growth may be based on income, labor and land which every one knows and which are adequate. However, nowadays society had changed, such as scientific invention example, it can bring profit chance to business, creating job opportunities in global labor markets, such as smart phones, laptops, desktops, non-manual driving vehicles, electric energy cars invention etc. any kinds of new scientific invention products, they can bring new science products business chance, they must need to employ may manufacture labour, salespeople, transport workers,logistic store workers, admin staffs, transport workers, product invention staffs , marketing promotion staffs etc. different job positions to let global human can have chance to find these jobs to do in order to earn income. Moreover, any kinds of scientific product inventions , which can bring many new jobs positions chance to let global unemployed people have chance to work and earn income.Also, any kinds of new scientific products invention may create many new jobs chance to global and solve unequal wealth and income allocation problem to global human, even businesses have chance to sell these new scientific invention products to sell to global buyers to earn more profit.

I mean that " new products invention" may help global societies to reduce unemployment challenge and it can bring long term economic growth in global labour market view. Moreover, when any kinds of new product inventions, such as battery energy vehicle, non-manual driving auto vehicle or public transport tools, home washing machines, televisions, radios, fans, smart phomnes, laptops, electronic book reading tools, internet invention etc, different kinds of new scientific product inventions, they can bring " consumption opportunity" to let global consumers have chance to buy any kinds of new scientific inventionw which can also encourage global consumption rate raises in order to increase global wealth improvement rate speed rises up rapidly. So, global wealth rising rate whether which is rapid or slow, it depends on whether how many different kinds of new scientific products invention may be confirmed to sccess to sell in global business market.

Hence, investment on invention, which may be tangible evidence to create economic growth in the distribution of income , wages and profits between global labor, scientific inventions of products sellers,and global scientific inventions of products consumers. They have close relationship to be influenced to increase economic growth speed whether they are rapid or slow from " global scientific new products inventions". If human product invention scientists can attempt to research how to invent any kinds of undiscovered new kinds of products inventions, for example, if global any kinds of scientific product invention scientists can attempt to invest time to invent 100 kinds of new scientific products inventions in order to provide global human have chance to buy to use. Then, these 100 different kinds of scientific invention products may help global new invention of scientific products sellers to provide many different kinds of new jobs vacancies to let global unemployed or job seekers have chance to work and earn income.

So, global unemployed rate will have chance to reduce in global societies. Moreover, they can also help these new scientific products sellers to bring " earning profit chance", even these global " new product invention scientists who have earn product invention royalty income chance after they can invent any kinds of products in success.

Finally, global consumption market growth rate will be influenced to rise up, when in the year, there are 100 new kinds of new scientific products invention have been already sold to let global consumers have chance to choose the kind of target of scientific product to buy to use. So, global new economic growth rate speed , it can rise up rapid up or slow down, it depends on whether the year, global has how many kinds of new invention of scientific products" have been invented to prepare to sell in global scientific products sale marketin macro economic view.

Hence, economic growth and human invention behavior, which have cloase relationship . The list of anti-growth factors could be extended perhaps however. Hartwell (1983) has pointed out that economies have always contained a mixture of three main systems for making production, consumption, and distribution decisions namely, administered and market free enterprise. It was the gradual freeing of man's entrepreneurial talents from the bonds of custom and command that finally resulted in the remarkable economic growth of the industrial revolution. However, in the twrms of human history, sustained economic growth is rare, and this suggests that several conditions (Needham's Packet), rather than memely one or two , have had to be met before it earns occur.

It is also the case, however, that its occurrence has at least in some respects made its survival more probable. HUman scientific investment has improved communications, such as smart phone, internet email and increased education (learning) chance, such as distancel learning, AI learning writing method, listening language learning method, reading e-books from smart phone, laptop channel method, which can chance traditional classroom leanring method to new scientific channel learning method or which can change traditional telephone or post lewtter communication method to nowadays sending email, smart phone calling, whataps new scientific tool communication methos.

ON conclusion, the free societies are influenced by any kinds of new scientific products inventions, Human had began to accept how attempted to buy any kinds of new scientific products inventions to use. New scientific inventions of products, which has bring more fashable of undiscovered new scientifical inventions of products choice to satisfy human ourselves daily new products invention using needs in our daily lives. SO, human scientists whose any kinds of new products inventions which will bring more chance to help global societies to create new social economic growth in global societies.

How ebooks influence reader behavioral change ?

What does human network job mean ? Why may human network job be popular? Why human network job behavior may influence economy ? Nowadays internet is popular to use. We can apply internet to find data , search any new things, even earn money. Why does internet may become huma network job source. For example, e-publish may be one kind of new human network job. Any authors may apply internet channel to help them to sell electronic or paper books from e-publisher web store. They may apply facebook, you tub etc. any online channel to promote themselves new books to let new readers to know whether when they may buy themselves favourable new topic books to read from electronic publisher web store.

Thus, future electronic publisher industry may help any authors to build internet network platform to help them to sell and promote to advertise their any one new electronic or paper book topic to let global any one reader to choose to buy their any new topic books from electronic publisher web store easily and conveniently. However, it implies that electronic network platform author may be one kind of future new human network job in our societies.

How electronic network platform author job may bring economy benefit in macro economy view? A person can have few friends, contacts and still be very influential if these few friends and contacts are themselves highly influential, e.g. one author must not need to know any one reader in global society. When they like to choose any electronic books from electronic internet network platform. They may become the author's any one topic book buyer, when they feel the author's any one topic book is fun and attract they make decision to buth the strange author whose the topic book from electronic book publisher's platform web store conventiently in short time. Although, they are strangers, they do not know themselves , but the reader can understand what it way that made Google from writing platofrm to create new creative mind and typing network job method to replace traditional hand writing book method for global authors. It will be one kind of new human network writing job.

Hence, global any one reader can apply an innovative search engine , such as google.com to find whether whom author personal new topic books are value to read from internet. Then, the electroniuc publisher's web store may be new book store platform sale network to help the author to sell many electronic or paper books from electronic network platform in short time. So, internet may be future new network plaform to help global any one author to create network writing job absolutely. Furthermore, internet may be popular social media to help any one author to build goold relationship between his/her readers. It is one kind of new network, human network job. New authors do not need to buy many paper books to prepare to put in any one book shop warehouse. Their every book can print on demand to reduce out of book stock in any one book shop. They may choose to sell either electronic books or paper books both from any one book publisher web store. So, electronic network platform may be one kind of good writing channel to help human authors to create income and it can also help authors to bring new creative mind and new topic fun content books to let readers to know and buy to read from electronic publisher network platform.

Why does human behavior may be one kind of new human network job to bring global economic advantages. ALthough, it may be free income or without inocme, but the person does the network behavior, his/her behavior may be bring advantages to influence many other people's health. For this case, when a worker in a coffee shop in an airport gets a vaccination aganinst the flu, it does not only helps him or her stay healthy, but also helps the many travellers who might otherwise have been inflected if that workers caught the flu. So, the externality , the result implies the vaccination of even a part of a community conveys benefits to the whole community. For example, governments pay special attention to the vaccinations of school children, teachers, health mothers, and the elderly, categories of people particularly susceptible not only to catching, but also to transmitting a disease.

It is not accidential that governments are heavily involved with vaccination . When there are externalities, free market, fail to persuade individual incentives with society's their the worker's decision of whether to get a vaccine ends up attracting whether other people get sick. The workers might not fully take all these other people's potential suffering into account when making her or his vaccination decision.

As Stanford University does many suggestions, understand this and tries to help them make the right decisions and so providers free flu vaccines for its staff and students.

Small pockets of unvaccinated individuals can allow a disease to gain a spread more widely well-being. For example, parent weighing the costs and benefits of a vaccine for their child is not always thinking of the consequences of that vaccination to other people. THese are markets in which subsidizing or regulating behavior can make everyone better off. Because the reason for requiring that a child be vaccinated before enrolling in school is not just to protect that child, because each child's vaccination affects others via potential contagions.

Nowadays, although human had been technological success, e.g. internet invention brings economic online shopping chance to global business societies. COnsumer shopping method had been influenced to stay at homes to use internet to shopping by internet technological invention, even robot invention can bring global job model change to improve employee efficiencies and performance. However, whether technological invention can bring global economic development, such as America's economic growth whether it can be influenced to grow up by internet, or robot or e-commerce online shopping moedel.

ON conclusion, I believe that technology may affect consumer behavioral change because technology has changed not only how we produce and connect, but also allows more humans to create and test new objects and ideas, reducing the costs and risks of innovation, and product development, also in developing countries, for digitalization has also significantly impacted financial sector, e.g. facilitating online transaction, to e-commerce sector, e.g. advances in AI, machine leanring robotics. By 2025, we estimate that 50 billion devices will be connected to the industrial internet of things (IOT), while 70 percent of manufacturers are expected to use digital by 2022. However, I believe that what time is the most right to invest technology. During recession is the smart investing time , because a recession or economic downturn can be an unsetting time for investors and their finances. Stock prices often fall just as the economy starts to slow and workers get anxious about potentially losing their jobs, due to the slowdown, but recessions can actually be one of the best times to global manufacturers to make technological investment decision.

Intellectual consumer behaivor economic behaviors

What does intellectual human economic behaviors mean ? I believe that when we choose or decide to do intellectual behaviors, then our societies will be influenced to bring economic growth in consequence.I shall attempt to indicate pollution case to explain how and why eithet our intellectual or foolish behaviors may bring economic growth or recession in consequence as below:

On one hand, for air pollution social case aspect example, if we only consider to buy cars to drive for working aimr or holiday leisure aim. Then, our societies air will be polluted. Our health will be influenced to bad. Our car driving behaviors may cause global environment air pollution seriously. In long time, global air pollution will bring our bodies health to be bad. Although, ourselves car driving behaviors may bring our driving travelling leisure enjoyment and comfortable feeling in short time, also we so not need to pay public transport fare often, but we need to compensate ourselves health economic intangible loss due to air pollution , when cars number increases, dirty air will cause ourselves health to become bad.

In the result, we will need to pay more medical expenditure when we are old age, due to ourselves bodies will become bad, due to we breathe global dirty air every day, due to ourselves cars pollute air in long time, e.g. 10 to 20 years, even 30 more without limited air pollution environment. So, driving cars behavior may be one kind of human foolish behavior and our foolish behavior may bring ourselves future long time medical expenditure absolutely.

One the other hand, water pollution social aspect, if we often keep much rubbish to pollute sea, oil exploration processing pollute ocean , ships gas pollute ocean, then fishes will eat polluted food and drive dirty water, due to global ocean is polluted.

In fact, because human only to consider how to buy boats to carry on leisure enjoyment activities, or catch cruises to travel on the sea. Also, oil manufacturers only consider researching anywhere to find new oil exploration places to manufacture oil product, when their oil exploration processes pollute ocean . Consequently, global fishes drink polluted water or eat polluted food. They will have poison. SO, human will have high chance to eat poison polluted fishes, due to fishes are poison or are polluted.

So, human is doing foolish activities, we only hope to find oil exploration places to pollute ocean or we only spend money to buy ticket to catch ships to travel anywhere in global ocean. All of these human foolish behaviors will bring pollution to global ocean. On consequently, we will need to compensate to eat polluted or dirty or posion fishes, ourselves bodies health will be bad. In long time, we need have high chance to pay medical expenditure when we are old. So, pollution case may be one good example to explain how and why human foolish behavior may influence ourselves future need to compensate serious medical loss.

All of these human foolish behavior will bring pollution to global ocean. On consequently, we will need to compensate to eat polluted or dirty or poison fished , ourselves bodies health will be bad. In long time, we will have high chance to pay medical expenditure, when we are old. So, pollution case may be one good example to explain how and why human ourselves intellectual or foolish behaviors may influence future long time economic loss or economic growth or recession in micro and micro economic view.

On another water pollution aspect hand, if we often keep rubbish to sea, oil exploration processing pollutes ocean and ships‘ gas pollute ocean, then fishes will eat polluted food and drink dirty water, due to fishes will eat polluted food and drink dirty sea water because the global ocean is polluted seriously.

In fact, because human only consider how to buy boats to carry on any leisure water activities, or catches cruises to travel on the sea. Also, oil manufacturers only consider any where to find oil exploration places to manufacture oil products from ocean, when their pol exploration processes can pollute ocean. Consequently, global fishes drink polluted water or eat direct food. They will have poison. So, human will have high chance to eat poison fishes.

Otherwise, such as pollution case, it can influence inflation or deflation. Consequently, the reason indicates supply and demand theory. If air pollution is serious, then we will consider health issue, global cars demand number may be influenced to reduce, when global cars number demand will reduce, global car prices and supply number will need to change to fall down in order to attract or persuade global car consumers choose to make car purchase decision.

Hence, global car manufacture number and car price will be influenced to reduce, due to global air pollution issue. Consequently, deflation will occur because when the country citizen usually does not spend much extra saving money to buy car expensive goods. Money value will be low. Otherwise, if global car pollution is not serious, human considers to buy cars to enjoy driving leisure lives. So, global car demand is influenced to increase , also global car price will also influenced to increase.

Consequently, global human will choose to buy cars to drive. Due to we accept to spend extra saving to buy expensive car goods. Car sale price and supply may be influenced to rise up. Money value is influenced to reduce. Inflation may be influenced, due to global car consumers number increases, we would not have extra money to spend easily. Car expensive goods expenditure influences our spending habit to avoid to make car purchase decision more easily. So, human intellectual or foolish activities may bring inflation or deflation consequency in possible indirectly in macro economic view.

On conclusion, above pollution case explain that how and why human intellectual or foolish economic behaviors may bring inflation or deflation consequency as well as economic growth or recession consequency as well as any goods demand and supply increasing or decreasing consequency. It implies that human behavior may have indirect relationship to influence any goods demand and supply number to either increase or decrease result as well as any goods price will be influenced to increase or decrease in micro and macro economic view.

The relationship between social change and human behavior

Why does economic changes may influence human individual behavioral change? I shall attempt to indicate shopping behavior and staying at home behavior to explain their case and effect relationsip as below:

Human behavior can be influenced by economic change or economic change can be influenced by human behavior? Why does recession may influence consumers reduce shopping desire? In social recession suitation, it is possible that many people lose jobs suddenly, due to businessmen lose many customers. They need to make decision to reduce employees number in order to continue to keep businesses. Consequently, many firms (organizations) their employees may lose jobs. When they have much time, due to lose jobs, they will feel to avoid to spend too much time and money to go to shopping often. Many losing jobs people, they will often stay at homes.

So, they will reduce time to go to shopping, then non essential products won't their preferable choice purchase products. Hence, recession will change many losing jobs people their shopping or consumption desires to avoid to buy non essential products often . Usually when economic boom, many people have jobs to do because consumers number must increase when many people have jobs to do. Then, many people can accept to spend money to buy non essential products often. Many people feel spend time to go to shopping can satisfy their purchase of any kinds of new products useful psychology or desire. So, recession is one good example to explain it can influence many people do not like often to leave homes to go to shopping easily. Many people like to stay at homes, becaue they feel worry about spending too much shopping time when they leave homes. Their staying home time is one good negative shopping behavior example. So, economic change may influence human individual behavior changes , they have direct cause and efect relationship in behavioral economic view.

May human behavior influence economic change? Is it possible that human behavior may bring the country social economic change in macro economic or micro behavioral economic view ? I shall indicate publishing industry example. Do you feel that if there are many students feel learning is very important when they read many books or many of students feel interesting to read or they have reading new books in habit, then it is possible that the country will have many students like to spend time to go to any book shops to choose the books, they feel that they can help they learn new knowledge. Then the country will increase students number, they often spend time to visit any one book shop every week. Their visiting book shops behavior which may become their habits. So, the country will increase students number, they often spend time to visit book shops. Also, it implies that visiting book shops behaviors may be their behavioral habits.

So, when the country has many students often spend time to visit book shops , their visiting book shops behaviors may help any one book shop to raise books sale chance. So, the country's student individual often visiting book shop behaviors, their habitual visiting book shops behaviors must may assist help any one book shop to increase books sale number absolutely.

Consequently, any one book shop , its books sale bumber must be influenced to increase to increase because the country will have many students like or feel need visit book shops habit in order to choose any suitable books to buy to read at home in order to raise themselves learning effort. When the country has many bok shops often have many students visit their book shops, then their books sale number may be influenced to increase. It explain why student individual visiting book shop behavior may help any one book shop sale number increases also.

How human productive behavior may influence economic development

May any country which citizen behavior assist themselves country development? It is one cause and effect economic question. I mean that if the country itself citicen can not concentrate mind or energy to choose to do one kind of industry in order to let themselves country can bring the most benefit, then whether the counry itself economy can bring the most serious economic benefit. I shall attempt to indicate these countries themselves indistry choice to explain whether these countries themselves citizen productive behavior may help themselves countries to achieve the largest economic benefits. I shall indicate as below:

New Zealand farmer individual wine productive behavior

For New Zealand country example, this country concerns itself effort is foucs on farming agricultural aspect. So, this country has many farmers

concentrate on farming agricultural aspect. May New Zealanders choose to spend time to produce different kinds of wines, e.g. wine or red grape wine is for the people are eating meat, or they are eating dinner.

When these New Zealanders their behaviors choose to do farming or agriculture to grow and produce different kinds of taste of white or red grape wine drinking products job. Themselves grape agriculture behavior will influence these New Zealanders themselves, they can learn how to improve different kinds of grape wine drinking products in order to achieve every kinds of white or read grape wines taste improving aim during their white or red grape producing process.

Why can New Zealander every individual white or read grape wine producers improve their white or read grape wine taste more easily? In behavioral economic view, it can explain that why any one New Zealander white or read grape wine producer can be encouraged or excited or persuaded to concentrate nervous and energy and effort to learn how to improve their white or red grape wine products easily.

In fact, New Zealand is one agricultural food export country. It has good natural environment resource , e.g. land, seed to provide any one farmer to produce themselves any kinds of agricultrual food products, e.g. fruit, or wine food products. Because New Zealanders know themselves country has enough natural resource . So, in common, many New Zealanders choose to attempt to do farming agricultural jobs in order to export themselves any kinds of fruit or meat or wine products to overseas or sell to domestic in order to earn profit.

So, when these New Zealand farmers number has been increasing every year. This country farmers will feel themsleves competition between this New Zealand farmers themselves are serious due to they may feel New Zealanders choose to do agriculture businesses in order to export themselves different kinds of farming food to overseas or sell to local to earn profit.

Hence, when many New Zealand farmers feel that farmers number has been increasing every year. They will feel themselves competition is serious. They must need to spend much time and nervous and effort to research what method is the best how to produce the best taste of white or red grape wine products in order to let local or overseas wine buyers to choose to buy his/her producing white or read grpae products to drink.

Hence, in competition psychological view, may influence many New Zealand white or reaad wine producers had been beginning to change their learning behavior on researching what method is the best in order to produce the best quality of taste red or white wine products to sell in order to attract overseas or local white or read grape wine drinkers to choose to buy his/her wine products. Their behavior will focus on learning how to raising or improving white or read grape wine taste method more than only focus on producing a large number white or red grape wine products. They believe wine quality is more important to compare wine producing number. So, New Zealand wine producers themselves wine producers behaviors have been changing on concentrating on researching wine quality method aspect more then wine producing number aspect in behavioral economic view.

America high technological productive behavior

For America example, US is one high technological country, it owns many high technological knowledge talent inventors, e.g. computer science inventors. Hence, US must attract many diferent countries owning high technological computer inventors choose to go to US to develop their computer science profession career. Also, it seems that when many computer science inventors or professions choose to go to US to develop themselves computer science new career. In behavioral economic view, due to their leaving themselves countries choice, which may bring influence themselve country job behaviors need to be changed. They must need to adapt US new live. Because they will forgive their past computer science job. These computer science professionals need to spend time to adapt US new lives. They " past computer science job behaviors" will need to be changed to their new US any computer employer's new computer science job model.

Because their traditional computer science jobs needed to be forgot in their themselves countries. They will feel their old computer science job knowledge and behavior needed to change in order to let their US any one new of computer company employer feels satisfactory to accept their new working behavior in any one US computer organization.

So, on the other hand, many US computer company employer will feel that they must need time to accept any one new overseas computer science professions their working behaviors, their working attitude daily, because these foreign comouter science professional, their past computer working behaviors and working attitude must be different to US domestic computer science professions.

In behavioral economic view, these overseas computer science professions, their working behaviors and attitude must be needed to change in order to adapt any one US new computer company itself domestic or local computer science professional stafs themselves daily working behaviors and attitude because these overseas and local computer science professionals must need to team work together.

In behavioral economic view, it is only one way that foreign computer science professionals must need to change themselves past country traditiona daily working behaviors and attitude in order to cooperate with these US local computer science professionals in teams more easily.

Consequently, if these foreign compute science professionals can change their past working behaviors and attitude to let any one US local computer science professional feels to cooperate with them easily in short time. Then, the US computer company itself whole computer professional teams themselves efficiencies will be influenced to raised or improved by the changing past working attitude and working behaviors of these foreign computer science professionals. So, in behavioral economic view, only if US any one computer company hopes itself computer teams themselves efficiency can be raised or improved when it decides to employ foreign computer science professionals and US domestic computer science professionals. They need to work in teams together. They must need to let these foreign computer science professionals to know how to change their working behaviors and attitude to let their domestic computer science professionals feel easy to work together. Then, the US computer company itself whole team efficiency must be rasied or improved easily in short time.

China share market investing behavior

For China share market example, economic development depends on financial market. Because if many Chinese have interest to invest to carry on shares buying and selling activities in orde to learn how to earn shares interest and share profit when the China shareholder can make decision to sell himself/herself shares in the the high price, then he/she can earn money when he/she can sell the China company's shares in the high sale share price position.

If China has many Chinese like to spend time to carry on investing shares activities. Themselves shares buying and selling behaviors will influence China has many companies can increase fund from many Chinese shareholders in order to have enough money to expand or develop themselves businesses in China in long term.

Consequently, when China can have many Chinese like to attempt to carry on buying and selling shares investing behaviors in China share market. Themselves buying and selling shares behaviors can help many Chinese companies have effort to increase enough money or capital in order to continue to do their businesses in long term absolutely. So, it explains why when many Chinese become shareholders , they can assist China will have many companies continue to develop their businesses if many Chinese like to carry on shares buying and selling investing behaviors in long time in China financial investment market nowadays in behavioral economic view.

Why has any individual country have many people invest share behavior which can influence the country's macro consumption desire?

I shall apply shares market buying and selling investment behavior to explaiin why shares investment behavior which may impact the country's overal consumption desire as below:

In behavioral economic view, I assume that when the coutry has many people have interest to attempt to carry on shares buying and selling investment behavior, then their frequent shares buying and selling behaviors which may bring negactive consumption desire or shopping desire of these shares investors their consumer behavior.

The reason is simple, when the country has many share buyers number suddenly been increasing rapidly. Consequently, these large group share investors must need to spend much time to research any kinds of company shares variations, whether when their share prices will rise up of fall down in order to achieve buying the company's shares in the lowest price and selling the company's shares in the highest price level in order to earn profit.

Basic on this reason, they must need to spend much extra time to research share prices changing behavior every day, e.g. one working person will wait to leave his/her job, after he/she can spend time to gather data to research the day's share price changing behavior after dinner. So, the working person's right time may be his/her share price market research behavior. Before he/she may spend his/her night time to go to shopping after dinner, but nowadays, he/she will fogive to do his/her shopping behavior before dinner or after dinner at hight sometime. He/she will make decision to spend much night time to turn on computer to click on share market website to research his/her share purchase choice to investigate whether his/her share price whether it rises up or falls down at the moment in order to make his/her share buying or selling decision at ever night time.

I mean the when the country has many people are share investors, their shares investment behavioral spenging time which will influence many shops lose customers at might often because the country will have many people feel need to spend night time to turn on computer or watch television to investigate share price variation. So, the country will have many people / share investors choose to stay at home in order to carry on share price variation investigation behavior, they need to listen share market update news from radios or watch the share market update news from computer or TV at home every night. Consequenly, they must reduce times to leave themselves homes at night. So, their shopping behavior also will be reduced. Because these share investors feel need to spend time to investigate share price variation news at homes which can bring economic benefits (high opportunity benefits) when they choose to forgive to leave homes to go to shopping times (opportunity cost) every night.

On conclusion, it seems that when the country has many people are share investors, then their share price investigating behavior may bring negative shopping emotion at night. Consequently, the country's any one shop may lose many customers from this share investor consumer group in behavioral economic view. Hence, when the country's share investors number had been increasing rapidly, it will influence any shops lose many customers from this share investing customer group at night frequenly in short time, even long time in behavioral economic view, because their shopping desires or shopping emotion will be brought negative feeling when they make decisions to spend much time to listen radios or watch TV or computers share price update nes at night. Hence, share market will bring negative impact to influence consumer shopping desire or negative shopping emotion in behavioral economic view.

Can technology influence human shopping behavioral change?

Nowadays, technological development has reached mature stage, whether technological mature stage may bring positive or negative shopping emotion influence to global consumers. I shall aplly internet inventin or ecommerce shopping channel tool to explain whether internet technology can bring postive or negative influence to global consumer behavior in behavioral economic view.

Internet is a good technological tool, it brings e-commerce business chance. In fact, commonly, global has have many businessmen choose to use internet channel to carry on their products transactions between global online-buyers and their electronic websites. So, global many shoppers had begun to feel online shopping is more convenient to compare visiting shops shopping. Their shopping behaviors have been changed from internet technological tool. Global has many shoppers choose to buy any products from any overseas or local businessmen their web stores. They only need to spend time to find any businessmen their webstores to choose the most suitable products to pay visa to buy from their webstores. at homes. So, in general, global had have may shoppers had changed their shopping behaviors from visiting shops to visiting webstores at homes often.

So, it seems that internet technological tool had influenced global many shops disappear, but internet webstores will be replaced their actual shops on streets. Some of businessmen either they choose webstores to replace shops or choose websotes and shops both or still keep shops only. Hence, internet tool influences global businessmen have three kinds of products sale channels to let globa local and overseas consumers to choose how to buy their products.

However, in fact, many of global shoppers, youngers and olders had begun to accept to buy any products from webstores. They feel to spend time to leave homes to visit shops , their shopping behaviors will be wasted time to not essential part to their daily lives. Hence, since internet technological invention, it had changed many consumers their traditional visiting shops shopping habit to change to buying products from webstores channel.

However, on the one hand, internet creates webstores ecommerce shopping channel to let global many consumers do not need to leave homes to go to shopping. It brings negative visiting shops shopping emotion to global general consumers nowadays. But on the other hand, it also brings positive visiting internet webstores shopping emotion to global general consumer nowadays. So, it seems that global many consumers feel that they often do not need to spend much time to go out shopping. Many global consumers feel convenient and enjoy to choose any products to buy from different internet webstores, when the online buyer chooses the most suitable product, he she only needs to pay visa card to buy the product from the online seller's webstore conveniently at home.

Hence, online shopping can bring economic benefit to online buyers, e.g. avoiding walking time or spending transport fare to visit the shop to go to shopping, shortening or reducing shopping time to do another important matter.

On conclusion, global many consumers began feel online shopping can bring more economic benefits on shortening shopping time, avoiding transport fare spending aspect. So, online shopping will be popular shopping behavior for future long time. It may encourage global many shoppers can make rapid shopping decision in short time in order to carry on any products buying transaction to global any one online shopper in short time easily in behavioral economic view. So, global many businessmen had begun to build themselves one attraction webstore in order to persuade different countries consumers to choose to click themselves webstores from internet channel to buy any kinds of products in short time easily.

So, internet technology had changed consumers traditional shopping behaviors to build positive online shopping emotion as well as raise online sellers' any products sale chance easily in behavioral economic view.

Why and how human behavior may influence the country's economic growth or recession?

When one country has many people choose to do the same matter for one period, whether their behavior may influence the country's pvera; economic growth or recession . I shall attempt to indicate cases toexplain their relationship as below:

For flowing rubblish behavioral case example, do you feel that when the country has many people often flow rubblish on the streets, instead of their flowing rubblish behavior may bring streets dirty? But, their flowing rubblish behavior may explain that this country has people may have enough money to buy food to ear, or enough cloths to wear, enough bottles of water to drink, even they may have enough money to buy new television, radio, refrigeraters , washing machines, desktops or laptops electronic home products from old to new to use in order to satisfy their living needs. So, when they flow old electronic home products, their flowing old home electronic products behaviors may seem that they have enough money to buy other new home electronic products to replace old home electronic products to use at homes.

However, it seems thaat this country ought have many people have jobs to do. So, many of them, they can easy to make purchase decison to flow any old home electronic products and buy any new home electronic products to use

. Because this country has many people have jobs to do. So, they can often not use old home electonic products to become rubblishs to flow on streets after they had bought any kinds of new home electronic homes.

In fact, it also implies that this country's economy grows rapidly. So, many businesses can glow up rapdly. When they expanded their businesses, they must need to increase employees number in order to let they help themselves to raise productivity or serve their clients absolutely. So, when the country has many businesses can grow up, it seems that its economy must be better or it is improved to compare past. Due to many different kinds of home electronic products had been often bought to use by this country people in this period. So, this country's any streets can be observed that expensive electronic home products were flowed on streets anywhere. then, this country will have many electronic home products sellers can sell their home electronic products very easily. When this country has many people can find any kinds of jobs to do easily. So, due to unemploymen rate had been decreasing.

In behavioral economic view, as this many electronic home products rubblish country case, we can observe this country may have many people have jobs to do. So, consumption number has been increased long time. So, cheap food, or expensive home electronic products may be rubblish on any streets. This country's people , their flowing rubblish behaviors may be explained that many of people have enough jobs to do, so they have ability to buy any good taste food to eat or buy any kinds of expensive electronic home products to use. So, this country's economy may be improved for this long period. So, in behavioral economic view, when this country can have many electronic home products rubblishs are flowed on anywherer in streets frequently. It seems that this country will have many people have jobs to do, so it causes they often change old home electronic products or replaced them easily, when they have enough income to spend to buy any kinds of new home electronic products to use at homes easily. Moreover, their flowing old electronic home products behaviors also indicate that this country has many people their salaries may be increased in possible from their emplyers. When this country can have many different kinds of home electornic products are sold. It means that this country's electronic home products needs or demand had been increasing, due to many people have jobs to do and income increases to excite their living of needs also improve. Consequently, this country may seem have better economic improvement. We can observe from this country's electronic home products rubblish incrcasing incomc in thcis pcriod.

On conclusion, this country ought experience economic growth at this period. So, " flowing expensive electronic home rubblish increasing number " may seem that this country's economic growth is rapidly in this period, due to many people have jobs to do as well as salaries increase in this period.

Technology how impacts human behavior changing?

Technology how influences human behavior to bring changing? For example, online share purchase and sale transaction from smart phone brings share investor can do share buying or selling transation in any where and any time conveniently, non manual driving auto vehicle, bring car owner feels comfortable and spends free time to do other matter, e.g. reading, listening mucis in himself or herself car freely. electrical energy vehicle can help car owner to reduce air polluton and it can brings the drivers do not feel drive long time in any journeys in order to avoid air pollution for environmental protection responsible car drivers in our societies. Thus, they will drive long time in any journeys when they can drive electronic energy cars to replace oil energy cars.

However, online technology can also bring consumers can choose to stay at homes to buy any things from seller individual online webstore conveniently. Such as online technology can bring shoppers do not need to spend much time to visit shops to buy any things. They can choose any kinds of products from any online sellers individual online webstores conveniently at homes. Online technology excite busy consumers can make purchase decision easily as well as it can help online sellers sell any kinds of products from internet easily.

In behavioral economic view, technology can change human behavior to be improved, it can let human feels comfortable, more free time ro use, rapid making any decisions, such as apply smart phones to make share purchase or sale transaction decision, online shopping decision, even travelling any where decision in short time, when the traveller finds the most cheap hotel accommodation room price and air ticket price frm any travel agent online tourism webstore, then the potential travel customer can follow the online hotel accommodation price and air ticket price data to make decision when to buy the air ticket from the airline travel agent or make decision when to prebook which hotel accommodation room to go to the country to travel from online travel agent tourism webstores. So, technology can encourage global any country travelers to make anywhere to trvel rapidly. If the traveler can find the country's general hotel rooms and airline tickets prices had been decreasing more sightly. The traveler may make travel decision to choose the country to travel in short time, then he/she can prebook the country;s any hotel room and airline ticket to pay by visa fraom the country's any hotel and airline travel agent webstores., before one week, even one month or more easily. Hence, online technology can also encourage traveler individual frequent travel times to be increased, due to global travelers can find any hotel rooms and airline tickets prices from internet conveniently at homes. They do not need to spend time to visit any airline travel agent to enquire travel choice country's hotel rooms prices and airline ticket prices. They can compare global travel of countries choices ' all hotels rooms and airline agents air tickets prices to make prebook airline seat and hotel room decision before one week, one month even six months early.

On conclusion, online technology can encourage global travelers can make travelling any where and when traveling time desicions easily. It can excite tourism industry develops in long time. Also, such as electricity cars invention can encourage environment protection car owners do car purchase decision easily, because they can choose to drive electronic energy cars to replace oil energy cars in order to avoid air pollution occurs easily. So, electronic cars can increase electronic car purchasrs number, due to many of environmental protection attitude of car owners can choose to drive electricity cars to bring air cleans, even non -manual driving cars can encourage lazy driving and free time driving car owners to choose to buy non-manual (artificial intelligent) cars to drive , because they can spend much free time to read, listen music or do any matters in themselves cars, they do not need to drive cars, robotic (AI) auto driving machine is such one non-manual driver to help them to drive themselves cars confidently. So, non-manual driving cars can attract lazy and enjoying free time driving car owners to choose to buy to replace traditional manual cars to drive easily. Moreover, online share transaction can help any share investors to make share buying and selling decision in short time easily. When they can apply smart phones technological tool to carry on share buying and selling activities easily. They can observe any share rising or falling price suitation from smart phones in any where any any time easily. So, smart phone technology can help global any shareholders to make share purchase and sale transaction easily. So, technology can encourage human makes decision in short time rapidly.

How and why employees behaviors may influence economy development?

In behavioral economy view,I believe the country's any organizational employees behavior may bring indirect relationship to influence the country's long term economic development. I shall indicate past manufacture industry social development period to explain their relationship. For many countries' past business activities had belonged to manufacturing industry, such as US, UK past before 1980 year, it focused on steel manufacturing and steel manufacturing related machine products. So, US, Uk developed countries manufacturing industries may be past main country's economic income sources. I assume US , UK past had one million number different kinds of industries. They ought had about seven houndred thousand number organizational businesses were belonged to manufactured industry. They may include:

Steel manufacturing and steel related machine manufacturing, e.g. vehicle manufacturing, home appliances, e.g. washing machine, television, radio, refrigerate cooler, heater, air condition etc. different kinds of different kinds of steel -related manufacturing machine, they were manufactured from US, UK steel machine manufacturers. So, US, Uk the other three hundred thousand number industry may be general service industry, e.g. hotel service, restaurent, cinema, public transport service, tourism lesiure , wine bar, supermarket etc. different kinds of non-manufacturing industries business organizations were operated in UK, US past before 1980 year.

So, in UK, US developed countries industry development history, they ought have high percentage of businesses belonged to steel related manufacturing machine and steel products. Also, in the past before 1980 year, US, Uk business employers , they employed many workers are manufacturing workers. They needed to spend long time to work in factories. They were skillful workers, and they are trained to manufacturing cars, washing machine, television, heater, etc. even steel itself different kinds of steel related products to prepare to deliver to their shops to sell to US, Uk local or overseas clients.

So, I believe that past UK, US ought employ many employees, they belonged to skillful manufacturing workers, manufacture increasing steel machine or steel related machine number of products rapidly daily. So, if UK, US had had many of these manufacturing factories owned high skillful workers, then their manufacturing steel-related machine or steel both kinds of products number must be influenced to raise rapidly. Consequently, their steel machine manufacturing products would been exported to overseas or would been sold to local both markets , they may be influenced to raise sale number. They (these manufacturing workers) needed to be trained to know how to manufactur these different kinds of machine products in the efficient teams and they ought to be trained to raise their efficiencies in order to shorten time to manufacturing many kinds of steel related manufacturing machine or steel itself products rapidly. So , if their efficiencies and manufacturing performance was improved, these US, UK any one manufacturing worker and their teams ought achieve raising productivities significantly.

Hence, when past UK, US manufacturing industry development period, if these two countries' any manufacturing factories could have many manufacturing workers could be trained to be skillful and proficient manufacturing workers. Then, in past every day to these factories workers, they ought help their steel or steel related manufacturing employers to raise any kinds of machine or steel products number in every team. So, when past in the manufacturing industry development, US, UK could have many factories' manufacturing workers themselves steel or steel related machine products manufacturing skill could be trained to to improve to any kinds of these machine or steel manufacuring products quality as well as their products number could be influenced to raise by themselves skillful improvement significantly every day.

Then, what would be influenced to occur to past UK, US manufacturing industry period? In behavioral economic view, when these two manufacturing industry developed countries, such as UK, US , if they had many factories workers can be trained to improve their skill in order to achieve any kinds of steel or steel-related machine products quality could be improved as well as products manufacturing number could be also increased absolutely.

In consequence, past UK and US both countries ought increase themselves any kinds of steel and steel related machine products number to be supplied to themselves local shops to let local clients to choose any one kind of machine manufacturing products to buy easily as well as they could also export to supply overseas any countries to buy their different kinds of steel or steel related machine products to let overseas steel or steel related manufacturing machine product buyers, they can have many of these different kinds of these steel or steel-related different kinds of manufacturing machine from UK and UK these both countries easily to compare other countries.

On conclusion, I believe that past US, and UK macro manufacturing industry income GDP would increase significantly. So, they would have good economic growth performance because when many of these manufacturing workers themselves manufacturing effort could be improved. So, it explained when employees manufacturing abilities can influence economic growth indirectly.

Robots invention whether they can help organizations to raise efficiencies or inefficiencies?

In behavioral economic view, in any organizations, when the organization hopes its worker teams can raise efficiencies , the organization may choose to increase more workers number and/or it can provide training to improve these workets themselves skills in order to raise their efficiencies. For one warehouse example, when the warehouse increases many goods , they are needed to delivered these goods from the shelves to the delivering destination locations. If this warehouse supervisors feel these workers themselves goods delivery speeds are slow, which is possible due to this warehouse's workers number is not enough. So, this warehouse supervisor ought increase workers number in order to increase their goods delivery speed in order to deliver goods from the shelves to every indicated goods delivery destination in order to let any one lorry driver can transport the right kinds of goods and ensure the accurate goods number to transport to any one client home rapidly.

However, if this warehouse supervisor planed to buy several warehouse goods delivery robots to assist these warehouse workers to find the right kinds of goods from shelves and then deliver to the right destination location in the warehouse. So, these warehouse orkers can concentrate on counting the accurate goods number and ensuring the right kinds of goods in order to prepare to let lorry drivers to transport these goods to these goods of buyers themselvers homes rapidly. Consequently, in the first step, robots can concentrate on finding th right goods from shelves and delivers them to the right goods transportation of location destination. Then, in the second step, these warehouse workers can concentrate on counting the accurate goods number and ensuring the right kinds of goods in order to prepare to put them to the lorry. Consequently, when warehouse robots and warehouse workers can cooperate to work together, the most important, robots, can deal on finding the right kinds of goods and deal on delivering the accurate number of goods of job duty as well as these warehouse workers can only concentrte on counting the right kinds of goods number in order to avoid it has none any mistake of wrong kinds of goods and inaccurate goods of delivery number to be transported to the lorry and to deliver to any one buyer's home.

So, it seems that warehouse robots ought help any one warehouse worker to raise himself efficiency and avoid goods delivery of mistake occurrence easily as well as their help to warehouse workers that can let any one goods buyer feels their goods can be delivered to their homes rapidly. Moreover, warehouse robots can also help these warehouse workers to raise efficiencies because warehouse robots can help them to shorten goods delivery time between any one shelf and any one goods delivery destination of location in the warehuse because robots may help them to find the right kinds of goods from the right shelf in the short time. So, any one worker does not need to spend long time to seek anywhere is the right shelf location for the kind of goods when the kind of goods are needed to deliver to the buyer's home from lorry. Warehouse robots can help them to do this aspect of " finding the goods from the right shelf in short time job duty". So, any one warehouse worker only needed tospend less time to do the counting of any right kind of goods number and ensuring the right kind of goods job duty. Consequently, this warehouse 's any one worker, his any one kind of goods delivery time may be reduced, because robots' assistance and they may have more confidence to avoid mistake to deliver the wrong number of goods and/or the wrong kind of goods to any one goods buyer's home.

On conclusion, it seems that warehouse robots ought may help any one warehouse worker to raise efficiency for any one team in the warehouse as well as the warehouse any one supervisor does not need to spend much time to observe any one worker individual performance for " goods delivery job duty aspect" because their goods delivery job duty that had been replaced to do by these several warehouse robots. Robots can achieve the more accurate of right kinds of goods and the right number of goods delviery job performance to compare any one of human warehouse worker themselves right kinds of goods of delivery and right number of goods of delivery job performance. So, when robots can participate to cooperate with this warehouse's any one worker to do their goods of delivery job duty in this warehouse every day. Then, robots can raies any one of supervisor individual confidence in order to let they do not need to spend time to observe any one of worker individual whose goods of delivery job performane. They can concentrate on supervising any one worker whose goods transport to lorry in the final step in order to avoid to deliver wrong goods number and / or wrong kind of goods to any one goods buyer's home every day. Consequently, this warehouse's overall teams of their delviery of goods performance many be improved by robotss' participatin to goods of delivery task as well as this warehouse's oveall teams themselves efficiencies may be influenced to raise by robots' goods of delivery task participation.

Why social behavior may influence organizational strategy needs to be changed ?

Why any organizations need to know whether nowadays social behaivor how has been changing in order to implement the kind of the most right strategy to achieve the profit aim pursue in possible. I shall indicate nowadays ecommerce or online, customer shopping behavior to explain above question concerns they ought have close relationship between social behavior and organizational strategic choice or organizational behavioral changing need.

On nowadays ecommerce business, or online shopping model, this kind of shopping model in global many young and old age consumers like to apply internet tool to choose any country sellers website stores in order to stay at home to buy any kinds of products from themselves webstores in global societies.

In fact, online shopping model had been popular for long time above to twenty years. Most of global sellers will make decision to design themselves webstores in order to attract global many online buyers to choose to buy their products from themselves webstores. So, it seems that social consumers purchase behaviors had been changed to online shopping from internet invention.

Hence, social consumers purchase behavioral changes may influence any organizations' strategies need to be changed from visiting shops purchase strategy model to online purchase strategy model, if the seller still concentrate on concentrate on considerate how to design itelf , but neglects to considerate how to design itself webstore, e.g. how to design attract product photos to put on itself webstore, how to arrange sale price information location to be putted on webstore and visa card payment location on itself webstore in order to let any one online buyer can feel very easier to buy itself any kinds of products from itself webstore. Then, its potential online buyers will be influenced to increase number when they can find this online seller itself any kinds of products photes and every kinds of product sale price information and visa card payment channel locations easily from itself webstore.

So, it implies that nowadays any one seller ought need to design one webstore to let any one online overseas and domestic consumers can have chance to click itself webstore to choose any one kind of product to buy conveniently when he/she does not hope to leave him/her home to go to shop, because nowadays social shopping behaviors had been influenced to change when internet invention, them it gives another online purchase method to replace visiting shops purchase method to global any one buyer in nowadays societies.

So, if nowadays any one seller still concentrate on how to design itself shop display in order to put any kinds of product on shelf in order to let any one visiting shop customer to find the kind of product to buy, but it neglects to change to choose to pursue another new technological shopping method, such as webstore purchase method in order to implement effective strategy to design the most right webstore as well as in order to attract global overseas and local consumers to find itself webstore easily from website and find its any one kind of product phots and sale price and visa card payment button in order to choose to buy itself any kinds of products in the short time. Consequently I believe that the seller will lose many customers from overseas and local when its other same or similar product sellers choose to design themselves webstores in order to let global any one product buyer can buy themselves any one kind of product when they can pay visa card to buy their products from them webstores conveniently when they stay at home habitly. Then, the seller will lose many global potential customers in long time.

On conclusion, in behavioral economic view, any consumer behavioral social changing, which will influence any in order to avoid customers number loses significantly . In future time, organizations need to make rapid decision in order to implement the most reasonable and the most useful strategy in order to avoid global potential customers number reduces or lose them in long time. So, social behavioral changing environment ought influence any global organizations need to decide how to change themselves strategies in order to avoid customers loses significantly in future time.

How and why human behavior may influence economic growth or recession?

May ourselves daily behaviors influence our global societial continue economic growth or recession? Do they have cause and effect close relationship between human behaviors and global economic growth or recession? I shall apply behavioral economic theory to analyze and explain whether ourselves daily behaviors and our global societial economic growth or recession which have close cause and effect relationship as below:

Every country itself economic development must depend on any business activities, otherwise, any kinds of business activities must need ourselves business activities or behaviors in order to achieve any business activities as well as achieve the country's overall economic development in macro view.

However, any country's overall business activites or behaviors which must depend on any kinds of individual businessmen, themselves employees daily working behavior or activity or performance in order to help them to attract or increase many clients number to acieve " earning profit" aim. So, it seems that any individual business, itself overall every department individual working behavior is one main factor to influence the company's overall business performance.

For agricultural fruit and meat food farming industry example, such as New Zealand is a farming main target industry country. It had had many New Zealanders were daily themselves own farming businesses for many years. Their farming businesses include growing fruit, sheep, cow, pig pork, meat etc. food sale business. If the New Zealand farmer owned a large size farming land, then he will choose either growing fruit or feeding sheeps, pigs, cows to be meat to to transport to New Zealand supermarkets to help them to sell to their farmers meet to New Zealanders in order to earn profit. Thus, if the New Zealand farmer owned large size of farming lands, then he needs to employ many farming employees (farming workers) to help him to carry on farming business daily tasks, e.g. picking up friuts, feeding pigs, cows, sheeps to eat food daily. These daily farming jobs are very important to influence this New Zealand farmer's meats or fruits sale number whether they can be easy or diffcult to sell in New Zealand supermarkets , if these farming workers can own encough farming knowledge or skill to know how to pick up fruits method and make judgement to know whether it is right time to pick up the kind of fruits from the trees , as well as know how feed this pigs, sheeps, cows to eat food in order to let they are better health. Consequently, their farming behaviors which can let these animals can provide the best taste and enough meat from these animals to let New Zealander to buy to eat from New Zealand any one supermarket. Even these New Zealand farming workers can know whether the kinds of fruits, e.g. oranges, apples, gapes etc. fruits whether they ought be picked up from the trees at the right time. Consequently, they can make judgement to decide to pick up any kinds of the best taste fruits to let any one New Zealander to buy to eat from any one supermarket in New Zealand. Otherwise, if they do not make judegement to know whether the kind of fruit ought not be picked up because they still need longer time to continue grow up to increase fruit size and better taste from the trees in order to let any one fruit buyer can feel better taste when they eat this kind of fruit later. If they can buy this kind of fruit to eat later, then this New Zealand farmer's his fruit buyers can buy the best taste of this kind of fruit to eat from an yone supermarket in New Zealand. Consequently, many New Zealand supermarkets will choose to buy any kinds of fruits from this farmer fruit supplier when they feel this farmer's fruits can provide more better taste fruits to compare other farmers' fruits.

Thus, due to New Zealand is one farming main income source country. It's any kinds of fruits and meats need to be export to overseas to sell , instead of local sale. It's GDP percent is very high to whole country 's overall income source. So, any one New Zealand farmer individual and any one farming worker individual working behavior will influence its economy whether it is influenced to grow or recession possible. Moreover, it also seems that farming workers' farming knowledge and skill will influence themselves farming daily activities to achieve the aim of the number of increase or decrease to any kinds of fruits whether they are better taste or the number of increase of decrease to any kinds of meats whether they are better taste to supply to any one New Zealand fruit or meat buyers to eat from any one New Zealand supermarket. So, it implies that any one New Zealand farming worker individual farming behavior may influence any kinds of fruits or any kinds of meat taste because they are transported to any one supermarket to sell in New Zealand.

Consequently, if New Zealans had many farmers can teach god farming knowledge and skill to let their any one farming workers know how to decide judgement to decide when it is right time to pick up any kinds of fruits from trees , or how to grow them on soil in order to let they can grow rapidly. Then, many different kinds of fruits can be provided to let any one New Zealanders can eat the best taste of fruits when their fruits are supplied to any one New Zealand supermarkets. Even, if they knew how to feed foods to pigs, cows, sheeps to eat daily. Then they can be more health and they can provide the best taste of meats to let any one New Zealanders can buy their meats from any one New Zealand supermarkets. Moreover, their fruits and meats can be transported to overseas to let any one country fruits or meats buyers can choose any kinds of New Zealand meats and fruits to buy to eat from themselves countries supermarkets. Then, many overseas fruit and meat buyers will perfer to choose New Zealand any kinds of fruits or meats to buy to compare other countries fruits or meats to buy when they go to any one local supermarkets.

On conclusion, it seems that New Zealand farming workers themselves farming behavior may influence their farming employers any kinds of fruits or meats sale number and income because their farming task behaviors must influence whether their fruits or meats taste are the better taste or worse taste to compare their other local farmers (the farmer competitors) whose fruits or meats taste. If tthe farmer's any one farming worker can be trained to learn how to know to feed animals skill and when is the most right time to pick up any kinds of fruits from trees or how to grow them on the soil methods. Due to these farming worker individual farming behavior may influence his different finds of fruits and meats sale number to be increase or decrease, so these any one New Zealand farmer must need to depend on any one farming worker whose farming working methods, if their farming working behaviors can be the best to influence any kinds of fruits to grow rapid or any kinds of pigs, cows, sheeps animals grow up rapidly , then their sale number may be increase significantly and their taste can be improved to let any New Zealand or overseas meat or fruit buyer to buy to eat to feel from any one New Zealand or overseas supermarkets, then New Zealand's agriculture industry must be influenced to increase. In the world, any one fruit or meat buyer must choose to buy New Zealand's fruit and meat to eat in prefer to compare other countries' fruits and meats. So, New Zealand's GDP may be influenced to raise from any one New Zealand farming worker individual farming working behaviors.

Reasons why human behavior may influence economic recession or growth?

Can ourselves daily behaviors or activies influence ourselves countries' economic growth or recession? I shall attempt to explain the reasons why they have direct or indirect relationship between human behavior and economy growth or recession as below:

I shall indicate environment pollition case to attempt to explain above question. Our societies had been experiencing servious environment pollution challenge. However, environment pollution , such as air pollution is caused by air planes and vehicles emission by air planes and vehicles emission as well as water pollution is caused by plastic rubblish, or dirty water or oil or gas chemical material, these both kinds of pollution ought may bring economic recession and this both kinds of pollution are caused by human ourselves daily foolish activities.

I believe human behavior and economy and pollution which have cause and effect relationship. I shall analyze this environment pollution case to explain why they have case and effect relationship between human foolish behavior and environment pollution and economic recession as below:

When global societies had many people like to buy cars to drive to bring emission to fresh air on the roads as well as many manufacturing factories will bring emission to pollute fresh aair in their manufacturing processes. Factories and cars will bring air pollution , due to factories need to pollute fresh air in order to manufacture many products and car owners need to drive their cars to go to offices or leisure places. Their cars will also bring emisson to pollute fresh air. On consequence, car owners themselves frequent driving behaviors and factory workers themselves frequent manufacturing behaviors may bring environment pollution. Technology or human behavior whether may influence economic growth or recession. Moreover, air planes also brings emission to pollute air when they are flying in sky. Also, when ships bring oil pollution or sea plastic rubblishs bring pollution to global oceans.

In fact, manufactuers and cars owners, such as factories workers manufacturing behaviours ans car owners driving behaviors and pilots driving air planes flying behaviors and ships transport behaviors, which may cause plastic rubblish, oil or gas emission to sky or sea or on the road to cause ocean and air pollution is serious. However, human ourselves need to buy cars to drive to satisfy ourselves driving leisure or enjoyment, travelers need to catch air planes to travel to enjoy leisure needs, factories workers need help factories to manufacture many products to sell to customers to satisfy their using needs. oil exploration needs to find lands to explore new oil lands.

All of these business and leisure activites may bring serious air and water pollution. However, due to serious air and water pollution will bring earth warming challenge , such as some countries temperature will be influences to rise up to 40 degree or higher br earth warming. However, earth warming is caused by air and ocean pollution. Pollution must be caused by human ourselves, driving cars leisure and factories manufacturing business activities. Hence, if human decided to continue to do these foolish behaviors, we only pursue to manufacture different kinds of industrial products or drive cars to enjoy leisure aims, but we also neglect ourselves behaviors may bring environment pollution. Then, earth warming or earth temperature will be influenced to rise up absolutely in long term. Moreover, if our future earth will be influenced to bring serious high temperature effect by human ourselves these foolish behaviors.

On consequencey, warth warming will bring serious economic losses in possible because when ourselves earth temperature had been influenced to rise up to 40 degree or high. Ourselves health will be caused poor, due to we will feel difficult breath, we must need often tried and hard to work, due to our nervous and health will be influenced to poor by pollution and earth warming effect. Also, we need to pay more money to see doctors when we had long life. Then, our societies will lose may strong labors to help manufacturers to work, e.g. factories will reduce workers number to help manufacturers to produce more different kinds of products, due to workers health is general poor. Due to lacking enough workers to manufacture products, our societies will begin to reduce enough supply number of products to sell to global consumers to satisfy their use needs.

On conclusion, in behaviroal economic view, our societies will lose many labors due to their bodies are not health by air and water pollution. Global economic and business activities will be influenced to worse by global workers reducing number reason. So, economic recession will begin to occur in possible when pollution reaches the serious level.

Can human behavior may help economic growth? Why human behavior and economic growth have close relationship? I believe that productivity growth in different industries, how the shares of wages and profits, how taxation affects growth, how inventions which can bring global economic growth, create working chance, sale income chance, consumption chance, productivity chance, wealth chance. These factors may bring global short term or long term economic growth. All of these factors hace close relationship between human invention and economic growth. I shall explain as below:

For any kinds of things inventions example, are best regarded as a form of investments, and their volume depends in like manner, on their expected profitability. Investments opportunities are recreated by inventions investment. However, inventions may not be economig growth factor, but there is a high profitability that prior circumstances will bring them about, so learning from human past prior experience is important not just in scientific or engineering matters, but in other fields, such as business and social organization. So, research and development, such as human invention behavior which has chance to bring long term or short term economic growth.

I mean that human invention may be one kind of investment opportunity to bring global economic growth in possibility, because human new knowledge learning behavior may attribute to global new business invention chance to bring unlimited economic growth chance in nowadays society. Hence, human can not neglect to create ourselves " invention mind or invention behavior" in order to help global economic growth more easily. SO, human invention may be one kind helping global economic growth new investment opportunuty, which is created from " human learning behavior". IN fact, an improvement in investmednt opportunity method may be created by human " any kinds of new inventions behavior". SO, nowadays society, any kinds of new inventions of product, whcih ought help global societies to bring economic growth chance.

The theory of economic growth may be based on income, labor and land which every one kknows and which are adequate. However, nowadays society had changed, such as scientific invention example, it can bring profit chance to business, creating job opportunities in global labor markets, such as smart phones, laptops, desktops, non-manual driving vehicles, electric energy cars invention etc. any kinds of new scientific invention products, they can bring new scientifical products businessess chance, they must need to employ may manufacture labour, salespeople, transport workers,logistic store workers, admin stafs, transport workers, product invention staffs , marketing promotion staffs etc. different job positions to letglobal human can have chance to find these jobs to do in order to earn income. Moreover, any kinds of scientific product inventions , which can bring many new jobs positions chance to let global unemployed people hace chance to work and earn incoime.Also, any kinds of new scientific products invention may create many new jobs chance to global and solve unequal wealth and income allocation problem to global human, even businesses have chance to sell these new scientific invention products to sell to global buyers to earn more profit.

I mean that " new products invention" may help global societies to reduce unemployment challenge and it can bring long term economic growth in global labour market view. Moreover, when any kinds of new product inventions, such as battery energy vehicle, non-manual driving auto vehicle or public transport tools, home washing machines, televisions, radios, fans, smart phomnes, laptops, electronic book reading tools, internet invention etc, different kinds of new scientific product inventions, they can bring " consumption opportunity" to let global consumers have chance to buy any kinds of new scientific inventionw, which can also encourage global consumption rate raises in order to increase global wealth improvement rate speed rises up radidly. So, global wealth rising rate whether which is rapid or slow, it depends on whether how many different kinds of new scientific products invention may be confirmed to scceed to sell in global business market.

Hence, investment on invention, which may be tangible evidence to create economic growth in the distribution of income , wages and profits between global labor, scientific inventions of products sellers, and global scientific inventions of products consumers. They have close relationship to be influenced to increas economic growth speed whether they are rapid or slow from " global scientific new products inventions". If human product invention scientists can attempt to research how to invent any kinds of undiscovered new kinds of products inventions, for example, if global any kinds of scientific product invention scientistis can attempt to invest time to invent 100 kinds of new scientific products inventions in orde to provide global human have chance to buy to use. Then, these 100 different kinds of scientific invention products may help global new invention of scientific products sellers to provide many different kinds of new jobs vacancies to let global unemployed or job seekers have chance to work and earn income. So, global unemployed rate will have chance to reduce in global societies. Moreover, they can also help these new scientific products sellers to bring " earning profit chance", even thes global " new product invention scientists who have earn product invention royalty income chance after they can invent any kinds of products in success. Finally, global consumption market growth rate will be influenced to rise up, when in the year, there are 100 new kinds of nre scientific products invention have been already sold to let global consumers hacew chance to choose the kind of target of scientific product to buy to use. So, global new economic growth rate speed , it can rise up rapid up or slow down, it depends on whether the year, global has how many kinds of new invention of scientific products" have been invented to prepare to sell in global scientific products sale market in macro economic view.

Hence, economic growth and human invention behavior, which have cloase relationship . The list of anti-growth factors could be extended perhaps however. Hartwell (1983) has pointed out that economies have always contained a mixture of three main systems for making production, consumption, and distribution decisions namely, administered and market free enterprise. It was the gradual freeing of man's entrepreneurial talents from the bonds of custom and command that finally resulted in the remarkable economic growth of the industrial revolution. However, in the twrms of human history, sustained economic growth is rare, and this suggests that several conditions (Needham's Packet), rather than memely one or two , have had to be met before it earns occur.

It is also the case, however, that its occurrence has at least in some respects made its survival more probable. HUman scientific investment has improved communications, such as smart phone, internet email and increased education (learning) chance, such as distancel learning, AI learning writing method, listening language learning method, , reading e-books from smart phone, laptop channel method, which can chance traditional classroom leanring method to new scientific channel learning method or which can change traditional telephone or post lewtter communication method to nowadays sending email, smart phone calling, whataps new scientific tool communication methods.

ON conclusion, the free societies are influenced by any kinds of new scientific products inventions, Human had began to accept how attempted to buy any kinds of new scientific products inventions to use. New scientific inventions of products, which has bring more fashable of undiscovered new scientifical inventions of products choice to satisfy human ourselves daily new products invention using needs in our daily lives. SO, human scientists whose any kinds of new products inventions which will bring more chance to help global societies to create new social economic growth in global societies.

Why ought any kinds of businesses need to invest in technology to offices when businessmen began to do businesses? The reason is simple, such as any offices need email to communicate to let different departments staffs can contact to do any tasks in short time. So, email can replace telephone calling communication channel between departments in offices. Moreover, for paper files, electronic files may replace to keep to save any office confident documents or general memos, letters, reports etc. documents. So, paper printing number may reduce. Even some businesses began to sell their products from online webstores to let customers to pat visa to buy their products from their webstores conveniently. Hence, computer technology is essential to nowadays any kinds of businesses offices.

The best are developed with the entire project-focused organization in mind. For example, a question on resourcing could involve looking a cariety of systems and files with no way to automatically generate the rught combination of data. Hence, any business offices ought need a single, centralised database which keeps accounting, project and even HR information and can integrate data when required.

ON the office investing in technology web-based system with mobile access benefit, due to investing globalization and pressure on fee rates means staff are in the office less frequently than ever. A web-based system means data can be accessed from PCs and networked laptops with no other software needed. So, instead of offices can apply laptops and intra-internet communication technological tool, which can also offer the option of a mobile applications suite which means personnel working on -site can enter timesheet and expense reports from laptops, even when not connected to the central data base. This helps minimise time delays, streamlining the billing process and improving cash flow. So, office mobile online site technology may help thme to bring real- time , easy access benefits. For exmaple, if a staff is still making decisions based on information that is seven or eight weeks old, the staff will be surprised by the power of having real-time information at the staff's fingertips. At any time this will give the staff an accurate "snapshot" of the health of the staff's project, enabling the staff to take preventive action if the problems arise before it is too late.

This visualisation ensures that all key stakeholders can identify project problems immediately they happen . It's also an ideal way for directors or other managers to grab headline information before a short notice meeting, for example, all of office laptop, mobile intra-internet, onsite technology may help to ensure more targeted decisions and better project control. Hence, office technology may help any business offices to save more time deal urgent tasks daiuly. It means that office technology may help any offices to save much time in long term.

For some businesses office technology may help their businesses to manage on projects to achieve rapid finishing in short time, such as all projects of harbour construction business aspect, some projects may face complex to prolong time to finish. SO, defining a discipline as " complex project management assumes that one can find projects cause of complexity". Also, any the harbour business projects do not really exist. The term project is a contract used to describe a particular human activity. Hence, if the harbour construction company managers can let its all harbour construction managers to apply mobile onsite technology, intra-internet communication channel to do daily communication tasks in short time between their different construction teams. Then, these new harbour onsite mobile intra-internet communication technology ought help all onsite harbour construction managers can supervise all harbour onsite workers to construct all harbour construction projects in short time efficiently and effectively.

Sp, on-site mobile intra-internet communication technology may be future construction industry which a kind of essential onsite mobile intra-internet communication technoogy.Moreover, on-site mobile intra-internet communication technology can bring future construction industry on time to save cost and construction quality improvement benefits. Due to increasingly construction industry and clients demand more for less and this is in a traditionalty high risk industry. The problem of construction and its relatively slow pace of change seem to stem from its competive building living demand role in providing building buyer value. With its attendant professions, it is often too remote from the customers‘ experience of their buildings.

When if the construction company really knew how to add value for building clients? What if the construction firm could improve productivity among those using the building? How much is that worth? What if the school could improve performance of students in shcools and the recovery of patients in hospitals? Such improvements represent much cost benefits that could mean that the building pays for itself. However, nowadays building technology can bring these key benefical features to any construction companies, such as value success are committed leadership providing the vision, suitable values and effective shared processes.

How office technology brings intelligent thinking to office staffs? Finally, I beleive that if the company can invest technology in office. It will bring intelligent thinking to office staffs in order to improve efficient and performance, because investing in office technology , which is a way to reduce risk without going over the top through effective use of the company networks. Why can office technology working environment can help staffs to bring intelligent thinking in order to improve performance and raise efficiency?

The reason of office technology working environment can excite staffs their intelligent thining to be raise. What's lacking is a way of mitigating against these risks and doing so cost- effectively. Because more recently, a new stage has been reached where office staffs rely not only on their technical and business knowledge, but now have methodologies and tools so sophisticated that they can forward predict and control any office projects to finish before due date more easily.Hence, with good technical knowledge, sound business underatanding, a good way of methodologies, and training in the very latest software technology to hand, these are the not investing in office technology staffs, those who still find it impossible to deliver projects successfully more easily before any their office projects finishing due date. What needs to be addressed to change this situation? The main factors critical to improve office staffs performance and improve efficiency, the non-investing in office technology working environment ought to changed to invest technology to office working environment in order to excite staff individual working emotion to bring raising efficiency, even improve performance effectiveness.

ON conclusion, any offices need to invest technology to offices in order to bring " improving technical skill to staffs their working environment", because they need to know that skill does not equate to competence , and there fore, a competence and therefore a competency based assessment is essential so that a prospective office employee knowledge and understanding, attitude and skills can be evaluated. So, technological office can help managers to evaluate office employee individual job skill more easily in order to make decision whether skill is high or low to let high skillful staffs can continue to be trained to work in offices as well as fire the low skillful staffs. So, when the office can attempt to spend more money to invest to its office working environment, it means that the organization should be investing in training for permanent staffs in the scarce skills working markets. A small investment in office technology can reap significant benefits further down the live, such as planning for skills scarcity on investing nowadays office technological working environment.

Can robot technology encourages consumers shopping ?

Why may knowledge influence economic growth? Have they close relationship between knowledge and economic growth or recession in behavioral economy view? I shall attempt to indicate evidences to explain these two questions as below:

IN fact, human development had been experiencing from agricultural stage to industrial manufacturing stage, till to nowadays, service section stage,e.g. hotel tourism leisure development, and technological development stage, e.g. computer and robot development. All of these stages, which are created by ourselves knowledge, it means that how we decide choice, what social development direction will be caused. It it is true, it seems that global human knowledge may influence how our social future continue development. Our social economic growth or recession will be brought to influence from knowlege

indirectly.

It is focus on " behavioral economic concept" Economists define scarcity as the condition of wanting more than we can get with available resources. Scarcity is a fact of life. So, human can arrrange ourselves resources in a lot of different ways, such as watching TV, buying a book, a car or traveling, but at any given time, ourselves have a fixed range of possibilities. SO, scarcity also describes the world on a collective level. As a society, we can produce only so many things, and we have to decide how those things are divided among many people. But, when social development, knowledge is very important to cause human (scientists) choose how to decideto invent any new things in order to satisfy human unlimtied need and using desire. So, the total quantiry of available knowledge does not diminish as more and more people acquire it. So, ourselves every behavioral decision in life involves weighing the trade off between costs and benefits . We look at our options and decide whether it is worth giving up in order to get the other.

Economists explain this time cost of choice the " opportunity cost", opportunity cost is the value you could gained by choosing your next best alternative, the opportunity you have to pass up in order to take your first choice. Why may ourselves behavior have relationship between opportunity cost and economic growth? For computer invention example, when scientists feel compute products will be future human needs daily, for student learning using need, office tasks needs, wathcing movie, listening music leisure need,even playing game need. So, scientists had chose to spend time and resource and labor to invent computer products , they forgave to spend time and resource and labor to invent other products. They computer invention is their opportunity cost, includes time, money, resource, labour, knowledge, mind on computer scientists , they had forgiven to spend these resources to research how to invent other kinds of new products.

However, when computer new products had been invented in success, e.g. desktop, laptop, can be popular to be accept to provide to global computer users to use. This kind of computer invention , its users number had been increasing, manufacturing computer number will be influenced to grow, due to computer invention will help developing and developed countries GDP growth rapidly since 1980 year , the earily first stage of computer invention had been experiencing during our global technological development history.

So, it implies that computer scientists had been confirmed to do right choice decision to forgive to spend resources, time, money and labour and knowledge to research how to invent any kinds of new products. They make right decision to research how to invent new computer products,even improve desktop to laptop and smart phone , hand carrying smart phone and computer both functions new products to satisfy computer users daily using needs. It is truw opportunity cost to computer scientists case. Also, when past, our scientists do right choice to invent this kind of computer product, this kind of computer products can bring global eocnomic benefits, such as government can increase profit tax form computer sellers, offices can use computers to reduce employees number, when computers can help offices to save much document, clerical employees number may be influenced to reduice, tasks can be simple from complex tasks, spending tasks time may be influenced to reduce by computerization of office, factories can apply computers or robots to replace workers to manufacture any kinds of products, such as cars, waching machine, rice cookers, radios, fans ,television etc. different kinds of electrical products. So workers number may be influenced to reduce and wage expenditure must be reduce.

Hence, new knowledge may help global societies to bring economic growth, such as past scientists had decided to forgive to spend time, resource, money, labor, skill, knowledge to research how to invent any kinds of new products, it is possible that they have some different kinds of new products concept choices, computer concept is only one kinds of choice among these new different kinds of new products invention concepts. However, they need to choose only one kind of new product invention among of these different kinds of new product concept choices, because they have not enough resource to provide to them to invent in the past. Finally, they evaluate the weigh and cost between computer invention conept and otehr new products invention concepts. In fact, computer is one kind of "the bringing much economic benefits" new concept invention product choice.

I believe that if computer will be continue improved in order to bring more economic growth in prossible. SO, scientists need to spend more time, resource, money, labor, skill, knowledfe to research how to continue to improve traditional computers to bring more using functions, in order to help global differernt industries to reduce resource, time, labour , money aim to bring reducing cost spending expenditure benefits to global industries , due to societies had been experiencing " knowledge social stage". If societies need to apply computer technology to assist our societies can continue develop, when our societies' different industries, such as service, manufacturing, even agricultrial sectors, e.g. robots may help farmers to predict when it is right time to grow vegetable, or replace farmers to grow vegetable, fruit in farms to provide human have enough food to eat, or robots can help hotel to clean rooms, serve clients, robots can help cinemas to sell tickets, robots can help manufacturers to product new products in factories. So, technological products may help any kinds of industries to reduce employees number, improve efficiencies and productivities and reduce wages expenditure economic cost benefits.

Production possibilites economic concept knowledge indicates about who produces which goods and why. The fact that millions of people and firms around the global coordinate their activities to provide consumers with the right combination of goods and services seem like magic. In fact, coordination doe snot happen by chance, nor does super-planner tells every one where to go and what to do. Instead, the global production time is a natural outcome of people every acting in their own self interest to improve their own lives. Economists call this coordination mechanism the " invisible hand", an idea that was first suggested by economic thinker Adam Smith.

To get some insight into the who and why of production, such as shirt production case, most shirts are made in China, and other countries when factory wages are low.

Have AMerican workers become worse at making shirts over the last two countries? Definitely not, In fact, as are better than American workers at making shirts. INstead , each good tends to be produced by that country, company, or person with the lowest opportunity cost of producing that shirt kind of product, such as scientists make cooperation decision to invent computer products together, they can earn high invention royalty income, computer sale and manufacturing number increases, governments can earn more profit tax, different kinds of service, manufacturing industries can reduce workers nummber, wage expenditure, improving performance economic benefits . So, countries and firms and persons need a specialize in making goods for which they have the lowest opportunity cost. THey than trade with one another to get the coordination of goods. They want to consume, such as computer manufacturing , if IBM and Microsoft both companies can cooperate to research how to improve themselves traditional model of laptops and desktops to create new improved and more using functions laptops and destops, e.g. small size, more new using functions, clear colour and easier visible screen, or small book cover design, new computer model. I believe that the resulting, gains from themselves computer trade can be shared much that every computer buyers ends up better offer, global computer users will choose to buy and use these both IBM and Microsoft future new computer invention products to compare other kinds of computer manufacturers.

In production possibilities frontier economic concept, it explains why IBM and MIcrosoft ought cooperate to manufacturer computers, their cooperation can bring more economic benefits to themselves and global computer users, e.g. more computer functions, reducing sale price, reduce computer workers manufacturing wages, and computer manufacturing workers number, increasing computer manufacturing and demand number, increasing profit to themselves and government profit tax income, increasing buyers number, offices can improve effeciencies and employees perofrmance, reducing manufacturing cost expenditure, improving student learning ability, etc. different kinds of global economic benefits. Hence, in production possibilities frontier economic concept, IBM and Microsoft ought make cooperation decision in order to bring global economic benefits. In fact, computer manufaturing industry is one competitive market, it is one in which truly informed, prices taking buyers and seller easily trade a standardized good or service. IBM and Microsoft need to cooperate in order to win their computer manufacturing competitors , if they hope to earn in global computer manufacturing top leader position. Otherwise, if IBM and Microsoft do not choose to cooperate to invent new kind of computer products, their traditional computer products will be not popular to be accept to use to compare their computer manufacturing competitors. Because, future computer trends to cheap, more using functions, small size, light weight , clear visible and touch feeling screen. in order to attract computer buyers choices more easily.

On conclusion, it is possible that scientists invention knowledge may bring eocnomic growth indirectly. Their invention choice or invention decision may assist our future economy development rapidly or slowly. Hence, knowledge is one invisible hand to influence global economy either it can bring growth or recession in possible.

Can human behavior is influenced by insurance product

Can human behavior be influenced by insurance product? I shall attempt to indicate insurance cases to explain cause and effect relationship between them as below:

People in developing countries are ofren highly explosed to risk, enjoy little social insurance from government or welfare support. This assumption will explain how and why our behavior may be influenced to change easily by insurance product. A standard finding in development economic is that demand for even actuarially fair weather insurance or health insurance or saving or retirement or education kinds of indurance is surprisingly low. So, when the country has many people feel they can not have enough insurance protection to avoid losing job risk. Not enough insurance suppoting , this factor may influence human behavior may change easily when economic recession occurs. For example, in share market case, when the share buyer feels he has no enough insurance to protect his lives, although he has job to do, he won't be influenced to reduce to buy many share numbers and avoid to do share buying and selling transactions easily when he feels economy will occur recession as soon as possible.

Hence, it seems that not enough insurance factor may influence share market buying and selling transactions number reduces in possible. Hence one should expect more "behavioral firms" in poor countries.When in rich societies. The consequence of wide-spread present bias may be some workersadvantage of employer match programs for retirement saving, in poor countries, this may lead to bring high return investment opportunities for a wide range of firms. Hence, developed country, such as US, UK firms, they will prefer to provide enough saving insurance or medical insurance or accident or education insurances to let workers feel more financial saving feeling in order to let they do not want to change job easily.

Because they do not want often train new workers to do their positions, they need to spend long time or waste time and human resources to do training new employees tasks. They avoid to spend long time training expenditure and training time to teach new employees. SO, these developed countries firms can accept to spend more saving , health or accident or education or retirement insurance products to persuade excellent skillful workers to stay to work till to their retirement ages.

So, firm's insurance expednitur e may be one kind of employee behavioral performance method to avoid employees leaving number increases rapidly. Hence, it seems even any kinds of insurance products, e.g. health, accident, medical, saving and retirement insurances, they may influence employees or share buyers feel psychological safety to do or not do changing new job decision or share buying and selling decision easily in behavioral economic view.

Why can insurance influence employees feel psychological safety refers to individual's shared beliefs about the safety of interpersonal risk-taking in the workplace (Kessel at al. 2012). A psychological safe work environment enables employees to feel safe at work in order to grow, learn, and contribute in a rapidly changing world, as well as to achieve job performance improvement (Edmond- son & Lei, 2014).

So, it seems that insurance ought persuade employees choose to stay long time in present firm or it ought imporve employees performance when the firm achieves insurance program to satisfy employee individual financial protection psychological need in organizational psychological view. MOreover, insurance firms also need to innovate their different kinds of health, medical , accudent, saving and retirement insurance products in order to let every organization to do the most suitable insurance product to satisfy the firm's all employees financial safe psychological need to raise the insurance firms themselves competitive effort in firms insurance clients market. Hence, it seems that insurance products may influence our social employee behavior or social share market behavior both.

ON conclusion, share product may be one main psychological safe product to influence human behavior in nowadays economic society. It can influence organizational development and financial investment market development both in behavioral economic view.

Can non-manual driving cars dominate traditional car market

Nowadays, non-manual driving car invention may influence traditional car market development. In car development history, human had been habitly driving gas energy cars, but since battery energy cars invention, it can influence environmental protection car buyers feel gas energy cars may pollute global air. So, many different countries car buyers begin to choose to buy battery energy cars to replace traditional gas energy cars to drive. For example, US, Uk, China , they haver many big cities, their different cities living car buyers had begun to choose to buy battery energy cars to replace their old gas energy cars to drive to different destinations from their living cities every day.

So, it seems that nettergy energy cars had been beginning to replace some old gas energy cars in some countries cities, e.g. China Shanghai large cities, US, New York, Washington large cities, UK London large city. However, it brings these questions: Can non-manual driving cars may dominate future traditonal gas energy cars market? Because, cattergy energy cars bring environmental protection advantages to reduce air pollution.

So, battery energy cars may influence nowadays many gas energy car buyers to choose to buy battery energy cars to replace gas energy cars to replace gas energy cars to drive to avoid air pollution problem serious occurrence in our future societies.

In car market demand and supply view, I assume that if future many gas energy car owners accept to battery energy cars can reduce air polution continue influences our health when we often breathe dirty air due to gas energy cars' emission.

Hence, I estimate the demand number of battery energy cars pollution will be influenced to increase by air pollution. If future global air pollution will continue seriously influence global human health, it will influence global many car owners make choice either not buy any cars to drive, they will choose to catch public transport tools, e.g. bus, tram ,ferry, taxi, underground train etc. to go to anywhere or they will choose to buy battery energy cars to avoid gas continue pollute air to influence our health. So, it seems that battery energy cars will replace traditional gas energy cars to cause gas energy cars demand number decreases and battery energy cars demand number increases.

The other questions concern: Can battery energy cars influence future non-manual driving cars demand number reduces? Can non-manual driving cars replace battery energy cars and gas energy cars to dominate global car market?

In fact, non-manual driving cars may let many lazy car drivers or car buyers do not need to drive their cars, robots may help them to drive cars when they are sitting in themselves cars. So , they may read books, lsten music or sleep when their non-manual driving cars are still running on the roads. Although, non-manual driving cars can let many lazy car drivers feel comfortable and free when they are sitting in themselves cars. But non-manul driving cars can let they feel not safe, when robots help they to drive cars.

It means that their lifes are dominated by robots. However, traffic accidents may occur in any time, if robots help them to drive their cars in whole road journey time. So, they will feel more dangerous to compare they drive themselves cars on road busy time. Moreover, non-manual driving cars also need gas energy. So, non-manual driving cars still cause air pollution when many non-manual driving cars are being driving on the roads.

Hence, non-manual driving cars can also let environmental protection drivers feel that they can cause air pollution when they are driven on the roads by robots. Otherwise, battery energy cars must not pollute air , because they are using battery charge energy to replace gas or oil energy. Moreover battery energy cars won't let many car drivers feel safe to drive themselves cars on the road, due to they can still drive themselves cars and they won't need robots to help them to drive cars on the roads.

On conclusion, it seems that battery energy cars can attract many car buyers to choose to buy more than the kinds of both non-manual driving cars and gas energy cars. In supply and demand view, if future non-manual driving car manufacturers hope to raise sale price and demand purchase number. Unless, they can reduce their future any kinds of non-manual driving manufacture number to less than battery energy cars sale number to let future non-manual driving buyers feel that they can not buy any kinds of non-manual driving cars easily if they make purchase decision to buy them leter. Then, any kinds of non-manual driving cars prices may be influenced to raise to sell more easier when car buyers feel their supply number will begin to reduce to sell in global non-manual driving car market. However, future battery energy cars will be non-manual driving cars main competitive choice target to global car buyers. So, non-manual driving cars will be difficult to dominate the primary car choice tool to car buyers in future global car market. Human behavior how influences tourism development.

How economic changing environment may influence traveler leisure choice? I shall attempt to apply demand and supply economic theory to explain their relationship as below:

Life -style economic environment changing factor may influence household or family traveler lesiure behavioral change, such as trip choice, e.g.anywhere trip destination choice. For exmaple, in US family traveler trip choice focusing on the self-rent car driving or self car driving journey choice role, which is in the larger dream / nightmare pattern dominating AMerican life and thought, space, romance and technology,the automobile occupies to general US household family travel behavior.

So, in general , if every US household family income reduces, when unemployed people number had been influenced to rise, due to social jobs reduce, it will influence many US families do not choose self-driving cars trip or renting cars driving lesiure arrangement in themselves whole journey. THey will choose to pay to travel agents to help them to arranage whole trips, travel paskage may influence free travel bus transport tool arrangement which can replace them self-driving car trips or renting car self driving car trips arrangement, when US is experiencing recession to influence many American either loses jobs or reduce salaries. Because many American like to buy cars to go to anywhere in their holidays. SO, driving cars may be their life style behavioral habit.

Life style factor is as activity pattern may chance as an individual adapts to a change in the environment. Life style changes will socioeconomic, and technological chance, increasing or decreasing real income, increaing or decreasing working hours, and new consumer technology, e.g. online e-ticket purchase may help global travelers make booking airline seat decision among different travel e-ticket price comparison from e-ticket agent web-stores in short time. So, many travelers feel not need to visit travel agents to buy paper tickets. E-ticket purchase method wil influence any one traveler whosetravel trip choice demand and travel destination choice demand both change rapidly in short time when they can know where travel destination e-ticket

price is more cheap, e.g. US, UK , China different cities e-price price. So, e-ticket purchase method may influence traveler travelling destination choice changes easily in short time. For example, a traveler plans to travel to US , Washington, New York large cities trsips, but when he finds UK , London large city e-ticket price is cheaper to compare US large cities e-ticket price in August from UK any one e-ticket travel agents webstores. Then UK any one e-ticket seller may influence the traveler makes final e-ticket purchase decision to travel to UK , London large city to replace US trip plan in short time. So, e-ticket sale method may change global travelers their trip plans change rapidly in short time. I mean that travel e-ticket purchase technology may influence global traveler trip destination changing choice in short time to compare walk-in visiting travelling agents paper ticket booking airline seat choice in nowadays society.

However, tourism and destination markcters should utilize different marketing tactics to content and retain existing traveler customers encourage new and prospective ones. So, economic environment may bring impact to global traveler behavior of destination familiarity or trip choice, destination image, safety and security, travel motivation, travelling attitude changes. Tourism is any country's overall encourage's main leisure activities supply of services to compare other kinds of lesiure supply. SO, any countrics' dedtination's success in attracting tourists is dependent on the quality of essential benefits that it offers attractions, facilities and accessibility.

Rational choice theory proposes that consumers seek to maximize their utility by calculating the costs and benefits of alternative available to them (Glimcher et al. 2005, Scott 2000). So, they explained that any one traveler is rational choice decision maker , they must compare travel ticket price, and travel agent trip leisure service arrangement package , e.g. restaurant food choice, hotel room choice, visiting anywhere destination choice ,traveling transport tools choice,and price, destination leisure playing satisfactory feeling etc. cost and benefit comparison elements to make final trip destination choice decision.

So, whether the traveler income is increasing or decreasing, it can not influence the traveler's trip destination choice decision changes very easily. Any one traveler must calculate all related trip elements, e.g. food, hotel room expenditure, leisure expenditure, air ticket price, rental cars price, public transport tools fee etc. different elements to make final trip destination choice because every traveler is general rational leisure consumer, they must compare all costs and benefits related to the country's any one city (travelling destinations) in order to arrange themselves real trip destination in the several travelling spedning days in the travelling county. For tourism destination re-opening in post- COVID-19 Pandemic case example, despite the existing pressure from health-related risk-and additional challenges (e.g. rising oil prices, inflation, political disruption). All of these factors may bring long time negative emotion individual economic pressure feeling to influence global every tourist's psychology. Positive emotion destination feeling to the country may be influenced to bring negative emotion destination feeling, e.g. US , New York, Washington cities may be influenced to let global tourists feel negative traveling destination emotion feeling after COVID19 Pandenic occurrence. So, disease risk.

Human knowledge how influences economy

Why may knowledge influence economic growth? Have they close relationship between knowledge and economic growth or recession in behavioral

economy view? I shall attempt to indicate evidences to explain these two questions as below:

IN fact, human development had been experiencing from agricultural stage to industrial manufacturing stage, till to nowadays, service section stage,e.g. hotel tourism leisure development, and technological development stage, e.g. computer and robot development. All of these stages, which are created by ourselves knowledge, it means that how we decide choice, what social development direction will be caused. It it is true, it seems that global human knowledge may influence how our social future continue development. Our social economic growth or recession will be brought to influence from knowledge

indirectly.

It is focus on " behavioral economic concept" Economists define scarcity as the condition of wanting more than we can get with available resources. Scarcity is a fact of

life. So, human can arrange ourselves resources in a lot of different ways, such as watching TV, buying a book, a car or traveling, but at any given time, ourselves have a fixed range of possibilities. SO, scarcity also describes the world on a collective level. As a society, we can produce only so many things, and we have to decide how those things are divided among many people. But, when social development, knowledge is very important to cause human (scientists) choose how to decide to invent any new things in order to

satisfy human not limtied need and using desire. So, the total quantity of available knowledge does not diminish as more and more people acquire it. So, ourselves every behavioral decision in life involves weighing the trade off between costs and benefits . We look at our options and decide whether it is worth giving up in order to get the other.

Economists explain this time cost of choice the " opportunity cost", opportunity cost is the value you could gained by choosing your next best alternative, the opportunity you have to pass up in order to take your first choice. Why may ourselves behavior have relationship between opportunity cost and economic growth? For computer invention example, when scientists feel compute products will be future human needs daily, for student learning using need, office tasks needs, watching movie, listening music leisure need,even playing game need. So, scientists had chose to spend time and resource and labor to invent computer products , they forgave to spend time and resource and labor to invent other products. They computer invention is their opportunity cost, includes time, money, resource, labour, knowledge, mind on computer scientists , they had forgiven to spend these resources to research how to invent other kinds of new products.

However, when computer new products had been invented in success, e.g. desktop, laptop, can be popular to be accept to provide to global computer users to use. This kind of computer invention , its users number had been increasing, manufacturing computer number will be influenced to grow, due to computer invention will help developing and developed countries GDP growth rapidly since 1980 year , the early first stage of computer invention had been experiencing during our global technological development history.

So, it implies that computer scientists had been confirmed to do right choice decision to forgive to spend resources, time, money and labour and knowledge to research how to invent any kinds of new products. They make right decision to research how to invent new computer products,even improve desktop to laptop and smart phone , hand carrying smart phone and computer both functions new products to satisfy computer users daily using needs. It is true opportunity cost to computer scientists case. Also, when past, ou scientists do right choice to invent this kind of computer product, this kind of computer products can bring global economic benefits, such as government can increase profit tax form computer sellers, offices can use computers to reduce employees number, when computers can help offices to save much document, clerical employees number may be influenced to reduce, tasks can be simple from complex tasks, spending tasks time may be influenced to reduce by computerization of office, factories can apply computers or robots to replace workers to manufacture any kinds of products, such as cars, washing machine, rice cookers, radios, fans ,television etc. different kinds of electrical products. So workers number may be influenced to reduce and wage expenditure must be reduce.

Hence, new knowledge may help global societies to bring economic growth, such as past scientists had decided to forgive to spend time, resource, money, labor, skill, knowledge to research how to invent any kinds of new products, it is possible that they have some different kinds of new products concept choices, computer concept is only one kinds of choice among these new different kinds of new products invention concepts. However, they need to choose only one kind of new product invention among of these different kinds of new product concept choices, because they have not enough resource to provide to them to invent in the past. Finally, they evaluate the weigh and cost between computer invention concept and other new products invention concepts. In fact, computer is one kind of "the bringing much economic benefits" new concept invention product choice.

I believe that if computer will be continue improved in order to bring more economic growth in possible. SO, scientists need to spend more time, resource, money, labor, skill, knowledge to research how to continue to improve traditional computers to bring more using functions, in order to help global different industries to reduce resource, time, labour , money aim to bring reducing cost spending expenditure benefits to global industries , due to societies had been experiencing " knowledge social stage". If societies need to apply computer technology to assist our societies can continue develop, when our societies' different industries, such as service, manufacturing, even agricultrial sectors, e.g. robots may help farmers to predict when it is right time to grow vegetable, or replace farmers to grow vegetable, fruit in farms to provide human have enough food to eat, or robots can help hotel to clean rooms, serve clients, robots can help cinemas to sell tickets, robots can help manufacturers to product new products in factories. So, technological products may help any kinds of industries to reduce employees number, improve efficiencies and productivities and reduce wages expenditure economic cost benefits.

Reference

Hartwell, R.M. (1983). The origins of capitalism. A Methodological Eassy. in Pejovich (1983).

Needham, J. (1963), Poverties and Triumphs of the Chinese scientific tradition, in Crombie (1963).

Investing in office technology can bring what advantages

Phaal, R., Farrukh , C. & Probert , D. (2004). Technology roadmapping- A planning framework for evolution and revolution. Technological Forecasting and social change, 71, 5-26. htpps:// doi. org/10.101016/ S00401625(03)00072-6.

CHAPTER SIX

Can technology help countries development

Online teaching education

Future, online teaching method will be popular to be applied to teach to any university, even secondary and primary schools. Because internet service is free charge to any students in any countries. Many different age students who can know how to apply internet as well as internet studying is very convenient to any students who can to internet to learn or study in home or public library or school library conveniently. Teachers do not need spend much time to teach students in classroom. They can use internet to teach teachers by face to face seeing and talking to their individual student from every student's computer. So, students do not also often spend much time to go to school to learn. So, developing any fast speed and time saving and talking and listening online teaching methods will be popular needs to any UK primary and secondary and university students in the future. It will be one new technological teaching method to change the traditional classroom educational method in UK and schools. For example, when one UK student who had left UK and is living in another country long time. If any UK school did not provide online teaching service to any UK students. It means that the UK citizen can not choose study himself/herself any UK school if who still hope to study any UK course when who is living in another country. Even one foreign student who does not go to UK to study, if he/she can find any UK primary or secondary or university to study from online. Then, the UK school won't lose one foreign student, due to it does not provide online teaching method to any foreign students. So, online Technology educational learning method will be one popular learning method which is enhanced, supported, mediated or assessed by the use of electronic media. Technology also enhanced learning may involve the use of new or established technology and/or the creation of new learning material. It may be deployed both locally and at a distance (i.e. a combination of traditional and e-learning approaches), to learning that is delivered entirely online. Online learning technology characteristics (features) include identification of a project lead for each area of any learning strategy, identification of two " quick win" for example lecture capture, electronic submission and feedback.

How can online technology enhance learning at UK any schools? It will include these several aspects to analyze. On identifying, prioritizing and innovation hand, online technology is a process for resourcing, prioritizing, acquiring and evaluating school software and hardware for UK any school needs. On staff development learning plan and a student skills development plan hand, UK schools need to establish a base-line policy on the standard (minimum) technology enhanced learning expectation for education each program and module and a mechanism for updating the schools' policies. On evaluation and research hand, a mechanism for engaging the owners of the technology enhanced learning strategy with best practice in the sector including contributing to and benefiting from pedagogical research and the evaluation of the student experience to UK any school.

Thus, UK schools can apply online technology to develop on educational aspect, such as digital literacies and appropriate technical skills that equip UK students for life-long learning, graduate level employment and professional practice, be empowered to learn how to learn with online teaching technology, using online technology to engage in interactive, creative and co-constructed learning with the potential for online learning in an interdisciplinary and international context, using online teaching technology to engage in learning with and from people from anywhere in the world, be supported on placement and in workplace learning through mobile applications and other supportive technologies that facilitate their online learning when away from the classroom, having access to innovative methods of online learning teaching and assessment that are the foundation of a research-lead academic environment, engaging with UK schools in developing , implementing and reviewing the technology enhanced learning strategy. Thus, in the future, it is important to build a capacity to the online education strategy to adopt future learning innovation and student individual online learning need (demand) to UK any school online teaching trend.

There are many examples where UK academics working in isolation or in small UK teaching organizations or classroom learning groups have developed teaching innovation that have a positive impact on UK students' academic experience , but these have remained isolated to particular modules or occasionally program. The aim of education researching online learning process is to identify the good online teaching innovation that is being developed and to prioritize those that have the potential to make a significant contribution to improving the academic student experience at UK any schools. This online teaching process will need any UK schools which can plan how to apply limited resources necessary to achieve online teaching. In addition, the online teaching research process would evaluate and prioritize large scale educational software and hardware requests for primary, secondary and university students' requests. An important part to this process will be to ensure the integration of online educational products and packages that school staff and students regular use to make routine working and access as seamless as possible.

Decisions about school administrative online technologies should not be taken in isolation before assessing the impact on UK teaching staff. In addition, a range of techniques such as, online expert facilitation, coaching and peer support will be used to support individuals, groups or longer academic units, who are learning on major technology enhanced online learning projects. Staff engagement may also facilitated through incorporating technology that is used in teaching staff research and/or professional activity that can be cooperated into their teaching.

Online learning technology can develop UK students skills, UK schools need to understand how UK students understand technology and learn with it, therefore the digital literacy strategy needs to be considered as part of the overall strategy as well as the relevant skills development in UK employability strategy. So, in the future, online learning strategy will make it clear that students will develop technical skills the appropriate level for graduate employability and professional practice. Also, in the future, the online technology can enhance learning working group to discuss external development, that are of educational strategic importance, understanding and evaluating current best practice and research and understanding and evaluating the online educational strategic contribution that pedagogical research and student feedback can have on online educational strategy, policy and practice. The e-learning unit is responsible for informing and educating. This could be done by, for example, providing a short digest of relevant information for each meeting and by setting aside a proportion of each school meeting to discuss a topic of particular online educational strategic interest to every school. Academics that have not got a specialist interest in online educational technology enhanced learning will need relevant information at an appropriate time. This could be provided at a school department or faculty level and this will have clear links to the staff online teaching development plan. Hence, online educational development strategy will influence any UK educational school technological improvement in the future.

Environmental protection technology

Why does environment technology valid to UK businessmen and government to develop? Nowadays, global air and water pollution is serious. Even, UK has many farming is polluted by the water and air pollution. It will influence UK farmers' income if whose farm land (natural resource) is polluted by water or air (natural resource). Even it will influence UK citizen will encounter food shortage if UK farmers can not grow any fresh and health food to provide the enough food numbers to eat every day. Moreover, air and water pollution will influence UK citizen drink the polluted water and breathe the dirty air to live every day. This natural resource (air and water challenge) will influence UK citizen health to cause illness , even death every easily. So, UK government can not neglect the natural environment pollution challenge. The environmental protection technology will help the UK and development countries to solve the challenge of climate change to avoid or reduce farming, foods, or vegetable or fruits or rice, pork, livestock numbers loss threats, i.e. the development and deployment of low carbon energy technology, including technology for the efficient use of energy. The commercialization of low carbon energy and energy efficiency technologies in the UK, with a specific focus on the demonstration and deployment phases of bringing low carbon technologies to UK market.

The UK Government needs to deliver a low carbon economy and to meet UK ambitions emission reduction target. So, low carbon and environmental protection technology researching and development will reduce the carbon intensity of energy production as well as reduce energy demand, towards meeting the contributing UK's ambitions production as well as reduce energy demand, and renewable energy goals. The use of energy (including transportation fuel) and the UK's targets on climate change, for example, by helping the UK make a step change in increasing deployment of renewable energy, improving UK energy efficiency and helping low carbon technologies reach the market. The development of low carbon technologies, and to realize the benefits of doing so in terms ensuring security of energy supply for the UK future economy development.

In UK, private sector investment in technology innovation in the low carbon energy sector will other sectors of the economy. So, in UK energy technologies are likely needed to be developed to avoid dangerous climate change, or an acceptable cost. So, in the future, UK government will need to consider to research environment protection and low carbon energy technology. The activities will reduce carbon emissions, or have the potential to reduce carbon emissions on the longer term, through the use of energy technology will accelerate development and deployment of low-carbon energy and energy efficiency technologies will capacity in the demonstration and deployment of low carbon technologies. Innovation in the energy sector is the only way to identify, develop and reduce the costs of new and improved technologies for the extractions, generation, distribution and use of energy. It has long been an important means of achieving the UK's energy policy aims of a secure and affordable energy supply, as well as to develop the environmentally friendly technologies that are required in UK response to climate change, i.e. nuclear, wind or water, sun energy technology, which is future new energy technology is suitable to research to create to apply instead of current electricity energy.

How global warming influences UK agriculture growth. Scientists have also been fighting the use of chlorine in municipal water systems to kill various strands of bacteria. Chlorine reduces by about 80% the number of alimentary tract diseases relative to polluted, unchlorinated water. A relatively new genetically modified agricultural products. They were partly successful in Europe, such as UK (some countries banned genetically modified products) in spite of the fact that neither history nor research supports their case. People began to modify plants as early as the beginning of the agricultural revolution (8000 to 10,000 years ago), when they started seed selection and who have continued ever since. The green revolution of the 1960 year brought about strains of grans and rice more resistant to a variety of local conditions. The effects have been that countries like India, which had suffered from recurrent famines over the millennia, became self-sufficient in food due to the resultant sharp increase in agricultural productivity. It was a real science and technology over the poverty dominating most of human history. But it is precisely the products of science and technology that ecologists are so deathly afraid of. In an interesting study in a quarter (28%) of clinically analyzed cases of obsessive compulsive disorder were cases resulting from the fear of global warming.

To destroy the modern, whether industrial or postindustrial, civilization, human have to destroy an important engine of economic growth, that is its energy sources. And this is what eco-warriors try to achieve under the banner of against global warming. Thus, UK government will have responsibility to attempt to research new technology to fight global warming challenge for itself farmer benefits and even global benefits both on the future.

Future Economist global warming technological protection economic influence opinion

Some future economists indicated reasons to explain why UK government and businessmen needed to consider how to develop natural environment protection technology to avoid global warming challenge to influence UK economy development. They indicated the anthropogenic (human-made) global warming resulting from the increase in "greenhouse gas". They offered their perspectives on the scientific valid of anthropogenic global warming phenomenon, its probability of occur and expected consequences and is dominated by technologists, economists and political scientists, who considered the need to make the horribly costly adjustments in energy generation and usage suggested by climate alarmists.

Many stress that global warming is primarily caused by other phenomena than human use of fossil fuels or human activities in general. They are looking at the activities of the sun and impact of the larger universe as the main source of global warming and stress that global warmings (plural) happen intermittently with global cooling. I shall explain why global climate warming will influence to the political and economics of the issue to UK country. For it is the latter, rather than the global warming itself, that will pose a challenge to the Western world, such as UK and the world at large in the future. Scientists concerned who should move forward with policy measures to avert the alleged disaster. They also apply manufacturing theories to support enough to frighten politicians into action and scare societies into acceptance of measures that would sharply reduce UK citizen their living standards. Otherwise, UK politicians had support that bureaucracies were established, money allocated and lobbies created dependent on the new kind of subsidies. In consequences, climate alarmism and resultant interventions in national economies and human activities have become the increasingly wide spread and increasingly cost reality. With the growing availability of money distributed, and even more promised, a range of benefit of the global warming machinery has been on the increase. So, if UK government did not concern how to innovate new weather protection technology to avoid climate change adverse (poor) influence. It is possible that billions of dollars of UK public money are needed to spend on research global warming challenge because global warming will influence UK agricultural industry. UK agricultural industry is one important export income source to raise UK GDP income every year. If global warming become very serious to influence UK weather to be bad to cause UK farmers who can not grow good taste food and vegetable to supply to domestic and overseas food consumers to eat. Then, UK will loss much GDP income from local agricultural export sale. It seems global warming and agricultural production which has direct relationship to influence UK economy development in the future.

The main problem with climatology is that it must be based as already stressed on very many variables affecting climate and too few hard data necessity. Differences apply not only with respect to the scale of changes obtained, but even to their direction (rising or declining temperature). Some weather scientists indicated to concern global warming challenge. In consequence, it would be impossible to discover if and where errors were made not only in estimating relationships between variables but also in the quality of data used. (Hauser, J. Tellis, G. J; Griffin, A. 2006) They were comparing average temperatures measured some 30, 40 or 50 years ago by, say, 90 % weather stations in the countryside and 10 % stations in the cities with contemporary average temperatures measured by weather stations located today on 50:50 basis in the countryside and cities. Then, one could obtain the increasing temperatures without any real world climate or even weather changes. Comparability would be ensured if the same number of countryside-located and city-located weather stations had been compared for different periods. The alarmists intentionally mix up " temperature growth" with the trend of temperature growth. To give an example, if in the first decade the temperature grew by 0.5 % degree, in second decade it grew by 0.3 % and in third decade it grew by 0.1%, what was registered was a growth in the temperature, but certainly not a trend of growing temperature. A fourth decade should, on the basis of the trend, bring about no change in the temperature.

To conclude, scientists believed that global warming was caused by human's bad behavior more than natural environment influence. So, it is human's responsibility needs to solve this challenge, due to who feel earning profit aim is more important to protect natural environment, e.g. air and water pollution , due to manufacturing process is the main factor. So, UK has responsibility to attempt to research how to solve global warming challenge , such as it has many famous scientists who can devote their scientific skills to cooperate to solve global warming challenge with other countries' scientists. Some weather scientists also hypothesized that human may be at the end of the present warming period. If they are right, it would be bad for humanity, as warmer periods have always been associated with better conditions for economic activity. To sum up, scientists believed that global warming will influence human economic activity to be bad.

The psychology and political economy of global warming success to UK farmers

Climate alarmists were able to convince a large part of the Western public and a majority of Western politicians of the cause of fighting against the global warming. It supposes itself in an instinctive preference for collectivist solutions in economic and social spheres, with negative to disastrous consequences when scientists are applied in practice, so UK government needs to concern global warming challenge, due to it is possible that it will influence UK natural environment weather to be poor to influence many UK farmers' agricultural and vegetable and fruit and rice wheat etc. food growth successfully. What is the global warming influence to cause disease? For example, ecological alarmists and activists (eco-warriors) never admit they are wrong, they long pursued their fear mongering campaign against chlorine. Their success in branding DDT a dangerous substance had a negative impact on the malaria eradication campaign in poorer parts of the world. Alternatives to be have been far less effective and the result has been the resurgence of malaria cases and the manifold increase in malaria -caused deaths to the largest extent in Africa.

Automation technology in manufacturing industry

Nowadays, UK computer and space explore technology had reached the mature stage. It means that UK government ought not need to continue spend much resource to research these two kind technologies. Otherwise, the automatic manufacturing technology, e.g. human intelligence new product. It has need to develop because human intelligence machines will bring beneficial to satisfy human everyday life need, e.g. hospital patients' activities need, if the patent who can not walk easily, but the human intelligence machine can assist the patient walk to anywhere conveniently. So, he/she does not need to sit on wheel chair and apply the human intelligence machine man to help him/her to drive on the intelligence automatic driving vehicle to go to anywhere conveniently.

Otherwise, increased automation in low wage countries, e.g. China, Korea, Africa, Hong Kong etc. which have traditionally manufacturing firms, could use automatic technological manufacturing to bring lose cost advantage and potentially lose their ability of achieving rapid economy growth by shifting workers to factory jobs. So, UK government and businessmen needs to consider automation technology development, i.e. 3D printing manufacturing industry will encourage UK companies to move manufacturing process, closer to gain the biggest advantage from this 3D automation technology development.

A growing concern of premature de-industrialization in energy and developing countries could require new models and a need un-skillful the UK workforce. In the future, the best way toward for UK cities will reduce their exposure to automation is to boost their technological dynamic and attract more UK skilled workers. Automation technology progress can give UK manufacturers' employee benefits, such as long term healthy productivity improvement, raising productivity efficiency and product quality, macroeconomic and microeconomic effects of automation technological change, it's change will be beneficial to UK society, i.e. automation active labor market policies, which could help UK job seekers find jobs from training to incentive to support self-employment to create high technological job employment chance in UK society. So, raising science, technology, engineering and math subjects update skills level are needed to UK any universities, which can be increasingly important in UK society, these factors could complicate the ability of UK high automation technology education to adopt to the UK automation manufacturing technological change. A talent mismatch already exists in UK, with many well UK educated workers can find employment in lower-skilled jobs. To combat this, greater coordination will be needed between the education, training and employment sectors in UK society.

Why are high automatic technology product development models needed to research to UK any manufacturers? UK government and manufacturers need to consider how to achieve high technology product development models. According to Hauser et al. (2006) indicated the high technology (high tech.) development process, is influenced by the innovative process, bringing products on exception value which stimulate product market demand. Innovation provides products the specific basis for which world economies compete with each other on the global market. Able to find new solutions, innovations generate significant changes in existing markets, destroy them, or create new marketing (Hauser et al. 2006). So, UK manufacturers need to concern on any manufacturing high technology product development process because which can influence any new products development to manufacture to sell to any overseas or domestic both markets successfully.

What is high tech. product meaning? Mohr et al. (2010) argues that there are two reasons why it is important to clarify and specific high technology : (1) due to the impact of technologies on the economy, attempts are made to classify economic production and incomes ; (2) due to the impact of high tech. on the environment. Standard marketing strategies are being modified and adopted , therefore, it is necessary to know the products to focus on. Why UK manufacturers need to consider high technological product process. Nowadays, high tech. products are complex, advanced, requiring specific technical knowledge, which is technologically not discontinued and being produced at the companies which have twice as many technical personnel and invest twice as many in scientific research and development than other companies. Moreover, these products are time-sensitive as scientists are continuously searching for new approaches for invention of more advanced technologies which make all preceding ones lower-ranking. The most important, nowadays global consumers will adopt the particular technology. It means that global customers may delay adopting new high-tech. products and in order to mitigate the prolonged uncertainty require a high degree of education and information about the product and need post-purchase reassurance.

Anyway, nowadays customer individual needs in high tech. environments are characterized by sudden changes related to unpredictable fashion. Even, consumers concern about how to preserve new product' competitive technological standard is completely incompatible with technological uncertainty. The most important factor is the prevalence rate of any new products development process, which is influenced by slower than of traditional products. In many cases high-tech. automatic product market are being materialized slower than which are expected. The technological uncertainty challenges will exist in development process, such as uncertainty related to the timetable for development of the question whether the new product will be function as promised. In automatic high-tech. industries, the time requires for product development is difficult to predict as , commonly, it takes longer than expected , uncertainty related to unanticipated consequences and uncertainty about the product life cycle related to competition products. In conclusion, these factors will influence new automatic technology product development process unsuccessful, so UK manufacturers will need to concern on any high technological automatic product's manufacturing process.

Future economists predict automatic technology how to influence future UK economy

Before, all over the world presented picture of demonstrate in London on the occasion of the meeting of the G20. Some economists indicated disastrous economy consequences will occur to any one of Western country , such as UK, so if any one of Western country did not consider automatic technology development to itself country. They indicated one example, such as material incentives to produce disappeared throughout Russia and, when Society leadership called off the experiment, the country faced industrial output reduced to 10% of what had been registered in 1914 and agricultural output reduced to such low levels as to cause widespread famine.

Why would UK encounter disastrous economy consequences if UK government did not encourage manufacturers spend money to invest to innovate automatic technology industry? According to a variety of anthropological studies, a collectivity is unable to operate efficiently with everybody giving talent workers have chance to devote whose best effort to manufacture any high technological products, e.g. human intelligence vehicle or airplane. Hence, economic incentives are needed to UK manufacturers to invest high technological automatic industry development. Because the economists predict UK will have many talent worker numbers, their number will be more than a certain number of normal effort workers, due to UK technological education level is very excellent to provide to train many young technological manufacturing students to find this kind of high technological manufacturing job. So, the high technological manufacturing job seekers will increase and it won't decrease to UK job market in the future.

Assuming that UK high technological automatic manufacturing workers who would desire only to introduce changes in the workings of the international economic order and policies of countries participating in the present economic order rather than change the order itself, what will be UK manufacturers their specific economic preferences in the future? It implies tnat either concentrate on spending more investment to automatic high technological development, e.g. human intelligence automatic high technological products or still concentrate on spending more investment to common traditional technological products.

However, UK was a developed Western country which had had strong automatic high technological development effort very long time. Otherwise, it compared to some developing countries, such as Asian China, Hong Kong, Korea etc. Asian countries their future economic growth rate will show un- surprising , different patterns, so the Asian countries has weak effort to invest high automatic technological product development, such as human intelligence technological development. The catching-up process suggests low economic growth rate in the high automatic technological product development to the Asian developing countries in the future.

Hence, the future economists predict that it views as probable successors of the Western world economic leadership if any Western country , such as UK manufacturers who prefer to invest to any high automatic technological products development , e.g. developing on human intelligence automatic technological products more than traditional common technological products development. On the one side, but it seems important to stress that two very poor countries among the challengers-China and India-are examples of countries that changed their institutions and economic policies from no or little economic freedom to more economic freedom. Because there two countries whose governments prefer to lend loans to encourage their country manufacturers prefer to invest high automatic technological products manufacturing. On the other side, attitudes toward foreign direct investment (FDI) have undergone change since the 1960 s and a large majority of less developed countries, e.g. China and India are now competing strongly among themselves and with developed market economies for direct investment from multinational companies. So, UK will face China and India high automatic technological product competitors in the future. And in fact, all countries that joined Western developed economies did that without much (if any) external inflow of public resources. It is right time that UK government needs to lend loans to encourage domestic manufacturers to invest high automatic technological products to raise whose international high technological products sale effort to win its future competitors. So, machine resources will be increased demand to o UK manufacturers if who chose to spend machine resources to innovate to manufacture any new and high technological automatic products to raise human daily life needs in the future. It means that it is right time UK manufacturers need buy much machines to prepare to manufacture many future high technological automatic products when these machine prices are low. Because the future global machine prices will possible be raised if many China and India manufacturers will also buy many machines in the future. For example, USA government had provided much financial support to assist sugar cane producers to develop their businesses. And they are dependent to a much larger extent than sugar cane producers and sugar processors in the USA on government. Without very high subsidies to renewable energy generation, they would not have survived at all. So, USA government had been the first country which could lent much financial assistance to encourage domestic renewable energy generation manufacturers to develop high technological energy manufacturing business. So, UK government needs follow USA to lend financial assistance to encourage domestic high technological automatic industry development.

Future economists also predict China and India will be competitors for future leadership in the global economy, special high technological products. China has been the media and analyst's favorite for quite some time. Quantitative projections have seemingly supported such expectation. Such as China and India had manufactured many high technological new space rockets products, ocean war large ships etc. Moreover, China has become one of the major world trade players in the early twenty-first century.

Many long-term forecasts, assuming similarly high economic growth rates in the decades ahead, predict that China will surpass the USA in terms of aggregate GDP somewhere between 2020 and 2030 or later, say between 2030 and 2050 year. The future economists conclude on the basis of these predictions that China will not only pass the USA in aggregate product (GDP), but its economy and economic policies will influence the rest of the world to a similar extent that the USA does at present.

I stressed a very important point, namely that the UK future high technological automatic product competitor China and India, namely that economies not only grow, but in the process change their structure. China and India have been industry very rapidly (the first transition) and building the physical infrastructure that accompanies industrialization changes to technology in the future. However, at a certain per capita GNP level the two countries, such as China and India will face another structural shift when which technological development will reach the mature stage in the future. China and India had been primarily historical pattern of economic development because the shift in the role of engine of growth from industry to services is to a much greater extent a qualitative shift. Both higher and different skills are required. And, even more importantly, interactions generating ideas driving the highly human-capital-intensive service economy require a much freer environment, not only in the economic area. Chinese exports have been heavily labor-intensive. This being the case, they contributed to the expansion of industrial employment, offering for the first time in the history of China a taste of (very modest) prosperity to more than 100 million new industrial workers and their families. This is the major component of the success accomplished by Chinese economic growth. Richer trade partners create room for more trade, so the Chinese should hope that intra-South trade, that is, trade between the emerging economies of Asia, the Middle East, Africa and Latin America, will open up new and growing opportunities. I presume that if Western economy , such as UK did not developed high technological automatic industry to stable their social welfare, so thoroughly slowed down their economic growth.

Will it allow China to accomplish the transition to a mature, innovation, service-sector-based market economy? It has allowed the economy to industrialize much more successfully, even if the labor shift from agriculture to industry has not yet been completed. But it is a long way off the next major test: the second high technological industry transition of the economic structure to China. Bear in mind that Russia attempted it twice and failed at both attempts.

But even, assuming that China at some point in the future does succeed in accomplishing the second transition, will it be able to supersede the USA, for example, as the main global high automatic technological innovation center if it wants to become the No.1 global high technological industry economy? Given the nature of the centralized state and its stability to collect financial resources , China's ability to increase research and development expenditure to high automatic technological products and to hire a mass of researchers, engineers, technicians and other specialists should not be doubted. This process in already taking place.

But , again, Soviet Russia already exceed the USA in the R&D/GDP ratio in the 1970s, long before the communist collapse, with no effects on its innovativeness. Inputs matter less than outputs, quantity in the innovation process mean much less than quality. The latter characteristics depends importantly on economic, civic and even political institutions. Otherwise, independent India had three options open to it in 1946s. It could pursue spontaneous economic development, with some state intervention to be sure, along the lines of basically free market capitalism; it could turn the clock back and try to recreate the rural-agricultural and handicraft based. The dominant way of thinking was Society -style priority to industrialization and , within industrialization , priority to heavy industry. In other words, not textiles and clothing, which has been developing well in India since the mid- nine teen century, but production of sewing machines and , even better, production of machines the produce sewing machines.

The results were only to be expected. The heavy stress on the expansion of capital-intensive heavy industries in a very poor country quickly strained the ability of the Indian economy to generate adequate savings. Moreover, some of these industries were above the level of industrial competence of an underdeveloped economy. Thus, the amount of required resources (capital, skilled labor) was usually larger per unit of output than in the same industries in more mature, richer industries economies. In another view point, India will develop light industries, just as any other poor country with a great deal of unskilled labor, had a comparative advantage and no less importantly, an economy in which, due to their low capital/labor ratio, light industries could employ many more people, spreading prosperity more widely in a poor country. So, it explain that why China will have more effort to develop heavy high technological industry in the future. Thus, India got less economic efficiency, less employment than in a spontaneously developing economy, less ability to compete internationally in light industries suitable for an underdeveloped economy and finally got heavy industry unable to compete even on the domestic market and, therefore requiring no less heavy a dose of protection. Overall India got an underperforming economy, in particular in its relations with the rest of the world.

To conclude by comparing the performance of the traditional sectors of the Indian economy and the performance of its modern, human -capital-intensive subsector of manufacturing and skill intensive service sector. The latter both employ workers with high-and medium -high skillful level (in branches ranging from computer software and biotechnology and pharmaceutical high technological light industry). India is ahead of China in terms of the output and export of such products and services. Thus, it implies that UK ought concentrate on developing high automatic heavy high technological industry, e.g. human intelligence technological products because these industry is not better development to other many countries' strong effort , such China and India large population countries.

Developing countries cities technological

competitive investment factor

Some economists predict developing countries every city in the global 750 is projected to have a larger future technological economy growth. But the diversity of developing countries' economic performance is large. Developing economy cities, such as China, Japan, Hong Kong, Korea cities can grow rapidly by acquiring capital and technological know-how and putting them to use by their rapidly growing urban labor forces. Even, these developing countries cities' rapid technological development can impact to US labor market supply.

Due to future rapid technological development to these developing countries, the result will cause developing countries cities, such as Asia China, Hong Kong, India cities economy growth will rapidly. Otherwise, developed western countries cities, such as US, UK, Canada, Australia, Span, Germany etc. countries lie close to the technological frontier have stable urban populations and more limited investment and job creation opportunities. It will influence these developed countries' economic growth is slow than the developing countries. Due to developing Asia countries cities will prefer to invest more technological development to compare to developed countries, such as US, UK, Canada, Australia, Span, Germany etc. countries. Therefore developed countries, such as US, UK, Canada, Australia, Span, Germany etc. countries tend to grow more slowly. It seems developing Asia countries, such as Hong Kong, China, Korea etc. countries urban and central cities economic performance within developing countries will be better than developed countries, such as UK, US urban and central cities within five years.

Thus, I suppose that future developed countries, such as US the speed of technological development will be slower to compare developing countries, such as Hong Kong , China, Korea, India etc. countries. Then, it will bring this question: How to solve developed countries, such as US, Washington, New York etc. cities future economic slow growth challenge? For future developed country cities, such as New York, Washington etc. large cities' technological investment and location decision, it will need understand that diversity is essential. Various factors can have an impact on US country intra-national urban cities performance, including sector structures, agglomeration benefits, infrastructure quality. For example, US country central government needs have tolerance of diverse performance, land supply and US city governance plan. It aims to raise US central and urban cities' future economic performance. Moreover, US country will need to concern above issues to arrange how to improve central and urban city economic development . Specially, it will need to concern technology innovation to encourage many overseas technology investors to anticipate different kinds of technology products innovation, e.g. human intelligence machine, mobile, computer etc. high technology products. It aims to absorb different countries' new technological knowledge of different kinds of high technological products to excite US domestic or foreign countries consumers' desires to choose to buy many different kinds of high technological products to raise US GDP growth in US technological product sector industry in the future.

What are the trends impact on rural America's future economy?

Some economists indicate that there are five trends reshape to impact rural America' future economy. They include that digital economy will shift future America rural economy. US quality of life will change a lot, the US rural economy will stay uneven, US commodities will compete in global markets and will give less benefit to US rural economy and US new products will revolutionize US agriculture economy.

The first aspect impacts to US agriculture economy, the US future rural economy stays uneven. Growth will concentrate in 4 out of 10 rural places and they have scenery, a retail hub, or one next to a city in US. The impact on rural America includes some rural places will try to manage growth , but many places on a quest for new economic engines. Thus, it will bring these questions to US rural economy impact, such as : Who will be US businessmen clients? The struggling farmers? The struggling farm-dependent country? The booming mountain area? The rural area transforming into city?

The second aspect impacts to US agriculture economy, due to US commodities will compete in global markets if it will bring a smaller benefit in US rural economy. Then, US farm scale will cut costs and competition fewer US farms and places will depend on farm income. What is the impact of commoditization on rural America? There are more farms depend on area jobs and it creates a new imperative to add value. What is the impact of commodity on US clients? The need for competitive commodities remains, but the payoff for added value is rising and community impacts are important.

The third aspect impact to US agriculture economy, new products will revolutionize agriculture. Major, shift from commodities to products, spurred by biotech, means two agriculture in the future and two rural America . Hence, US future agriculture determination the rural economy will be declined. A future new US agriculture supply chain integrator will be caused from the traditional farming supply chain procedure the change to outsourced contractor farming supply chain procedure, such as: In beginning, from farmer will outsource supply chain contract to processor, then contract to distributor and contract to food retailer final step.

The fourth aspect impacts to US agriculture economy, what will be two agricultures impact to the US future economy? The first US agriculture impact will be US commodity agriculture. It focuses on production capabilities, farming foods production will be thin margins maintained with technology and big sale. The second US agriculture impact will be product agriculture. It focuses on consumer needs, farming foods production margins will be protected by capturing value and building business relationship. Thus, it will bring these questions concern what the impact of product agriculture which can influence to US economy. How to apply biotechnological agricultural techniques and farming product application to raise US farming productivity? How to build world class agricultural (farm) producing chains that benefit to US farming produces production method? How can US faming foods producers participation or lead in product chains?

In the fifth aspect impacts to US agricultural economy, it is digital economy impacts US rural agriculture. Future diversity economic base can encourage US farming product agriculture to enter rural digital agricultural service consumption sector to change US agricultural consumer individual shopping habit. What will impact to US farmers? Digital agricultural economy will bring these questions: Who will lead in broadband digital agricultural technology? How to launch e-markets and businesses and how to cooperate with US rural farmers? What will impact on US agricultural on natural resource management aspect and on how to US commodity to build amenity strategies?

However, rural America's future will be shaped by policies that will encourage agricultural technology adoption, it will enhance farming worker skills, it will improve rural quality of life and it will ensure access to capital to bring US agricultural economy growth.

According to John G. (2016) indicated that " a point forecast is that GDP per capita will rise well under 1% per year in the longer run, with overall GDP growth of a little over 1 to 12%. The main drivers of slow growth are educational attainment and demographics. First, rising educational attainment will add less to productivity growth than it did historically. Second because of the aging and retirement of baby boomers, employment will rise more slowly than population which in turn, is projected to rise slowly relative to history." Thus, it seems that some economists believe education and born rate will influence future US employment method. They assume that the employment and growth ratio will rise and unemployment ratio will deadline of US will increase birth ratio and future there are many young people (students) can have chance to accept high education degree to raise whose education level to prepare to enter different kinds of high educational jobs market to work in the future.

Considering a more growth accounting perceptive on productivity growth. According to the analysis in Fernald (2015) which uses a multi-sector growth model for the projections. It indicated that although, the details differ and if bases projections on TFP data since 2004, it also implies a preferred point estimate of 1.6% per year in US over this short period. The " fundamentals" of labor-productivity growth (namely, growth in total factor productivity , TFP) have exceeded the actual realization for reasons that reflect the unwinding of dynamic of labor quality and capital depending associated with the great recession. Thus, how to raise labor quality which concerns how to raise educational level to young people in any country will be one labor economic challenge in US in the future.

Fernald (2015) also explained " the shortfall" in productivity growth relative to fundamentals reflects, at least in part, the unwinding of two dynamics associated with the great recession. He indicated that first, at the end of the great recession business had a lot of capital relative to labor, which has attended the need of add capacity to meet demand in recent years. In contrast to the outsized growth in capital deepening from 2007 to 2010 year, we have seen capital "shallowing" since 2010 year. Second, businesses fired low-skilled workers during the recession, which raised labor quality in 2007 year to 2010 year period. As these potential workers have been rehired, the growth rate of labor quality has added less.

Thus, on the one hand, when one country encounters economic recession, many employers will like to employ high educational level and high skilled labor to raise productivity. If US encountered economic recession, but it had none (lacked) enough high educational level and high skilled knowledgeable workers to be supplied to the labor market in US. Then, US will encounter long term economic recession period, it can't shorten economic recession period. Thus, US will need to let many US young people have effort to study to prepare enough high educational level knowledge to do different kinds of professional or high knowledgeable or high technological jobs in future US labor market.

However, US high knowledgeable labor can also assist US businessmen to raise productivity growth. Due to labor quality could be grown by high educational and increasing number of knowledgeable workers. On the other hand, moreover, if there are many US young married parents who will either choose not born any babies for next generation or choose born only one to four children. Then, future US will have a small numbers of young people to be supplied to primary schools, high schools, even universities to study. It also means the university level graduate student numbers will decrease also. So, low birth rate factor can also influence the high knowledgeable labor numbers to be supplied to future US labor market.

So, I recommend that US government needs to encourage many young parents choose born next generation and provides student loans to lend to poor families to support whose children can have more chance to attempt to go to high schools or universities to study in the future.

US development practitioners are increasingly aware of the role that US social and political structures play in future shaping US's development paths and results. In this context, US macro social analysis needs to understand the ways in which power relations act to circumscribe the opportunities available to poor US people to improve their situation. For example, US donor organizations need to understand of relevant US social structures, such as informal institutions or other relevant US social practices in US.

This provides an entry point for understanding the broader US political environment or challenges in a particular sector or process. Furthermore, any US donor organizations need to place greater emphasis on the analysis of livelihoods and economic opportunities and their relationship to reduce the unequal of gap between rich and poor US citizen in US societies . Thus, US government needs to encourage donor organization participants choose to do the reasonable donor behavioral to aim to reduce the unfair donor spending to the unneeded donor assistance beneficiaries. To let us socio-economic has more balance chance to every US poor citizen in US society. So, it can also raise average every US poor citizen feels better quality of life in US society.

How does the rise of US exports to East Asia factor influence US economy change? Export have become an increasing important source of revenue for both national and regional forms in the United States. How does the primary growth market for US exports to influence US economy growth? I recommend the developing nations in East Asia will the developing nations in East Asia will soon rival today's industrial nations as the most important US trading partner . In view of the rapid growth of US exports and their geographic shift toward developing nations.

Some economists indicates that two tends in recent US export performance are particularly notable. First, US exports have increased rapidly relative to total US output, development with important implications for the entire economy. Approximately 130,000 US firms employing over 10 million domestic workers, export their products (US Bureau of the census,1993). Second, the geographic distribution of US exports has been shifting dramatically. The industrialized nations of the organization for economic cooperation and development (OCED) account for about 57% of all US exports . However, in recent years of the start of US exports to major trading partners in East Asia. America has been rising and now accounts for 26% of the total. Thus, economic policymakers can no longer make trade related decisions without considering their effect on US exports to East Asia market.

From 1981 to 1987 year, two factors temporarily stemmed the rising tide of 1980 year. First, the US dollar began to appreciate significantly in 1981 year as the United States enacted a restrictive monetary policy and an expansion fiscal policy. From 1981 to 1985 years, the dollar rose almost 50%, thus making US exports more expensive relative to foreign products (Hakki & Whittakersand J, Gregg Whittaker, 1985. " The US dollar recent developments, outlook, and policy options". Federal reserve bank of Kansas city, economic review, Sept./Oct., pp.3-15.) Thus, future US will need to make good international export and import trade relationship with Asia countries, e.g. China, Hong Kong, Japan etc . countries to raise GDP income.

Education factor influences US future technology labor market change?

In the past, there fundamental forces have shaped US work labor market, includes an increase in the returns to education. General education upgrading and the large numbers of female need to work. How educational attainment, demographics and human capital will be predicted to influence US future labor market. Some economists believe education is useful to influence US future labor market. They indicate the social returns to education policies today depend on the relative prices that labor of different educational levels will command in future US labor market; current US labor market trends appear to leave a large group behind; less educated males. The rationale for social policies target specifically to this population is strengthened if predicted future outcomes in US labor market will lead this less educated male group numbers to fall down.

How to supply educational level components to influence future changes in US labor supplied? It can change in the size of the US working age population, it can change in hours worked conditional on being of working age, and it can change in the skills (effective human capital units) to US workers of different education levels, gender and age . In US , the labor is supplied by both highly educated men and women increased substantially relative to the supply of labor by the less educated. Among US males this is largely , due to an increase in educational attainment; highly educated US males did not differentially increase their supplied compared to less educated males nor did their experience differential increases in their human capital policy in US. For US females, some economists found large increases in the labor supplied by US working age women that are due to both large increases in hours worked and increase in educational attainment. So, I assume that future US will have many high educational level female labors to work in US society.

Today, human history is at the beginning of a growth industrial revolution. Developments in genetics, artificial intelligence, robotics, nanotechnology, 3D printing and biotechnology will be popular to influence US future job market change. For example, smart systems, product-homes, factories, farms or cities with help to solve problems ranging from supply chain management to climate change. The rise of the sharing economy will allow US human to monetize everything from their empty house to their car.

Due to the future patterns of consumption will change to trend high technology life enjoyment, it will cause production and employment will also change to employ high technological production labor. As entire industries adjust, most US occupations are changed to high technological manufacturing industries. When some US jobs are threatened by others grow through a change in the skill sets required to do them. a key element in understanding how the benefits and burdens of the growth.

Nowadays, the current technological changes of humans and machines , but rather an opportunity for work to truly become a channel though which human recognize full potential. As US is a high technological developed country. I assume many US employers will choose to act to be the first high technological and invention manufacturing leader to encourage which labors need to learn high technological production methods to prepare manufacture any new technological products to sell in the future US domestic or foreign both markets. Thus, it is possible that future high technological manufacturing labor numbers will be shared large go e.g. 50 to 60% future total US labor market.

How can future US labor market affect job creation and productivity growth? US future economic growth requires factor reallocation across US firms and continuous replacement of technologies. US labor market influences US economy dynamism by their impact on the supply of a key factor, skilled workers to US new and expanding firms, US growth -favoring labor market includes portable pension plans and health insurance united to the current US employers, individualized wage-setting and US public income insurance systems that encourage mobility and risk taking.

US future economic growth arises as production shifts from less to more successful firms though the reallocation of factors of production . US labor market can advance restructuring. Overly regulations tend to create a system in which a large share of economic activity occurs in US small firms without the ability to grow. US labor market should be organized to promote potential high growth US firms, especially through decentralized and individualized wage setting, portable jobs.

In the future, US will have many key importance of high growth firms. US capitalism entails a process of creative destination. New ideas continuously challenges act structures, giving rise to structural transformation as successful innovations and new products firms and industries will arise and obsolete ones will decline in US society.

Martin , J. P. (2012) studies pointed to high-growth forms (sometimes known as gazelles) as the main drivers of this process. In the US , an estimated 1% of firms creation 40% of all new jobs and 5% create almost 70% of new jobs. A review of the studies of US firms growth reveals some common findings . US high-growth firms are crucial to net job growth, generating a large share of all net jobs . This is particularly pronounced in recessions, when US high-growth firms continue to grow when other US firms deadline. US small firms are over-represented among high-growth firms, but these US firms come in all sizes . A small subgroup of large high growth firms are major job creators. Such as US high -growth firms are younger on average, US young and small high high-growth firms grows, not through mergers and acquisition and make a larger contribution to net employment growth than do US larger and older higher growth firms, high growth firms are present in all industries. Through they are slightly overrepresented in service industries in US.

Some economists predict that future US will be a flexible labor market, the marginal product of labor and the average wage in an industry should tend toward equally across US firms. Taking advantage of a legislative change to raise cost to US employers a study measured the gap between the marginal product of labor and the average wage in an industry before and after the reform. The gap increased after the legislation, which suggests that the legislation reduced allocative efficiency. Their studies have suggested that total factor productivity could increase by as much as 30% in China and India of they were to attain the US level of allocative efficiency across firms within individual industries. The result implies that plants with low total factor productivity are too large and plant with high total factor productivity are too small relative to the US benchmark of allocative efficiency.

What is allocative efficiency meaning? It occurs when the mix of product produced matches consumer preferences (where marginal benefit equals marginal cost). There products and services are the most profitable, thereby promoting economic growth other research also indicate a strong quantitative effects of strict employment protection legislation on the rate of reallocation in US industries experiments. By relaxing employment protection rules to US developed countries, such as UK, UK etc. with the strictest legislation could increases their reallocation rate by an estimated 50% in the most dynamic sectors, those that benefit most from flexibility.

The effect appears to be particularly strong on the entry-exist margin, which is arguably, especially importation for creative destruction. In future US, if manufacturing industry can have high technological production method to achieve reallocation rate to efficiency to every manufacturing industry. It can have benefit to economic growth, due manufacturing process can be move efficient to avoid cost. Also high technological manufacturing reallocation rate innovation method can influence the future US number of jobs lost in contracting or existing US firms as well as the number of jobs gained in new or expanding US firms in future a certain period divided by the average number of existing jobs. So, US high technological manufacturing reallocation rate innovation method will bring disadvantages to cause many contracting or existing firms job lost, but it will also increase the number of jobs gained in new or expanding firms in US. Thus, if future US manufacturing industry can have high technological reallocation rate innovated successfully. It will raise many new job chances in new or expanding firms in US, but it also have chance to cause many contracting or existing firms job lost or the same time.

What will expected to impact of future computerization on US labor market outcomes? Some economists estimated, about 47% of total US employment is at risk, due to that US wages and educational attainment will exhibit a strong negative relationship with an occupation's probability of computerization. They indicated that the poor performance of global labor markets across advanced economies has intensified the debate about technological unemployment among economists more recently. Indeed, over the past, decades, computers have substituted for a number of jobs, including the functions of bookkeepers, cashier and telephone operators (Bresnahan, 1999, MGI, 2013).

Although the extent of these developments remains to be seen, estimates by MGI (2013) suggests that sophisticated algorithms could substitute for approximately 140 million full time knowledge workers world wise. Hence, when technological process throughout economic history has largely been confined to the machine of manual tasks, requiring physical labor, technological progress in the twenty-first century can be expected to contribute to a wide range of cognitive tasks, which until have largely remained a human domain. Of course, may occupations being affected by these developments act still far from fully computerization, meaning that the computerization of some tasks will simply free-up time for human labor to perform other tasks. Nonetheless, the trend is clear: computers increasingly challenge human labor in a wide range cognitive tasks (Brynjolfsson and Mc Afee, 2011).

Thus, it seems that future US computerization job trend will influence some US traditional labor hand made manufacturing industry to divide some part job duty to let computerization work. However, it will not cause many US manufacturing labor to be dismissed. It can still keep some US manufacturing labors to US employers' needs in the future.

Popular science, technology , engineering and mathematics kind of labor supply will be increased demand in US.

Science, technology , engineering and mathematics workers will drive US innovation and competitiveness by new ideas, new companies and new industries in US. However, US employers frequently concern the supply and availability of this kind of workers. Over the past 10 years, growth in this kind of jobs was three times as fast as growth to general jobs in US. This kind of US workers are also less likely to experience joblessness than other kinds of workers. In the future, science, technology, engineering and mathematics workers will play a key role to grow and raise stability of the US economy.

Bureau of labor statistics, ESA calculation 2010 and 2018 year. indicated these kinds of technology, science and engineering workers had been increasing 7.9% from 2000 to 2010 year growth as well as these kinds of workers had been increasing 17% from 2008 to 2018 year growth. Otherwise, other kinds of workers had been increasing 2.6% from 2000 to 2020 year growth as well as these kinds of workers had been increasing 9.8% from 2008 to 2018 year growth. Hence, these kinds of science, technology and engineering workers increasing rate and increasing level are more than other kinds of workers both twenty years.

The other occupations include positions, such as educators, managers, technicians, health-care professionals or social scientists. The science occupation divides four categories: computer and mathematics, engineering and surveying, physical and life science four categories. The reasons why these kinds of jobs will be trend popularly. We define these kinds of degree holders as persons whose primary or secondary undergraduate major was in a science, engineering or technological field. To using similar logic to what we used in our occupation selection, we exclude business, healthcare, and social science majors.

The US department of commerce, economics and statistics administration analysis showed that a science, technology, engineering and math. (STEM) degree is the typical path to a job related to those kinds of degrees or more than two-thirds of the 4.7 million (STEM) workers with a college degree has an undergraduate (STEM) degree. However, this does not necessarily mean that (STEM) field or their jobs . For example, only 35 per cent of college educated computer and mathematic workers have a degree in computer science or math. Thus, these past data explained that it is possible US science, technology ,engineering and mathematics employers will increase needs and why many US students choose to study these subjects in US. Thus, future US economic growth will depend on developing these kinds of science, technology ,engineering and mathematics industries.

Increase development in genetics, human intelligence, robotics, nanotechnology, 3D printing and biotechnology technological industry

In US future, these kinds of jobs will be needed to increase development in genetics, human intelligence, robotics, nanotechnology, 3D printing and biotechnology. For example, smart systems homes, factories, farms grids or cities will help tackle problems ranging from supply chain management to climate change. The rise of US economy growth will allow US people to monetize everything from their empty house to their car in US. These new technological products development will change US patterns of consumption, production and employment adaption are also be changed by US corporations, US government and individuals.

Why will the technological revolution be broader socio-economic, geopolitical and demographic drivers of change to influence future US social economic and consumption pattern change? Future US most occupations will also be changed. When some traditional old jobs are threatened by redundancy and other new technological jobs will grow rapidly, existing jobs are also changed in the skill sets required to do them. The debate is between some economists foresee limitless new job opportunities and foresee massive dislocation of US jobs. In fact, the reality is highly specific to future US high technological production industry, region and high technological occupation in question as well as how US production workers can be raised themselves ability to actions the upgrade level of high technological production ability from various stakeholders to manage high technological production method change.

Overall, this is a modestly positive outlook of US high technological production employment across future most high technological production industries with jobs growth expected in several sectors. However, it is also clear that this need for more talent in certain job categories is accompanied by high skills instability across all job categories. Combined together, future US net job growth and skills instability result in most US businesses with face major recruitment challenges and talent shortages, a pattern already evident in the result and set to get worse over next five years in possible.

The question is how US businesses, government and individuals will react to these new technological job changes, due to talent shortage, mass unemployment and growing inequality challenges will encounter in future US society.

The current technological revolution does not need become a race between humans and machines , but rather an opportunity for work to truly become a channel through which US people recognize their potential. So, if US traditional low manufacturing skillful workers lack talent to learn new skills to prepare to do future new technological manufacturing jobs, such as 3 D printing, robotics, nanotechnology, biotechnological high technological products manufacturing jobs. Then, it will cause increasing of unemployment rate to some not talent US low manufacturing skillful workers. So, US government or high technological product industry employers need to consider this future unemployment challenge will be caused by high technological products manufacturing changing influences. It seems high technological development will cause these low manufacturing skillful workers unemployed rising numbers as well as high manufacturing skillful workers human capital shortage global challenges will exist.

In the future, the driver of changes to influence US demographic and socio-economic growth. They may include: changing work environments and flexible working arrangements. It means new technologies are enabling workplace innovations , such as remote working, co-working spaces and teleconferencing. Rising of the middle class in Asia markets. It means the world's economic center is shifting towards the Asia developing countries.

Some economists predict that Asia will be projected to account for 66% of the global middle class and for 59% of middle class consumption by 2030 year. In addition, climate change, natural resource will be constraints to a greener economy. It means that climate change is a major driver of innovation as organizations search for measures to help adjust to its effects. As global economic growth consumers are needed to lead to demand for natural resources and raw materials, over explanation implies higher extraction most and degradation ecosystem and these challenges will also impact US employment changes needs. All US government also needs to concern future global economic change influence.

Some economists believed the interplay between entrepreneur , innovation and economic geography growth in the United states of America have close relationship . Because future innovation is the driving force of growth in the knowledge economy to US . They assumed that if future US entrepreneurships chose to act as new firm formation, which will prefer to accept any new technological innovation to manufacture any new technological products and reallocate any new resources to apply to concentrate on manufacturing any new technological products within firms. For example, Bernard, et al. (2006) find that one third of the net increase in real U.S. manufacturing output between 1972 and 1997 is due to the net adding and dropping of products by surviving firms, a contribution that dwarfs that of net firm entry and exist. Clearly new firm formation is only one dimension of innovation and existing firms account for a large share of total research and development (R&D), in many industries such as pharmaceuticals. It seems US any industries will need spin off of existing operations and the acquisition of independent start-ups are now important dimensions of new process and product development. Thus, innovation is an important factor to influence US economic growth in the future.

However, it will have challenges to US different industries when the causal connections between entrepreneurship, innovation and growth arises. For example, US employment growth of large, middle and small sizes of entrepreneurships will be strongly positively correlated with US any new firms formation, but this doesn't necessarily imply that entrepreneurship causes growth . There may be one factor that causes US employment growth and US firms formation to co-vary, and it is hard to find instructions that affect US firm formation, but have no independent effect on US employment growth.

The interpretation of the correlation between US employment growth and US firm formation relates to old debates in US economic geography about whether US workers follow US firms, or US firms follow workers or there are mutually reinforcing feedbacks between US firms' and workers' locations decisions. So, some economists believed that, US any domestic geography economic growth will possible be caused by these factor , such as either US geography firms innovation factor or US geography high technological workers high level productivity factor or

US geography firms innovation or US geography high technological workers high level productivity both combining factor. But the challenge will cause, it assumes that future many US entrepreneurships choose to innovate to manufacture whose products. Although, many high technological manufacturing workers employment chance will be raised, but it also cause many low technological manufacturing workers employment chance will be reduced as the same time. So, it is difficult to keep high technological and low technological both workers who have same fair employment chance as the same time in the future US society if US planned to achieve the future knowledgeable innovation economic society.

However, to achieve this innovation dream, the economists give opinions to US government which will need to encourage the foundations of US entrepreneurial policy and distinguish four broad actors: (a) individual agents who identify business opportunities and choose to exploit them. (b) new formed businesses which innovate using new knowledge and other resources, (C) the economy including all institutions that influence economic growth, and (d) US society is as the collection of all agents who are the ultimate beneficiaries of wealth creation. Within this organizing framework, US entrepreneurships will be easily shaped or changes the overall business climate to achieve knowledge economic society in the future.

The role of intangible assets influences the regional economic growth in US.

What are the four big factors of intangible assets? Some economists indicated they include knowledgeable capital, human capital, social capital and entrepreneurs capital. Nowadays, globalization and increased competition will cause new types of pressure to influence US economic growth. So, US companies need have flexibility, the ability to immediately adapt to market developments, and pro-activism in creating future markets. The relative importance of physical growth: However, soft production factors, that is those related to personal knowledge are becoming more important to influence US future economic growth, which regards to human capital and knowledge as driving factor of economic growth in industries developed countries, such as US.

All these soft production factors can be grouped in what is known intangible assets. These assets can be defined as non-material factors that contribute to enterprise performance in the production of products or the provision of services, or that are expected to generate future economic benefits to the entities or individuals that control their deployment (Akerlof & Kranton , 2000).

Whether it has a close relationship between these intangible assets and US regional economic growth? Some economists had researched to have more reliable quantitative statistical information to do report in above four big factors how to effect on US regional economical growth influence. Their report indicated that returns from human and social capital are taken as homogeneous for US all regions. They also indicated these two sets of questions in their report. The first one, dealing with knowledge accumulation, addresses, among others the following issues:

(a) How does innovation and knowledge accumulation occur within firms and hoe does it impact on economic performance?

(b) What is the role of universities in regional, national and global knowledge accumulation processes?

The second set of questions addresses the key knowledge diffuses over space and how this diffusion impacts on economic performances.

In particular:

(c) To what extent knowledge diffusion is conditioned by spatial proximity?

(d) What is the impact of knowledge accumulation and diffusion on economic performance?

They indicated to answer these questions, having reliable measures of how innovation process occurs, of the actors that take part in it and the mechanisms that are in place is important. They pointed out that the systemic nature of US regional intangible asset demands indicators that grasp two kinds of capabilities: network capabilities , i.e. connectivity, both intra-and-inter-regional and organizational capabilities, as well as their dynamic in US. These indicators have been applied to the study of linkages and relationships between US firms and between US firms and US universities, highlighting the mechanisms through which those actors contribute to the processes of knowledge accumulation, generation and diffusion.

They also found results: How does knowledge accumulation occur within US firms and how does it impact on US economic performance? They included collaborations with competitors are most commonly undertaken at early stages of the development projects, those with buyers and suppliers are more likely to result in the introduction of new products and processes: At the same, it has been highlighted that, regardless of the industry, the most innovative firms, i.e. those more able to absorb knowledge are more likely to participate in collaborative networks.

Thus, US future entrepreneurships need to offer knowledge accumulation opportunities for US regional firms and research institutions to benefit and contribute to global network of US expects to achieve rapid regional economic growth. US's entrepreneurships also needs to explore organizational innovation, those US firms whose structure enables learning by doing, using and interacting by relying, among other things on parallel development teams. Semi-autonomous work teams and reduced management layers are more likely to introduce new products to the future US domestic and foreign both markets.

What is the role of US universities in US regional, national and global knowledge accumulation processes? US universities can heavily influence US regional, national and global knowledge accumulation processes. For instance, when collaborating with multi-national enterprises, they may affect simultaneously the three level. Their report had highlighted interesting results on the local impact of universities: when it has been found that top ranked departments are significantly associated with partnerships involving spatially close industry partners, it has also emerge geographical proximity, is nt the main driver of collaboration choices. These are found to depend largely on US firms' networks and universities' specific characteristics. Among other things, the cultural traditional of academic institution has been shown to influence the ability to collaborate with industry and commerce research.

Networks characteristics have emerged as crucial in determining academic knowledge transfer: the better the access to international networks, the higher the patenting activity, have the knowledge transfer to US industry. This implies that the set of tools of knowledge based economic development should include not only research and development, but also clever ways of supporting academic research network.

To conclude, if US expected research development can assist economic growth. Then, US academics universities and companies both need to co-operate to carrying on experimenting any kinds of research and prepare to assist any US product innovation more easily. So, the intangible asset, not as scientists, technology, US universities' and firms' research fund which is an conditional factor to influence US regional research and development economic growth in the future.

Social factor impacts US technological development growth.

Has it relationship between social influence and economic environment in future US? For example, the social factors that are positively correlated with the economic growth (i.e. the expected years of schooling and the life expectancy) and respectively, the factors that are negatively correlated with US future economic growth (i.e. the US population or risk of poverty and the unemployment rate).

The improvement of the US future economic environment will be an objective of the macroeconomic policy on short, medium and also long term. The importance of social factors upon US future economic growth, considering that the future used macroeconomic indicator, GDP per capita, is not most proper measure for the future US nation welfare. Due to GDP per capital fails to take into consideration some specific sectors of the US social economy, such as the black market.

Until recently, some economists rely on culture is as a possible determinant of economic phenomena. However, in current years, better techniques and more date made it possible to identify systematic differences in people's preferences and beliefs and to relate them to various measures of cultural environment suggest an approach to introduce cultural-based explanation that can be tested and are able to substantially understand economic phenomena.

The increased importance of social factors relies on a basic concept. Some theory is measured to economic growth which has wrong assumption. For example, the fiscal and monetary policies focused on increasing the national income, which lead consequently to economic growth. The reason most of economic opinions have been argued because whose opinions are based on a wrong hypothesis, according to which the nation welfare is based only on the level of income.

Can social factors influence US future economic growth? Human development history, global life expectancy has been experiencing these stages: from the industrialization process, the technologic progress, the medical evolution, the scientific research, these stages were also related to internal causes, specific to some developed countries, e.g. US developed country. Thus, the differences are significant and are linked both to US life expectancy level and the GDP /capita. Such as US population is less than China population too much. Although, US land area is near to China area. It seems US will encounter life expectancy level need to prepare its technological development to raise economy growth of opportunity. For example, Africa and Asia are still facing major economic and social issues. The access to a health life and medical services are still long terms objectives for countries with low life expectancy.

According to Harrison & Huntington (2000), the analysis of social factors helps understanding the human behavior with respect to consumption, savings, investment system, expectations and attitudes towards the economic circumstances, which also have a major impact on the economic growth. The evolutions of economic and social environment are needed for US future development. In order to eliminate the gap of living standard, outside resources and support US needs have good social indicators study plan to concern econometric model to rise poor people living standard in future US society between rich and poor people who are living in US. However, I believe the social factors include demographic and culture, population's structure factors which are one important social indicator to influence the distribution of the US social public income.

Barro & Sala-i-Martin (1996) defined culture is as the sum of symbols, meanings, habits values, behaviors and social artifacts which characterize a distinctive and specific human population group. For decades, economists and social thinkers debated the influence of population change on economic growth. Bloom et. al (2001) defined three alternative hypotheses: that population growth restrict, promotes or is independent of economic growth . Each hypothesis was sustained with strong arguments, and all the arguments mostly focused on population size and growth. The debates revealed other important issues, such as the age structure of the population, the way in which the population is distributed across different age groups.

The economists indicated that people's economic behavior varies at different stages of life, changes in a country's age structure can have significant effects on its economic performance. So, such as US, if it had a high proportion of children are likely to devote a high proportion of resources to their care, which would tend to depress the pace of economic growth. By contrast, if US's population falls within the working wages, the added productivity of this group can produce an increase in the economic growth. This is how the combined effect of this large working age population and health, family, labor, financial and human capital policies can create cycles of wealth creation. On the other hand, if US a large proportion consists of the elderly , the effects can be similar to those of a very young population; a large share of resources is needed by a relatively less productive segment of the population , which likewise can inhibit economic growth in future US society.

Further Bloom et al. (2001) analyzed the three main mechanisms of population's structure for determining economic growth (labor supply, savings and human capital) and their dependence of policy environment. They indicated that a growing number of adults will only be productive of there is sufficient flexibility in the labor market to allow its expansion, and macroeconomic policies that permit and encourage investment, people will only save if who have access to adequate saving mechanisms and have confidence in domestic financial markets and the demographic transition creates conditions where people will tend to invest in their health and education, offering great economic benefits, special in the modern world's increasing sophisticated economies.

It seems future US labor market will need a growing number of adults to supply , a stable domestic financial market to encourage US people have more confidence to save money in banks, a stable health and education sector industry can encourage US people have confidence to invest to do this kind of health and education service industry. Instead of population of working age factor will influence US economic growth. However, US people living culture will also influence US economic growth. For example, if it has a trend that there are many US young people like often go to shopping in relax time, because who feel shopping is their young group entertainment in the year. Then, the year US GDP growth will be possible raised, due to there are many US young people prefer to spend for shopping expenditure suddenly in the year. In conclude, in social environment of cultural and population of working age size will influence US future economic growth.

Online tourism industry influences US future online industry economy growth.

Today, US online tourism sale industry has always been one of America's great home growth industries. Today, more than 8 million Americans are employed in travel and tourism. For example, US domestic South Carolina, hospitality and tourism has been as the largest local industry, providing tens of thousands of families directly or indirectly with jobs. Predicting global tourism consumption needs work be increased. US will experience in a changing economy, tourism industry will provide job security to many Americans as well as the service -oriented nature of many travel positions and these jobs are difficult, if it is impossible to outsource.

Many people accept to buy air tickets from online sale channel. Will future America government play an important role to influence future US online air ticket tourism sale method to raise online travel consumption behavior? However, some have questioned in recent years whether US policies have harmed the ability of the tourism industry to expand. One of the most frequently discussed concerns involves American visa policy, when European Union allows tourists from 26 European countries and almost all of the America and Australia to visit without a visa. America policies require some travelers from friendly countries, such as Brazil, to travel thousands of miles from home to attend the in-person interview needed to secure a tourist visa. Although, the US White House has taken steps to reduce rise wait times in recent years, in some parts of the world, like Vietnam and Turkey, the US tourist visa application process can be a multi-month process (US Travel Association , 2014).

Will the visa waiver program impact driving increases in US impact driving increases in US tourist volumes? Some economist analysis found that when a typical country joins the visa waiver program, it sees a notable increase in the number of countries who chose to visit the US in the immediate years. That follow over the course of its first five years in the US visa wavier program, the number of tourists arriving from a participating country rises by 16.4%. Also their analysis indicated to expand the visa waiver program to some countries would result in $7.66 billion in additional tourist spending within a five year period. It would also create at least 50,000 American tourism jobs within 5 years. Purchases of products and services by visitors contribute foreign significantly to job creation and economic growth in US international travelers to US purchased more than $180 billion amount . In addition, tourism generates a trade surplus as foreign visitors spend more in the US. So, US enjoyed a $57 billion trade maintained a trade surplus in tourism every year. Some economists indicated that India is likely to contribute to the growth in foreign travel to the US . If India government can ensure which have enough numbers of foreign travelers are encouraged to choose to travel to US. In the future, India will be one important tourism cooperation partner to US. So, US ought achieve online travel sale strategy to promote to Indian to know what online travel advantages can give to them in the future, e.g. reducing time to buy air ticket, convenience, cheap e-ticket price, avoiding to lose air seat supply, more airlines choice providing. These are online e-ticket sale attractive characteristics to India online e-ticket sale market. Thus, US ought concentrate on promoting this kind of online travel sale service to India in order to raise US many airline e-tickets sale numbers.

The effects of population growth influence US economy growth.

Nowadays, China and India population growth rate are rapidly. Population growth can have several disadvantage effects on the economic expansion and performance to China and India. Does it influence cultural and sociological links between the following per capita income, rates, technological advancement , education aspects? China with 1.32 billion people and India with 1.1 billion people. Though, they each enjoy a large labor force advantage, several key economic factors have contributed to how the Chinese and Indian populations have grown and what differing effects that growth has had on their developing economies. Although, there two countries have high population growth rates, but the poor people has low standard of living.

So, when these two countries population sizes are large, but the standard of living will be low, and population will be reduced by either the preventive check (international reduction of fertility) or by the positive check (malnutrition, disease, and famine). It seems china and India governments think overpopulation challenge will cause social crime increasing, education competition, raising the job applicants number will increase, but the jobs supply number won't increase faster than job applicants number, and it will cause unemployment etc. social challenge in the future long term. So, why China and India governments will choose to control birth rates every year. However, in these developing countries, children are often as an economic asset, a tool to help increase agricultural production. Demand or need for large number of children is driven down by improvements in living standards and child survival and by the modern of economies. The movement away from agricultural production and into more modern industries in the manufacturing and services sectors need the necessity to have numbers of children to prepare to supply to China and India future manufacturing and services job markets.

However, US is a developed countries. The country main GDP growth source is high technological industry. Hence future children birth rate is not necessary to prepare to supply for manufacturing or service industries needs mainly. It seems US population birth rate is stable. So, overpopulation challenge won't be caused easily. Can population growth influence US economic growth? US is different to China and India. US's population growth rate is less. Hence, if US population growth rate can rise. It won't have overpopulation challenge. US needs have many young people number who can have high technological knowledge to prepare to have enough supply to do the future high technological different kinds of positions to build social economic growth in the future. Hence, US ought encourage young people choose to marry and to born next generation children to supply future different kinds of high technological jobs of needs to raise technological productivity and they (high technological manufacturing workers) will be the main production of factor to influence future US economic growth in the high technological manufacturing sector.

Thus, I believe the effect future US of population growth will influence US future economic growth as the same time. Also, it is the right time, US government needs to assist universities have enough afford resources, e.g. university fund, technological educational courses, lectures etc. to provide future US technological education students' needs in the future. So, it brings this question: What can determine US economic growth?

In global macro-economic influence, since 1973 year, per captia income growth in the US and other advanced countries has slowed to 2.2 % a year or almost half the 3.9% annual rate of the preceding quarter century . If the US had maintained the level of growth experiences in the 1950 year and 1960 year, real per capita income today would be about 71% greater than it actually is. In contrast, it has been estimated that eliminating the variability in US consumption since world war II would be equivalent to boosting current real consumption by only about 4.8%. If the choice is between long-term growth policies and further short-term stabilization policies long term clearly have the potential for higher benefits. Hence, what factors determine US economic growth (David M & Roy J, 1993).

According to traditional growth theory, the main determinants of long run economic growth are not influenced by economic incentives. Perhaps the reason why economists have neglected long time, to profession relied on a theory that offered litter scope for policy to influence important sources of growth.

High technology development can reducing income inequality growth.

Some economists found one key is that education and anti-discrimination policies well designed labor market and large and/or progressive tax and transfer system can all reduce income inequality . In many OECD developed western countries, income inequality has increased in past decades. In some countries, top earners have captured a large share of overall income gains, when for other income has risen only a little. Some see poverty as the relevant concern with the type of growth enhancing policy reforms advocated for each OECD developed countries and economic growth might have positive or negative side effects on income inequality.

OECD (2011), it first highlights differences in some income inequality across the OECD and the factors driving them, such as cross-country differences in wage and non-wage income inequality as well as in hour worked and inactivity. OECD developed western countries can be divided into five groups to their pattern of inequality. For example, in five English-speaking countries (Australia, Canada, Ireland, New Zealand, the United Kingdom) and the Netherlands wages are rather dispersed and the share of part-time employment is high, driving inequality in labor earnings above the OECD average means-tested public cash transfer and progressive tax.

It seems income inequality will influence the developed countries, such as UK, Canada, Australia, New Zealand , US etc. economic growth. Although, technology change and globalization have played a role to influence the distribution of labor income. Some economists believe that any countries' policies will also influence income inequality. These policies factors include: technological education policies can increase different technology graduation rates from upper secondary and tertiary education and that also promote equal access to a well-designed different sector technology labor market policy can reduce inequality.

A relatively high minimum wage narrows the distribution if labor income, but if set too high, it may reduce employment of inequality reducing effect. It tends to reduce labor earning inequality by ensuring a more equal distribution of earnings. Job protection reforms that make permanent and temporary contracts more even in their provisions low income wage dispersion of earnings is rather mixed, removing product market regulations can reduce labor income inequality by boosting employment, policies the faster the immigrants and fight all forms of discrimination reduce inequality, progressive tax policy play a key role in lowering overall income across the OECD developed countries.

However, the redistributive fair income level between low level income labors and middle level income labors and high level income labors impact of developed countries, e.g. consumption taxes and real estate taxes tend to be regressive tax policy. Hence, it seems that reducing income inequality can cause the more fair income distribution between the high income level and the middle income level and the low income level labors. Then, it will let the developing countries or developed countries , such as US citizens feel that who can get real social welfare fairly, due to high technology development can boost economic growth in US society.

Long term cheap medical cost trend factor influences US economic growth.

Some economists predict to make long term forecasts to reduce medical cost trends how will influence US economy. Also, they indicate short run cheap medical cost forecasts for first 1 to 5 years to reflect the particulars of specific groups, benefit packages, regional markets or cheap medical cost network providers and use their local cheap medical choice information and actuarial skills to improve accuracy and reasonability. They also oversight group review on the consistency of baseline assumptions with factor influencing future US patients‘ medical choice taste, medical technology trend component and historical annual percentage increase in medical costs, premiums, income and excess cost growth are found to influence future US patients consumption behavior. However, their research predicting expensive medical cost is the main factor to influence to reduce US patient numbers among of ward room sleeping environment, doctor loyalty, hospital entertainment and service facilities provision hospital cheap car parking charge service, cheap or free telephone call provision, hospital meal quality provision etc. different factors .

They suggest that how to reduce medical cost. They indicate many other factors, e.g. patient individual illness aging, physician supply, medical insurance plan benefit will affect the cost of a particular patient, group, organization or plan in a specific locality or over the short run. Also they indicated that additional analysis is still needed to determine if reliable estimates of separate medical insurance premiums, medical care payments, pharmaceuticals or other cost categories are possible to influence medical cost to be increase.

Hence, for long run US cheap medical cost will encourage or attract many patients prefer to pay medical cost to see doctors in US any hospitals or medical centers. Then, US hospitals or medical centers income will increase and US GDP income will also increase in medical service sectors in the future. It seems that long run cheap medical cost will influence US economic growth.

Long term cheap medical cost trend factor

influences US economic growth.

The next generation of US talent management practices and solutions will largely be driven by US economic evolution, demographic changes and technology advancements. These factors are dramatically influencing the way US people work, the way US companies are organized and the way talent is managed.

Some economists explained the key economic factors driving changes in talent management include: the knowledge economy is value to companies, talent is now a required strategic asset. Key changes in the future include a line between inside and outside talent that will result expansion of the talent management, globalization, such as European expansion is well-known top expansion prospect for global companies now include China, Russia and Eastern Europe and America and the rest of Asia. So , US government needs to know globalization can give what opportunities to US future .

Although, knowledge management or knowledge economy will bring advantages to US. However, it also bring disadvantages to this aspect, such as skill gap and structural unemployment will also influence US organizations structural unemployment and skill gap challenges issues will be caused between low skillful and high skillful workers, generational geographies changing will occur in US.

Although, baby boomer retirement has been top of mind for many years in the US, even more significant demographic changes are happening outside the US, where population growth rates and aging population will influence as local economies. Thus, the ability for organizations success will need global talent or effectively more talent from areas of abundance to scarcity is becoming a strategic issue to any US companies development , increased health and longevity mean that seniors are working longer enabling US organizations to keep experienced team members into their retirement years. But it also raise US workforce planning and generational challenges, workplace and diversity is increasing, a more diverse pool of talent affords new opportunity . Such as hiring workers raise productivity of needs, digitization of candidate or employee profiles can meet US business employment needs because employee talent data has been digitized and integrated into comprehensive talent profiles.

Techniques , such as attribute matching and recommendation technologies can be applied in talent management can be applied in talent management to find and match the most right candidate to do any positions in short time efficiently, with the increasing need of telecommunication in the US market penetration of smartphones and tablet devices a significant portion of the world's human potential will have access to rich web and application experiences from anywhere. Thus enables US organizations to source and collaborate on knowledge work with any part of the world into a global talent pool.

How can intellectual assets impact to US to change to knowledge economy? The information age moved the basis of economic value from products to intellectual assets, information and the talent that develops them. It is now widely acknowledged that intangible assets, with largely consist of know-how, unique intelligent property, and patent right, drive move than 80% of the valuations of publishing US publicly traded companies.

In future US knowledge economy, US leading edge organizations will have efforts to use into the talent and intellectual capital of not only employees, but also clients, partners and the public at large in an effort to create an extended electronic community. For example, client support portals where clients can answer each other's questions, which will reduce costs by expensive client support calls for US companies in future US knowledge economy environment.

Also, knowledge economy will assist US companies to be partner and customer innovation efforts easily. Such as P&G daily product company's ability to source more than 50% its new product ideas to external innovation, driving industry-leading standards for new product launch rates. In future knowledge economy environment, it is clear that US organizations will be increasingly deriving value from talent that is outside the company.

In future US knowledge economy environment, the link between employees within the US organization and those outside, it is also driving talent management changes, particularly around sourcing, strategic workforce planning and employees engagement . Given these changes, executives in leading US companies will be increasingly focused on talent management issues, recognizing that talent, wherever knowledge economy will give knowledge management method to any US organizations to build more competitive advantages in the future. However, knowledge economy will also bring structural unemployment to US society. Unfortunately, today's global talent market is largely inefficient and characterized by a high degree if competition relative to the redistribution of talent.

One result of this inefficiency is long period of skill gaps structured unemployment is a particularly different scenario in which section skills are no longer required, not just within a US particular company, but within US an entire sector. Structural unemployment may be the future result of cyclical boom and bust cycles, offshoring of partial. In conclusion, whatever the causes of future knowledge economy to US , the result is an uneven distribution of talent relative to the available jobs in US. In part of structured unemployment in US will be caused from knowledge economy influence. However, knowledge economy will also influence US future businesses speed increases, bandwidth increases and growth in mobile internet access during US encounters the knowledge economy influence in society.

The impact of educational quality factor influences US economic growth.

Schools can train skills of an individual and human capital for future businessmen need. It is not the only factor. Schools nonetheless have a special place, not only because education and skill creation are among that prime explicit objectives, but also because which the factor(s) most directly are affected by public policies. So, US is well established that the distribution personal incomes in US society is strongly related to the amount of education US people have had. Thus, any noticeable effects of the current quality of US schooling and the distribution of US people skills and income will become apparent some years in the future, those US students now in US school become a significant part of the future US labor force. Then, the question arises as: To whether are these skills correlated with US student's subsequent performance in the future US labor market and will the US economy's ability to grow ?

The quality of human resources are measured by scores is directly related to individual earnings , productivity and economic growth. A range of research results from the United States shows that earnings advantages , due to higher achievement on standardized tests are quite substantial . These studies typically find that measured achievement has a clear impact on earnings, after allowing for a differences in the quantity of schooling, age or work experience, and for other factors that might influencing US people earnings. In other words, for those leaving school at a given grad, higher quality school outcomes (represented by test scores) are closely related to subsequent earnings differences. So, it seems quality of education and individual income has direct relationship to influence US economic growth.

According, educational program that deliver those skills will bring higher individual economic benefits. Obviously, students who don't better in schools as evidenced by either examination grades or scores on standardized achievement tests tend to go further in school or university. By the same way, the net costs of improvement in school quality if reduction in rates of student repetition study. Then, it brings this question: Will education quality bring future economic return to US?

Early some economists' research found that personal and behavioral traits, such as perseverance and leadership qualities had a significant influence upon labor market success, including earnings. To answer above question, we need to know if US schools which generally have good student performance, it will influence socio-economic advantage improved performance, changes in school climate, teacher morale and commitment, school autonomy , teacher-pupil relations and disciplinary had some compensatory influence towards greater equity. In American, pupil socio-economic background and classroom climate appeared to be the most important predictors of achievement. So, it seems human development will influence US economic growth in the future. So, US development organizations seem better will then non-specialized educational organizations to design and deliver effective combinations of livelihoods and literacy.

Whether people who attain literacy actually make much use of it is subject to debate. On balance, however, literacy seems more used where economic development is better established. This supports the argument that same degree of economic and political improvement is necessary to sustain literacy. Then, US people will use their literacy skills where conditions make it useful or desirable for them to do so. However, schooling is a social process, and improvements in resources, technology and quality of student and teaching inputs should in principle to able to be enhance its overall quality. In a good number of countries, large increases in average real expenditure per student and other measures of school resources in primary and secondary schools over the last four or five decades have not remotely been matched by a comparable increase in average test scores.

What can be influenced from quality of education to US? Some economists suggest the earning can provide an important incentive mechanism, which can influence both the quality and motivation of teachers. If teachers' real average earnings had kept the same level with other professional groups over the period, the productivity impact of their earnings growth would literacy have been small. The first view point, in fact, however, in many countries teachers' earnings have increased considerably less sharply than those other groups. Teachers may feel worse off, because of their decline in status relative to other professional groups. This circumstance could well explain part perhaps an important part of the apparent lack of impact on learning outcomes of increase in real per student spending over time. One to teachers' general salary is low to compare other professional in the global society.

Then, it brings this question. Can quantity of education influence US economic growth? In this modern economic approach to investigating the determinants of educational outcomes has borrowed well established technique from other economic applications. The idea that there is a determinate relationship between (teacher number) inputs to a production process (teaching process) and the outputs(student examination results and learning performance) that subsequently bring has being been important in micro-economic analysis. If US schooling teaching possibilities are governed by certain teachers' quality between factors of production, e.g. teachers; teaching performance , teachers' supply numbers to every schools, teachers' educational qualification. So, the product function describes the maximum feasible output (student examination results and learning combinations) obtained from alternative combinations of these inputs (teachers' quality teaching performance, supply numbers, education qualification).

Production factors are powerful analytic tools, which have been applied to the analysis of most forms of economic production. Since the mid-1960 year, they have also been widely used in the economic analysis of education. Thus, in schooling educational organizations, teacher salaries will influence teachers' performance (production of factor) to be good or bad. If teachers' educational performance is good, then production of output (student learning abilities and students examination results) will be good usually. Otherwise, if their educational performance is bad, then production of output (student learning abilities and students examination results) will be bad usually .

In US society, if many poor learning performance students have been produced. Then, there will not many talent young people who can contribute to serve US society in different professional aspects. It means that they can not contribute US economic growth easily. Thus, it seems that US quality of education can impact US economic growth for long term and US universities, secondary schools and US government ought need to find methods how to raise quality of education for next generation of labor supply market.

Bio-medical industry factorboosts US economy.

In the future, the perspective of bio-medical industry will be an alternative growth scenario. So, US government will need to modest improvements in key policy areas to adopt bio-medical industry needs, e.g. more favorable coverage and payment policies for medical innovation, improvements in regulatory policy to create efficiencies in research and development process and improvements in policy to incentive R & D (research and development) create efficiencies in the R & D process.

As an industry rooted in science and advanced manufacturing, the innovation bio-medical industry is uniquely position to help maintain US leadership in new technologies and scientific to continue to create high quality, high wage R&D and manufacturing jobs and enhance America's global competitiveness in the future. Today, the US bio-medical industry supports a total of 3.4 million jobs across the US economy , including over 810,000 direct jobs:

contributes $189 billion in economic output and is responsible for about one in five dollars spent on domestic R&D by US businesses. Hence, innovation bio-medical industry will be one high value knowledge-based industries as a driver of US economic growth.

The reasons include: The first reason is such as , the US history, it has been the world leader in bio-medical research and development of new medicine over the past 30 years. It has been one leader of world class life science ecosystem and innovation among different countries in medicine development history. So, bio-medical industry will be a high technological innovation related activity of industry leader, as is measured by R&D investment, e.g. generation venture capital and share a total R&D employment in manufacturing industry. Next reason is that US bio-medical industry employs a total of 813, 523 worker amount. These workers lead a wide range of occupations that offer high wage, high quality employment. The total economic impacts of the industry, it is estimated (via the generally accepted methodology of input/output analysis) that supports nearly 3.4 million total jobs and generates nearly $ 789 billion in US economic output (National Science Board, 2014). Finally, reason is that US people concern life health issue, In addition to improving individual health and lengthening life ages, medical advances have contributed to substantial societal health gains, such as reducing disability and improving productivity.

According to two Universities of Chicago economists indicated the estimated economic gains from declining morality alone in the US from 1970 year to 2000 year had a value to US society of more than 3 trillion a year. Hence, US medical health need of patient numbers will increase, due to who have large needs for life health. Hence, quality of education can influence bio-medical industry development to impact US economic growth in the future.

Welfare economic theory, Kaldor-Hicks efficiency theory and Pareto improvement theory relationship

Economists explain that welfare economic theory, Kaldor-Hicks efficiency theory and Pareto improvement theory which have close relationship. Welfare economic theory means general social equilibrium. They indicate the demand of commodities must same to the supply of commodities when the commodity market stays in the stable level. So , when production is increasing, the manufacturers also need to keep their products supply and demand keep to the stable level and consumers' demand of their products must also need to increase as well as bank interest rate must be fallen in order to raise consumption desires. Also, the low bank interest can also excite investors' investment desires.

Such as to explain why the developing countries cities technological competitive investment factor can impact US and UK economic growth. Welfare economic theory means general social equilibrium. The economists indicate the demand of commodities must same to the supply of commodities when the commodity market stays in the stable level. Due to the future developing countries investors will invest much on developing new technological products research. So, these countries' economy growth will be possible faster than US and UK both developed countries because it is possible that the technological product investor number will decrease. So, US and UK government will need to attract and encourage many foreign developing countries' investor prefer to invest their technological products research to assist US and UK both developed countries to develop its economy. As Welfare economic theory means general social equilibrium. If US and UK government can give benefits to these developing countries' technological product investors, then these developing countries' technological product investors will prefer to invest to developed country US urban cities, such as small cities or farming location to build factories to manufacture their new technological products. Because , London, New York, Washington etc. large cities' technological investment and location where land supply is limited and offices and factories rents are also expensive. Otherwise, UK and US, farming location or small cities location where have much land supply to build large offices and facilities and the rent is much cheaper than US and UK main cities, such as London, New York, Washington etc. Even, if UK and US government and banks can lend low interest rate of bank loans or government loans to encourage foreign investors to do technological product research in its country. So, UK and US bank low bank interest rate can encourage US consumers prefer to buy any future new technological products, due to low bank interest rate can not attract who choose to save more money in US and UK any banks as well as US and UK bank low bank interest rate can also encourage foreign developing countries' high technological product investors to choose to invest in UK and UK , due to who can pay low bank or government loan interest to compare themselves countries or other countries.

As Kaldor-Hicks efficiency theory indicates the policy is suitable to be implemented if the policy beneficiaries' welfares can compensate to the policy benefactress. So, US and UK bank and government low loan interest rate policy is valuable to implement if benefactress, such as US and UK government which can raise economic growth as well as the US benefactress, such as the high technological product businessmen can sell many different kinds of high technological products from foreign developing countries' investors' assistance in US and UK both developed countries.

As Pareto improvement theory indicates that it can not carry on continue, due to the country has shortage of natural resources after the country improved its welfares to reach the maximum standard. The result will be caused, such as the country will reduce this group of citizen's welfares, if the country decides to continue to improve another group of citizen's welfares. So, future US and UK will have shortage of natural resources to supply to technological product manufacturers. So, the number of technological product production will be fallen , due to the shortage of natural resources are supplied to US and UK high technological product manufacturers. The only solvable choice is encouraging foreign high technological product investors to attract them to supply themselves high technological products any resources to manufacture high technological products and provide to US and UK high technological product sellers to help them to sell in US and UK domestic market or export to overseas market to earn income. Then, US and UK will earn raise GDP income from high technological product sale industry in the future.

Natural rate of unemployment

Economists believe why natural rate of unemployment will occur in any countries. They indicate that during economy condition keeps at the balance situation (condition), anyway any country government adopts any policy. However, the natural rate of unemployment won't reach to zero level as well as there are some people will still unemployed or it is possible that some people will be alternative employment between any time. Hence, it means that although US and UK is an developed country. It can not guarantee there are not any people unemployed , so the natural rate of unemployment will not reach to zero level.

So, it seems that US and UK current economy condition had kept at the balance situation (condition). Thus, even future science, technology , engineering and mathematics workers will drive US innovation and competitiveness by new ideas, new companies and new industries in US. However, US and UK employers frequently concern the supply and availability of this kind of workers. Over the past 10 years, growth in this kind of jobs was three times as fast as growth to general jobs in US. In the future the **Natural rate of unemployment of** US and UK science, technology , engineering and mathematics worker number must not reach zero level.

Anyway, in the future, the perspective of bio-medical industry will be an alternative growth scenario. So, US and UK government will need to modest improvements in key policy areas to adopt bio-medical industry needs, e.g. more favorable coverage and payment policies for medical innovation, improvements in regulatory policy to create efficiencies in research and development process and improvements in policy to incentive R & D (research and development) create efficiencies in the R & D process.

As an industry rooted in science and advanced manufacturing, the innovation bio-medical industry is uniquely position to help maintain US leadership in new technologies and scientific to continue to create high quality, high wage R&D and manufacturing jobs and enhance America's global competitiveness in the future. In the future the **Natural rate of unemployment of** US and UK of bio-medical industry worker number must not reach zero level.

Thus, if future US had enough job number which could supply to these high technological and bio medical industries of labors to do. However, the **natural rate of unemployment** must not reach at zero level and it does not represent its economy is poor because one developed country , such as US had been experiencing economy condition keeps at the balance situation(condition), so it's **natural rate of unemployment** must not reach zero level . Otherwise, the developing countries' economy condition does not keep at the balance situation (condition), so their **natural rate of unemployment** have more possible to reach to close zero level.

Industrial production and pollution economy

Economists indicate that it has close relationship between industrial production and pollution. When traditional products are manufactured, the air and water pollution will be caused in the economic activity. So, human needs to protect environment to keep health, the demand of investment of money reduces pollution and labor number will increase to achieve to reduce air and water pollution in natural environment. Thus, product manufacturers need to analyze which economic stage(s) will encounter shortage and find methods to solve challenge.

This **Industrial production and pollution economy** theory can explain why US and UK needs to plan achieve digital economy to shift future America rural economy. Some economists indicate that there are five trends reshape to impact rural America‘ and England future economy. They include that digital economy will shift future America rural economy. US and UK quality of life will change a lot, the US and UK rural economy will stay uneven, US commodities will compete in global markets and will give less benefit to US and UK rural economy and US and UK new products will revolutionize US and UK agriculture economy.

US and UK needs to plan digital economy to future agricultural production of the reasons include: The first aspect impacts to US agriculture economy, the US future rural economy stays uneven. Growth will concentrate in 4 out of 10 rural places and they have scenery, a retail hub, or one next to a city in US and UK. The impact on rural America includes some rural places will try to manage growth , but many places on a quest for new economic engines. Thus, it will bring these questions to US and UK rural economy impact, such as : Who will be US and UK businessmen clients? The struggling farmers? The struggling farm-dependent country? The booming mountain area? The rural area transforming into city? The second aspect impacts to US and UK agriculture economy, due to US and UK commodities will compete in global markets if it will bring a smaller benefit in US and UK rural economy. Then, US and UK farm scale will cut costs and competition fewer US and UK farms and places will depend on farm income. The third aspect impact to US and UK agriculture economy, new products will revolutionize agriculture. Major, shift from commodities to products, spurred by biotech, means two agriculture in the future and two rural America . Hence, US and UK future agriculture determination the rural economy will be declined. A future new US and UK agriculture supply chain integrator will be caused from the traditional farming supply chain procedure the change to outsourced contractor farming supply chain procedure, such as: In beginning, from farmer will outsource supply chain contract to processor, then contract to distributor and contract to food retailer final step. The fourth aspect impacts to US and UK agriculture economy, what will be two agricultures impact to the US and UK future economy? The first US and UK agriculture impact will be US and UK commodity agriculture. It focuses on production capabilities, farming foods production will be thin margins maintained with technology and big sale. The second US and UK agriculture impact will be product agriculture. It focuses on consumer needs, farming foods production margins will be protected by capturing value and building business relationship. In the fifth aspect impacts to US and UK agricultural economy, it is digital economy impacts US and UK rural agriculture. Future diversity economic base can encourage US and UK farming product agriculture to enter rural digital agricultural service consumption sector to change US and UK agricultural consumer individual shopping habit.

Thus, future US and UK agricultural production needs to concern how to reduce air and water pollution to influence natural environment clean quality as well as it needs to find what economic stage of agricultural production will be innovated in the future.

The future of job skills influence

I. Introduction

Technology innovation will change businss models to impact on the employment. Many of the major drivers affecting global industries are expected to have significant impact on jobs, ranging from significant job creation to job replacement and from heightened labor productivity to widening skills gaps. This global technology innovation brings this question: How will technology change impact on human job skills?

Economists predict that there are many industries and countries the most in-demand occupations or specialists did not exist ten or even five years ago and the pace of change is not to accelerate. They also predict that by one popular estimate 65% of children entering primary school today will altimately end up working in completely new job types that don't yet exist.

In such a rapidly employment needs change, the ability to anticipate and prepare for future skills requirements, job content and the aggregate effect on employment is increasingly critical for businesses, governments and individuals in order to fully seize the opportunities presented by these trends.

The World Economic Forum's Future Of Jobs Report seeks to understand the current and future impact key disruptions on employment levels, skill sets and recruitment patterns in different industries and countries. It indicates that human is today at the beginning of a fourth industrial revolution. Technological development will be in these fields , such as artificial intelligence and machine learning, robotics, nanotechnology, 3D printing and genetics and biotechnology. For building technology example, smart systems, homes, factories, farms, entire cities will help tackle problems ranging from supply chain management to climate change. Concurrent to this technological innovation is a set of broader socio-economic, geopolitical and demographic developments.

II. What will be future human employment trends?

The global workforce is expected to experience significant change between job families and functions. Across the countries are covered by the report, current trends could lead to a net employment impact of more than 5.1 million jobs lost to disruptive labor market changes over the period 2015 to 2020 year, with a total loss of 7.1 million jobs, two thirds of which are concentrated in routine white collar office.

Future of jobs survey, World Economic Forum indicated that the drivers of change , industries overall, share of respondents rating driver as top trend percentage. Such as demographic and socio-economic: changing nature of work, flexible work 44%, middle class in emerging markets 23%, climate change, nature resources 23%, geopolitical volatility 21% , consumer ethics, privacy issues 16%, longevity , ageing societies 14%, young demographics in emerging markets 13%, women's economic power, aspirations 12%, rapid urbanization 8%. Technological industry includes mobile internet, cloud technology 34%, processive power, big data 26%, new energy supplies advance technologies 22%, internet of things 14%, sharing economy, croud sourcing 12%, robotics, autonomous transport 9%, artificial intelligence 7%, advance manufacturing , 3 D printing 6%, advanced materials, biotechnology 6%.

Some economists also predict how the timeframe to impact industries, business models: The impact is felt already included: rising geopolitical volatility, popular mobile internet and cloud technology, advances in computing power and big data, crowdsouring, the sharing economy and peer-to-peer platforms, rising of the middle class in emerging markets, young demographics in emerging markets, rapiding urbanization, changing working environments and flexible working arrangements, e.g. online working style, climate change, natural resource constraints and the transition to a greener economy. Then, from 2015 to 2017 year period, our life will be impacted by these influences. Such as new energy supplies and technology development, internet , advanced manufacturing and 3D printing, new consumer concerns about ethical and privacy issues, longevity and ageing societies, women's rising aspirations and economic power.

Further, in the future period from 2018 to 2020 year. Our life will be impacted by these influences. Such as advanced robotics and autonomous transport, artificial intelligence and machine learning and advanced materials , biotechnology and genomics will be mature developed. Thus, these technological changes will bring these impacts of this human job question, such as: How to change in ease of recruitment?

III. How to change in ease of recuitment?

Given the overall, disruption industries are experiencing, it isn't surprising that with current trends, competition for talent in-demand job families, such as computer and mathematical and architecture and engineering and other strategic and specialist roles will be fierce, and finding efficient ways of securing a talent technological development for every industry. Thus a tangible impact to further adequacy of employees' existing skill sets can already felt in a wide range of jobs and industries today. However, if skills demand is evolving rapidly at an aggregate industry level, the degree of changing skills requirement. Within individual job families and occupations is even more pronounced. Even, those jobs that are less directly affected by technological change and how a largely stable employment outlook.

How can technological development influence occupations or jobs future changes? For example, the mobility industries expect employment growth is accompanies by situation, where nearly 40% of the skills are required by key jobs in the industry are not yet part of the core skill set of these functions today.

As the same time, workers in lower skilled roles, particularly in the office and administrative and manufacturing and production job families, many find themselves caught up in a cycle where low skills stability means who could face redundancy without significant reskilling and upskilling even when disruptive change many erode employers' incentives and the business case for investing in such reskilling.

Future of jobs survey World Economic Forum also indicated skills stability from 2015 to 2050 year industries overall unstable and stable percentage such as below:

Media, entertainment and information industry skills stability 65% and skills unstability 35%,

Consumer industry skills unstability 30% and skills stability 71%,

Healthcase industry skills unstability 29% and skills stability 71%,

Energy industry skills unstability 30% and skills stability 70%,

Professional service industry skills unstability 33% and skills stability 67%,

Information and communication technology industry skills unstability 35% and skills stability 65%,

Mobility industry skills unstability 39% and skills stability 61%,

Basic and infrastructure industry skills unstability 42% and skills stability 58%,

Financial services and investors industry skills unstability 43% and skills stability 57%.

Thus, economists predicted the future skills serious shortage industries included basic and infrastructure industry unstable skills was 42% as well as financial services and investors industry unstable skills was 43%. Both were the highest percentage of the unstable skills among of them. It implied that university students could choose these both kinds of subjects to learn because these kinds of both industries will be shortage of graduated student number of supply. Otherwise, the other industries will have higher stable skills supply to employment market. So, it brings this question: How can stable and unstable skills influence to different industries and global employment market and living quality? For example: efforts to place unemployed youth in apprenticeships in certain job categories through targeted skills training may be self-defeating of kills requirements in that job category are likely to be different in just a few year's time. Indeed is some causes such efforts may be more successful if businesses models were on future expectations. Thus, businesses will need to put talent development and future workforce strategy front and centre to their growth.

It is therefore critical that long term changes to basic and lifelong education systems are needed to complemented with specific, urgent and forced reskilling efforts in each industry. This entails several major changes in how business views and managers talent both immediately and in the longer term. Thus, if university students can choose to study these any one subject among of them. Their living standard will be raised in possible, due to it will have many these kinds of job skills requirement in the future. Finally, it is also possible that unemployed young students will find jobs more easily and it will reduce young people unemployment number and it will raise life standard of future young people if nowadays any country universities began to encourage young students to choose to study any one of these above subjects to prepare to study . Thus, these industries' future unstable skills shortage will be decreased to influence any businesses development to be better in the future.

Can technology influence global human life of standard to be fallen or grown?

Some economists predicted long term global economic growth will be remain till to 2050 year at least. There are based on a model that takes amount of projected trends in demographics, capital investment and technological process.

Will the shift in global economic power be continued by technology process factor? They give these reasons to explain why technology process can influence global economic growth as below:

The first reason, they feel future consumer online transaction market will trend mature that are becoming increasingly mature, sophisiticated and digitally technological process online transaction in popular. The second reason, emerging markets vary greatly in their institutional strengths and weaknesses and need to be assessed in a technological transaction way. These could also be major differences in institutional strengths between industry sectors within countries. Deep local knowledge that is updated in real time is critical here to manage businesses successfully in an emerging market environment, e.g. shorten online shopping transaction time and online product choice process. Having the right local partners to navigate online business through local political, legal and regulatory systems is also critical. Identifying and promoting local talent who understand local online business and social cultures better than any outside will also be an increasingly source of comparative advantage (As discussed in more detail in a recent PWC Growth Markets Centre Report, " Presence to prosperity"). The third reason, for larger western companies making strategic investments in emerging markets, part of their contribution could be to try to improve the local institutional framework. This could involve offering, appropriate technical assessment and advice to local governments in areas like corporate governance, fiscal policy and intellectual property rights protection. It could also involve investing in social and economic infrastructure (e.g. schools, roads, railways, power and water networks) where there are critical to a company's long term success in a region. Finally, there are existing markets in North America and Europe. There will remain very significant players in the global economy for decades to come. PWC report analysis shows average income levels will remain much higher than in even the best performing emerging markets for the foreseeable future. Advanced economics will also generally speaking, still be easier and lower risk places to do business given their political and institutional strengths. Thus, it seems that technological process will be the main factor to influence global GDP growth and human living standard in our future societies. It also means that the economists predict the technological process will be one main factor remain to influence global economic growth and rasing human living standard.

Developing countries will face stronger headwinds in the decades and because technological changes are rendering manufacturing more capital and skill intensive. So, it brings this question: How past, present and future of human living standard is influenced by technological process development? To answer this question , we need to assume that economic growth is a precondition for the improvement of living standards and lifetime possibilities for the " average" citizen of the developing world. Optimists would point to improvements in governance and macroeconomic policy in developing countries and to the still not fully exploited political of global economic technological globalization to foster new industries in the poor regions of the world by outsourcing and technology transfer . Otherwise, pressimists would feel rich countries control world economy, threaten to technological globalization and obstacles that late industrializers have to surmount given competition from China and/or America owned high technolgical development etc. countries. Thus, it also brings this question: What will be changed to influence past, present and future economic growth and human living standard by technological development?

It is a global technology structural transformation change issue, it means that the birth and expansion of new (higher technological productivity change) industries and the transfer of labor from traditional or lower : productivity activities to modern ones. Thus, this history change will occur from past industrialization, then it will change to present technological process and it will change to future artificial technological industry in the future.

I. Has it close relationship between climate change and technological process to influence human living standard?

Some economists point out global growth will be hindered by rising operational costs as global temperatues rise, with studies suggesting that a worst-case impact of a 1% reduction in GDP growth per year could be realized. Research also suggests that the impact will be disproportionately damaging to developing economies and only through a collective effort to enact strict carbon emissions policies can be the long term financial challenge of climate change potentially. If it was truth, it will bring this question: Can climate change influence to reduce human living standard to be fallen?

To answer this question: We need to know why climate change can raise economic cost to global societies. Generally, we know global warming is likely to impact global activity. Such as, the effect on growth and inflation , climate damage functions: quantifying the impact on activity, regional poor effects. Accessing the impact of cimate change is complex with uncertainty about both the degree of future global warming and the subsequent impact an global activity. There are clearly some benefits as well as costs as the planet warms. There is also the unknown of how technological process will respond and potentially alter the path of global warming.

II. Why can climate change influence effect on growth and inflation?

Climate change at varying levels of warming, the impact of rising temperatures will be widespread, in part due to the financial, political and economic integration. Global warming will primarily influence economic growth through damage to property and lost productivity, mass migration and security threats. For Hurricane Sandy example, which flooded much of New York in 2012 year, it caused economic damage such extreme weather events can cause. Rising sea levels will also likely harm economic output and businsses become impaired and people suffer damage to their homes.

In economy view point, using a production function, we can demonstrate the likely effort climate change will have on output. If we assume less capital stock is available , due to the damage inflicted from climate change, we would see a fall in the productive capacity of the world economy. Then, the world products: function as each unit of labor produces less output, lower labor productivity may not just occur , due to a lower level of capital stock. However, higher global temperatures may affect food security, promote the spread of infectious diseases and impair those working outdoor. Such factors are likely to cause greater incapacity and social unrest and as a result will reduce both the effectiveness (productivity) and the amount of labor available to produce output. The argument whereby the world's population is seen not to respond to climate change. It is possible that, preventive measures , such as flood defenses are put in pace in order to avoid the costs of climate change. It is a short-term economic cost to this action as resources are directed from more productive uses. It can include two aspects influence , such as food inflation and energy cost increasing , the reasons are as below:

On the one hand, inflation is likely to rise as shortage, particularly in agriculture. Climate change will cause agriculture supply shortage and food demand rising. Due to a reduction in output, but an increase in the general price level as a result of global warming. This leads human onto the possible, an inflationary effects of global warming on the agriculture world economy. Because agricultural yields are sensitive to weather conditions and as our climate becomes ever more extreme, more frequent droughts may reduce crop yields in areas where food production is vital. Higher global food prices will likely thus causes the pressure to global consumers. Then, it will lead global food consumers' living of standard to be fallen down because we need to save more money to buy food. So our entertainment and daily essential spending expenditure will be also decreased, due to saving more money to buy inflationary food.

On the other hand, energy costs will increase, due to climate change influence natural resource supply number of energy production to be shortage. Thus, it will bring higher energy costs are also likely to boost inflation. As our climate become more extreme, we are likely to demand greater energy to both our working and living environments during the summer and heat , then when we experience cold winters. Thus, if human lacks high technological process development to prepare to win climate change challenge influence, e.g. invention of renewable energy or new food planting or growing method which can adopt to grow or plant in bad climate in the future easily. Then, we shall face our living standard to be fallen , due to lacking technological development to solve climate change negative influence challenge in our future.

To conclude, I believe that human living standard will be fallen, due to we lack high technological process to prepare to solve climate change challenge, such as global warming, sea level rising, flooding, etc. natural crisis to cause food nature resource and energy nature resource supply shortage. Then, it will cause inflation of our essential product or food price rising seriously. Finally, as an effect, human living standard will be fallen.

Whether future technology can influence human living standard

I Can technology influence human habitable population dynamic change to impact living standard?

To explain above question, we also need to consider these questions, such as: What factors influence human population growth trends most strongly? How does population growth or decline impact the environment? Does urbanization threaten our quality of life or offer a pathway to better living condition?

Nowadays, human population trends are centrally important to environmental science because they help to determine the environmental impact of human activities. Rising population put increasing demands on natural resources, such as land, water and energy supplies. At the same time, pollution challenge will cause, due to human needs , spend or waste much natural resource to raise living standards, such as air and water pollution and greenhouse gas emissions, along with increasing qualities of water. Then, it will bring this question: Will technology influence environmental impact to human living standard?

Paul R. Ehrlich & John P. Holdren (1974) indicated one widely-cited formula is " I=PAT", which concerns population interacts with several other factors to determine a society's environmental impact as below:

Environmental impact = " population" x "affluence" (or
consumption) x " technology"

In fact, the question depends on assumptions about human preference. What standard of living is seen as acceptable , and what levels of risk and variability in living conditions will people tolerate? Many of these issues are not just matters of what humans want, rather who intersect with physical limits, such as total arable land or the amount of energy available to do work. In such instances nature sets of bounds on human choices (Joel E. Cohen, 1995).

To research whether technology can influence human habitable population dynamic change to impact living standard. We need to answer this question. How did industrialization alter population growth rates so sharply? One central factor was the mechanization of agriculture, with enabled societies to produce more food from available in inputs.

In our past agricultural society, as food supplies expanded, average levels of nourishment rose and diseases declined over succeeding generations. Improvements in medical care and public health services, which took place more in uraban than in rural areas, also helped people to live longer. So , death rates face in our nowadays technological society. After several decades of lower mortality, people realized that they did not have. So, many families decided to born many children to achieve their desired family size as well as birth rates began to fall as well because human was educated popularly in our technological society. Thus, in our technological society, it will cause expanded work forces, it can help nations increase their economic output, raising living standards for everyone. They also can strain available resources and services. Anyway, it also may cause shortages and economic discuption.

However, I believe pollutants, medical services, mortality and fertility factors can influence human living standard to be better or poor, instead of technology factor. But, I also believe technology will be one important factor to influence human living standard. I shall indicate these reasons to explain why technology can influence human living standard to be better or worsen and it has effort to reduce these bad factors causing to influence our future living standard.

The first reason, exposure to pollutants is a major factor contributing to infant motality and lower life expectancy in developing countries, e.g. China, India, Hong Kong, Korea. Thus, if any these developing countries lack enough technological environmental investments, such as providing cleaner energy sources and upgrading sewage treatment systems which can significantly improve public health. So, these development countries' population living standard will have negative impact if they lack technological environment investments to reduce pollution serious level to influence citizens' unhealth.

In second reason, increasing life expectancy is creating a public health infrastructure that can identify and repond quickly to disease outbreaks, families and other threats. For example, when severe alute respiratory syndrome (SARS) emerged as a disease that might cause an international epidemic. The health centers for disease control and prevention launched an emergency response program that required health departments to report suspect cases for evaluation, developed tests to identify the SARS virus, and kept health care providers and the public informed about the status of the outbreak. The United States and many other countries also reported their SARS cases to the World Health Organization. These types of close surveillance and preventive steps to control infection. Thus, it seems nowadays, countries need to invest or medical technology on attempt to invent more unique medical machines to avoid any unknown diseases existing.

The third reason, that drives population trends migration when includes geographic population shifts within nations and across boards. Migration in less predictable over long periods than fertility or morality since it can happen in sudden waves, for example, when refugees brings a war. So, slowly over many years, immigration often changes host nations or regions ethics mixes and strain society. Immigration often changes host 's or regions' ethic mixes and social services.

On the position side, it can provide needed labor (both skilled and unskilled). In my view point, if the country has good technology resources to provide skilled immigration labor to attribute their technological reource is one important factor (production of factor) to let immigration skilled laboe to contribute their effort to serve its country to raise productivity to develop its economy growth for long term. For technological process source countries, however, technology can assist immigration to attribute valuable talent. Specially, since educated and motivated people (labors) are most likely to migrate in search of opportunities.

II Human's history technological development

In human history development, through the early decades of the industrial revoluation, life expectancies were how in Weatern, Europe and the United States. Due to lack high technological medical invention. Many people died from infactious diseases, such as typhoid and cholera, which spread rapidly in the crowded, bad environment conditions that were common in early factory towns and major cities or were weakened by poor nutrition, due to lack high technological environment science resources to provide environment protection professionals to produce any new technological environment protection product to reduce air and water pollution. But from about 1850 year through 1950 year , a cascade of health and safety advances radically improved living conditions in industrialized nations. Due to technological environment industry protection development. Some this technological environment protection industry development brings these benefits to human, includes: improving urban sanitation and waste removal, improving the quality of the water supply and expanding access to it, forming public health boards to detect illnesses and quarantine the sick, researching causes and means of transmission of infectious diseases, developing vaccines and antibiotics, adopting workplace safety laws and limits on child labor, and promoting nutrition through steps, such as fortifying milk, breads and cereals with vitamins.

By mid-20 th century, most industrialized nations had passed though the demographic transition, as health technologies mere transferred to developing nations, many of these countries entered the mortality transition and their population. The world's population growth rate peaked in the late 1960 year at just over 2% per year 12.5% in developing countries. Thus, it seems health death chance from diseases and environment pollution importantly. It implies our environment pollution to influence our health will be serious, so we need continue to develop my technology on health and environment protection aspects to raise human living standard to avoid or reduce death chance increasing.

III Can food technology production shift diets, the type, combination and quantity of foods people consume, contribute to a sustanable food future?

Building on the United Nations Food And Agriculture Organization's food demand projections, it estimates that the world needs to close a 70% "food gap" between the crop calories available in 2006 year and expected caloric demand in 2050 year. It indicates the food gap stems primarily from population growth and changing diets. The global population is projected to grow to nearly 10 billion people by 2050 year, with two thirds of those people by 2050 year, with two-thirds of those people projected to live in cities. In addition , at least 3 billion people are expected to join the global middle class by 2030 year. As nations urbanize and citizens became wealthier, people generally increase their calorie intake and the share of resource-intensive foods, such as meats and dairy in their diets. As the same time, technological advance, business and economic changes and government policies are transforming entire food chains from farm to fork.

In human future, the demand of increasing technological agricultural production will increase to efforts to reduce the food shorten to close the food gap. However, relying solely on increased production to close the gap would exert pressure to clear additon natural ecosystems. For example, to increase food production by 70% , when avoiding further expansion of harvested area, crop yields would need to grow one-third more quickly than who did during the Green Revolution. In short, yield increases alone with likely be insufficient to close the gap. In the fuure, farming technology development will be applied to solve these challenges. Such as human plan use the globagrimodel farming technology to quantify the land use and greenhouse gas consequences of different foods and then analyze the per person and global effects of the three diet shifts on agricultural land needs and greenhouse gas emissions. Moreover, scienists estimate to apply farming technology to these diet shifts, if implemented at a large scale, it can close the food gap by up to 30%. When substantially reducing agriculture's resource use and environmental impacts. Thus, it seems farming technology industry will be increased demand to applied to solve future food shortage challenges to raise human living standard in the future.

In conslusion, due to human's history development, it proved in our past, we had been encountering agricultural production to industrial production . Then in the present, we are encounting technological production. In the future , we will encounter human intelligence technological production in possible. So, it implies "***future technology change will influence human living standard to be better if human continue consider to how to innovate medical health technology and agricultural growth technology and human intelligence technology and climate environmental protection technology and space technology research. Otherwise, human living standard can not be raised , even fallen if human is lazy and we do not continue to spend time and money investment to research these kinds of technological improvement.*** Thus, I think human ought continue to research these kinds of technological improvement to achieve human living standard to be better in the future.

Chapter 10 Can developed countries help global economic

Development

Defining developed and developing countries differences

What are the developed countries and developing countries

characteristics

What factors cause the differences between developed countries and developing countries? Do they have significant unique characteristics to be discovered to influence their differences? I shall attempt to indicate evidences to explain whether these are significant different unique characteristics between any developed countries and developed countries as below:

ON economic measurement aspect, low-and middle income economies are usually referred to as developing economies , and the upper middle income and the high income are referred to as developed countries. So, a developing country also called a less developed country or emerging market, it has a lower gross domestic product(GDP) than developed countries, with a less nature and sophisticated economy. The difference is between developed and developing countries. It may indicate that developed countries refer to the Sovereign (independent) nation/ state whose economy has highly progressed and possesses great technological improvement, as compared to other nations.

The countries with low industrialization and low human development indix are formed as developing countries. The World Bank classified the world's economies into four groups, based on Gross National Income per capita: high, upper middle, lower-middle , and low income countries. Least developed countries, landlocked developing countries and small island developing states are all sub-groupings of developing countries. However, it is not ensure that it is only all islands are developing countries, e.g. New Zealand may be one developing country or low developed country also. Experts have said the Guyana has one of the fastest -growing economies in the world.

The unique characteristics differences between developed countries and developing countries. They may include: developing countries are ususally poor, according to the Asian development bank, the major causes of poverty may include: Low economic growth, a week agricultural sector, increased population rates and a high volume of inequality. So, the features of developing countries, their common characteristics may include: low per capita real income, low per capita real income is one of the most defining because amony any developed countries , they may also include highly and lowly developed countries. For example, Norway is the most developed nation in the world. Switzerland is the second developed country in the world, Ireland is the third-most developed country. Then all of these nations may be highly developed countries , e.g. Germany, Hong Kong, China, Australia, Iceland, Sweden. So , it seems that New Zealand may be a lowly developed country to compare above these highly developed countries.

What factors assist the developing countries to become developed countries

However, the most developing countries in the world, they may include India, Brazil, China, Argentina is actually considered a developing country and characteristics of developing economies, high population is continue growing. Otherwise, China had began to use methods to discourage Chinese families to born more than one child in order to avoid population continue grows to bring social future burden.

Dependence on primary sector, e.g. Africa and India and New Zealand , they were still depending on main agricutural fruit, rice primary farming industry for themselves main GDP export income source as well as dependence on exports of primary commodities. So, developing countries should need focus on human development, it will remain the main focus of developing countriespost 2015 year. In this regard, the transition of developed countries to equitable and sustainable consumption will make in easier for developinf countries to pursue their human development goals in a more environmental susttainable way.

Hence, human development will may to help developing countries to develop more easily. It is future essential element to assist any one developing countries to be developed countries in success.

The unique characteristics of developing countries include that: Literacy rate is quite low as people are deprived of education facilities, the standard of living in developing countries is normally not very high. Otherwise, developed countries literacy rate is quite high , due to better education ayatem and life expectancy rate is more , due to better standing living. So, in general, the standard of living is very high to developed countries, e.g. UK, US , they have many the low income level or poor people still may have enough money to save in bank and the number of poor people is less in themselves countries, due to definitional discrepancies countries, such as Maxico, Greece and Turkey. India may be nowadays developing countries.

However, there are agrument or disagreement between developed and developing countries. The developed countries say that developing countries must stop burning fossil, fuels and other things that harm the atmosphere. Otherwise, developing countries argue that developed countries have developed by burning the fossil fuels. They say their development will be affected if they stop burning fuels. For Japan example, it is one highly developed country because ir is one of the largest and most developed economies in the world. It has a well-educated, industrious workforce and its large , affluent population makes it is one of the world's biggest consumer markets. Otherwisem New Zealand is not high technological and industrious developed country, it still depends on agricultural fruits, meats export farming industry for main GDP growth source. So, comparison New Zealand and Japan development speed, New Zealand is one lowly developed country. Otherwise, Japan is one highly developed country in nowadays our society. But, the comparison between New Zealand and China, China is still a developing country , but New Zealand may be one lowly developed country to compare China because Chinese government has repeatedly stated that China is the world's largest developing country, despite rapid economic growth over the past four decades. However, according to the 2018 survey, the United States is the world's most powerful country, following countries may include: Japan, Israel, South Korea, Saudi, Arabia, but the safest country may be Iceland because its crime rate is the least. Although, US, UK may be highly developed countries, but their crime rate may be high position. So, one highly developed country does not represent that it must have the most safest social living environment to let its citizen to feel safe to live. It may be any one highly developed countries themselves failure points.

However, environmental factors may also stop a country from developing because some places experience environmental issues, which can present them from developing, examples might be extremee flooding or desertification social factors may also stop a country from developing, e.g. high crime rate, high unemployed rate, low safe living feeling rate, low living standard, they are some parts of the world have issues that are caused by people to influence any countries continue to develop to be one developed country easily. So, all of these factors can assist any one developing country to become developed country.

What factors cause developed countries continue developed

What factors cause New Zealand to be developed country

in success

What factors influence New Zealand is still one lowly developed country? Can New Zealand fight itself country weaknesses to become one highly developed country? I shall attempt to indicate several evidences to explain what factors influence New Zealand can not develop to reach mature social development stage in itself nowadays society are below:

New Zealand is a small population country. It has only 4.8 million . However, there are many NZ people feel poverty to live. The causes of poverty in New Zealand. They may include: income inequality, lack of a simple fund support from government, lack of economic infrastructure, poor access to education, poor access to healthcase, opinion was evenly diviced on the primary cause of child poverty in NZ. Forty percent of NZ people said it was due to economic factors including unemployment, low wages, and rising living costs, the ever-increasing monthly power bills the the NZ government won't regulate or gone down.

However, in NZ, poverty is seen as relative, whereby those suffering deprivation are often struggling to feed their children, living in insecurce circumstances and unable to enjoy a satisfying social life easily to many New Zealanders. As a result, many NZ family members' health suffers and children fail to achieve a sound level of education. IN fact, there is poverty in the midst of prosperity in NZ. There is poverty amidst prosperity: There are around 682,500 people in poverty in this country or one in seven households, including around 220, 000 children .

In general, there are the causes of poverty reasons to any countries, they may include: lack of good jobs / job growth, lack of good education, the second root causes of poverty is a lack of education, a lack of social welfare, weather/ climate change, social injustice, lack of food and water, lack of government support. Although NZ may be belonged to one developed country. But, it is still staying on the lowly developed stage in long time development process. The main factors cause NZ is still one lowly developed country. They may include : lack of good jobs growth in order to let graduates can find good jobs to do and education level can not be improved . What factors cause NZ lacks good job growht and poor education improvement in long time?

In fact, NZ likes many developed countries, its witnessing a transformation in itself economy and employment opportunities. Its traditional exporting sectors , such as dairy, meat, forestry and tourism, remain important drivers of growth. So, NZ's main source of income, they are agricutlural products export, principally meat, dairy products, and fruits and vegetables , crude oil and wood and paper products are also significant. However, the impacts of poverty in NZ, because children in poor communities are three times more likely than the average child to be sick twice as likely to end up in hospital, and sudden unexpected death in infancy rates are more than 6 times higher for infants in the most disadvantaged areas of NZ. These harmful effects run into adulthood in NZ.

What are the most common jobs in NZ? The most popular carre was police officer. SO, when many NZ people hope to seek policeforce jobs. NZ will bring poor job growth development chance to let graduates have plans to develop other professional career in society. Many NZ graduates only consider policeforce jobs, it is one poor social job culture in NZ. However, NZ education is better than America in possible. NZ is definitely superior to the US, in the OECD nations indication, NZ is ranked 3 rd for education quality behinf Finland and Canada, the US ranks about 12 th . Why does NZ still be one lowly developed country in possible, when it can have superior education system?

In fact, NZ ranks highly on most indicators of well-being, but average social level of incomes are low , in general, inequality income were allocated and made NZ economy less developed in the face of shocks, due to low labour productivity factor, low labour productiviey is only partly explained by the farming main industry of the NZ economy and is primarily a consequence of low mulit-factor productivity growth within NZ other industries development, instead of farming industry as well as weak investment on other industries, e.g. technololgical, computer manufacturing , medicine life science drug manufacturing, construction, engineering, e.g. robotic manufacturing etc. different industries development. So, NZ neglects to consider how to develop other industries instead of concentrating on only development on agricultural industry.

However, economic geography is an important factor in NZ's poor productivity performance as the small size and remoteness of the economy diminish its access to global markets, the scale and efficiency of domestic businesses, the level of competition, and the ability to benefit from innovation at the global frontier. All of these many be the main cause weaknesses to NZ countinue development in success.

Moreover, NZ government lacks good policy to support its productivity growth, e.g. lacking to promoting international connections, none removing barriers to fixed capital investment to NZ domestic any industries development, instead of agricultural industry, accessing benefits of agricultural industry, accessingg benefits by improving urban planninf, enhancing competition and increasing investment in innovation and intangibles.

Hence, poor productivity technological improvement may be on main factor to cause NZ productivity growth is poor. It is main reason to cause NZ is one lowly developed country in long time, because global highly developed countries concerned high technological productivity is expected to be the main driver of income source , in particular via investment in technology and knowledge-based capital. So, any highly developed countries began to believe that economic growth from productivity improvements contributes to welfare through increasing the worker individual income that can be earned from each hour worked, providing individuals with the option to work lesss or consume moew job and service. Hence , NZ lacks high technological productivity improved to let any one talent NZ person can have chance to use his / her talent knowledge to do high technological jobs in order to attribute NZ society and to earn high hour income. NZ is only developing agricultural industry nowadays. SO, agricultural jobs wil be common jobs in NZ developed country. Hence, low technolgical productive improvement may be main factor to influence NZ to be one lowly developed country in long time.

What factors influence US and UK continue development

Why do US and US be a developed country? It has a high-income economy and a very high human development index rating. Ranking 13 th in the world. Today, the UK , US remains one of the world's great powers with considerable economc, cultural , military, scientific, technological and political influence internationally. Why are UK and US econome so strong? It's quality of life is generally considered high, and the economy is quite diversified . The sectors that contibute must be the US, UK 's GDP are services, manufacturing, construction and tourism . Moreover, UK and US are the world's largest economy by normimal GDP and net wealth and they are the second largest by purchasing power. Themselves nations's economy is fueled by natural resources, a well-developed and high productivity.

It seems that UK and US have a mixed economic development, developed through free market and global economy , which are regulated by their governments to prevent market failure easily.

What Factors Influence Social Development Speed

What factors cause why some countries can develop rapidly ? What factors cause some countries develop slowly? It would be hard to find a more fundamental conept for the social development and human development. The social development science is about human societies how we develop, so we had better have some idea to explain how and why what factors cause some countries can develop rapidly , e.g. US, UK, or what factors cause some countries can develop slowly, e.g. China, India. The reaons that there has been a question about the development speed to any countries , it has been an active and influential movement to insist that this was a human social development question. Why does Inida has many years history, otherwise, US has less many years histroy, what factors influence US can develop more rapidly to compare Inida? Even, India seems to be one developing country in nowadays society.

From sociobiology to social development psychology

What factors to India is facing to influence it can not succeed to develop to be highly developed country easily? Human cognitive mechanisms evolved in the Pleistocene, the period from about 2 million years ago, about 10,000 years ago, the end of the last Ice age, MOtivating this choice is the thought that substantial periods of development time are required for significant evoluntionary change, such as social need change, family need change, country need change. Much of Evolutinnary psychology has consisted of reflection on the different countries changing conditions that might have obtained during this perios, and the human development behaviors what would have been most favoured by natural selection given those conditions.

First of all to what influences human feels we need to develop, a lot of human behavior has roots that are far more ancient. Sociability , for instance, is not a uniquely human attribute. But significant changes in the nature of human sociality are evident over historical periods of tens or hundrends of years, presumably because they are due to cultural improvement, or raising human cultural quality , so our cultural improvement psychology influences why somc countrics can not develop rapidly, such as India does not consider itself Indian cultural level needs to raise significantly. Otherwise, US condiers itself American cultural level need to raise significantly. So, this cultural development reason may explain why India is still one developing country, although, its has many years history to compare US.

Social Development Psychology

Another important point about social development issus, it is the environmental factor, it is one picture to influence why some countries develop rapidly , but some countries still develop slowly. I don nor need to pursue that argument , since the focus will remain on the human development case, and no one could suppose that the social enviroment that human create for, among the other things, the production of new human social behaviors, is simply a consequence of genetically determined human behavior. For example, American hopes that it can create many talent people to help itself country to develop, so talent people development environment need can influence US can have many talent people to create to help itself country to develop to be highly developed country in short time, e..g. space science, life science etc.

I wished to emphasize particularly the ability of cultural evolution to transform the social development history to different countries issus. It seems clear that humans have learned in quite recent time to construct a remarkably social changing environment for the development for their young. So, any countries their future development, they must depend on how many talent young people, they can create. It is very important issue to influence any one country to develop to be one high developed or low developed or developing country. For that reason their introduction should be seen as representing major cultural improvemernt and social environment factors to influence any countries their future development speed. For this simple example, many further illustrate the point, they indicate that the mobile phone did not exist when I was a child. In fact, it is for hardly more than a decade that it has been for everyday life in developed countries. Ans whereas it may seem only more or less need for people of my generation, for those aged, say 10 to 20 , age, it is as unthinkable to deprived of one's phone as to wander the streets stark naked. Most teenagers move through the would, when this smart phone technological development, it can influence any one feels that it is essential product to our daily need. It is one cultural improvement factor example , it can explain why global many people feel smart phones are essential product to satisfy us need. It is not, therefore, merely behavior that has changed for those who have grown up with the mobile phone, but the social environment can bring indirect to influence any one , even old age feels smart phone need, when old age people can contact many young people , they must own least one smart phone for personal use. So, cultural improvement and social environment changing need both factors can influence any one country may make development decision in short time or long time, when the country people feel that they have urgent social and cultural improvement changing need rapidly.

What are the differences between developing and developed countries

I shall explain the difference between developed and developing countries characteristics as below:

Countries are divided into two major categories by the United Nations, which are developed countries and developing countries. The classification of countries is based on the economic status such as GDP, GNP, per capita income, industrialization, the standard of living, etc. Developed Countries refers to the soverign state, whose economy has highly progressed and possesses great technological infrastructure, as compared to other nations.The countries with low industrialization and low human development index are termed as developing countries. Developed Countries provides free, healthy and secured atmosphere to live whereas developing countries, lacks these things.

The characteristics between developing and developed countries may include as below:

Developed countries means that a country having an effective rate of industrialization and individual income is known as Developed Country. Otherwise, developing Country is a country which has a slow rate of industrialization and low per capita income. Developed countries have low unemployment and poverty, developing countries have usually high unemployment and poverty. developed countries have low infant mortality rate, death rate and birth rate is low while the life expectancy rate is high. Otherwise, developing countries have high infant mortality rate, death rate and birth rate, along with low life expectancy rate. Developed countries have better living conditions and high standard of living, but developing countries have bad living conditions and low standard of living. Developing countries have high GDP from industrial sector income source, otherwise, developed countries have high GDP income from service sector income source. Developing countries have high industrial growth. Otherwise, developed countries, they rely on the developed countries for their growth. Developed countries have high equal of distribution of income, otherwise, developing countries have high unequal of distribution of income. Finally, developed countries have effectively utilized to factors of production, otherwise, developing countries have ineffectively utilized to factors of production. Overall , any thing of developed countries are better than developing countries in nowadays societies.

Between developed and developing countries, one can identify a variety of differences. This differentiation of countries, as developed and developing, is used to classify countries according to their economic status based on per capita income, industrialization, literacy rate, living standards, etc.

What are Developed Countries?

They have usually these similar characteristics as below:

(1) Developed countries have industrial growth and enjoy flourishing economy. Developed countries experience marked development and growth in the areas such as transportation, business, and education. Developed countries are characterized by a low death rate and low birth rate as well. There is usually a very small gap between the two rates in developed countries.

(2) Developed countries are not characterized by shortcomings. They are well-developed in all fronts and are served well by water supplies, amenities, educational institutions, health care concerns. This is because of the fact that people are endowed with awareness about every possible aspect relating to human existence. The absence of shortcomings in the developed countries is possibly due to the fact there is a low birth rate in these countries. Nutrition is available in plenty to mothers and infants in developed countries.

What are Developing Countries?

They have usually these similar characteristics as below:

(1) Developing countries depend on the developed countries for help to establish their industries. They have only begun to taste the growth of the economy. Developing countries are in the beginning stages of development in the areas of education, business, and transportation.

(2) Developing countries are characterized by many shortcomings. These shortcomings include less awareness regarding matters relating to health, poor amenities, shortage in water supply, shortcoming in the area of medical supply, a higher rate of birth rate. The most important and worrying factor in the developing countries is the factor of poor nutrition. Poor nutrition to both mothers and infants is the main concern in the developing countries. Due to high birth rates, the probability of natural diseases is more in developing countries. Hence, the death rates are also eventually high in developing countries. However, since natural diseases increase by high rates in the developing countries, they will have a short population doubling time. In the case of developing countries, there is usually a big gap between the birth rate and the death rate. Infant mortality factor is influenced by the development

factor of countries. A developing country for that matter would have higher infant mortality than a developed country.

Overall, economists will differ their different characteristcs from these several aspects as below:

Developed countries display a high level of development. Developing countries: Developing countries display a lower development in different areas such as industrialization, human capital, etc. Developed countries have industrial growth. Developing countries depend on the developed countries for help to establish their industries. Developed countries enjoy flourishing economy. Developing countries begin to taste the growth of the economy. Developed countries experience marked development and growth in the areas such as transportation, business, and education. Developing countries are in the beginning stages of development in the areas of education, business, and transportation. Developed countries are characterized by a low death rate and low birth rate as well. There is usually a very small gap between the two rates in developed countries. In developing countries there is usually a big gap between the birth rate and the death rate. Hence, in overall, any aspects are worse, slow growth to developing countries compare to developed countries.

What are general their GDP difference

Developed Countries:

A developed nation is one that has a very high rank in industrial advancement, constructs its economy in light of innovation and assembling rather than agribusiness. The variables of production, for example, human and regular assets are completely used bringing about an increment underway and utilization which prompts a very high rank in per capita salary. A nation with a more Human Development Index (HDI) is viewed as a developed nation. It not just measures the financial improvement and GDP of a nation additionally its instruction and future.

Developing Countries:

A developing nation is those having a way of life or level of modern advancements well beneath that conceivable with money related or specialized guide; a nation that is not yet exceptionally industrialized. A country having less utilization of resources and low income per capita which leads to low GDP of a country.

Developed VS Developing Countries will have different development or growth speed to compare as below:

?Industrial Economies:

In developed countries, economy depends on industrial sector instead of agriculture sector. There is more development in industrial sector. In developing countries, mostly economy depends on agriculture sector and they are moving toward industrialization.

?Citizens:

In developed countries, citizens and well off and rich. In developing countries, proportion of rich citizens is very low.

?Unemployment:

In developed countries, there is no such issue of unemployment. They provide many employment opportunities to the citizens. In developing countries, issue of unemployment is there and it affects the economy of country very badly.

?Education:

The growth rate in education sector is very high in developed countries and they have best education systems. Whereas the growth rate of developing countries in education sector is low as compare to developed countries. While developing countries are following the education system of developed countries to achieve the standard.

?Technological advantages:

In developed countries, every place is full with technological advancements and they always try to make it better. In developing countries, there are many undeveloped rural areas and even urban sector have less technological advancements.

?Roads:

Developed countries have a very sound infrastructure by having better roads, railway tracks, airports etc. Developing countries don't have a sound infrastructure as compare to developed countries.

?Government:

There exists stable government in developed countries so that they make effective and reliable policies for better economic development. Developing countries have unstable governments and mostly try to following the policies made by developed countries.

?Health care:

In developed countries, good and better facilities for health have been provided to citizens. In developing countries, health care facilities are not so good and acceptable.

?Resources:

In developed countries, the natural and human resources are fully and efficiently consumed. In developing countries, many of the natural resources are still untouched and others resources are also not fully utilized.

?Income:

There is a high level of income as per citizen living in developed country so that they have high GDP and GNP. Developing countries have low level of income as per citizen living in country with unequal distribution of income as that have low GDP and GNP.

?High Human Development Index (HDI):

In developed countries, there are best education systems and better health care and high income level so this leads to high value and ranking of HDI. In developing countries, there are low income level and fewer facilities for health care and low rates of education so this leads to low or middle ranking in HDI.

?Life expectancy:

In developed countries, due to better health care the life expectancy has been increased and they have low birth rates as well as low death rates. In developing countries, life expectancy is not so high but has high rates of birth and death due to less facilities and education.

?Water and food supply:

In developed countries, safe and clean water is supplied with plentiful supply of food items and good housing condition. In developing countries, dirty and unsafe water is supplied with less reliable food items and poor condition of houses.

In conclusion, all our daily necessary need and social need to developing countries growth will be worse to compare developed countries in our nowadays societies.

How to measure the difference between developed and developing countries ?

The measurement factors between developed and developing countries may include as below:

(1) GDP factor

The classification of a country does not only depend on its income but also on other factors that affect how their citizens live, how their economies are integrated into the global system, and the expansion and diversification of their export industries. A developed country is one that has a high level of industrial development, bases its economy on technology and manufacturing instead of agriculture. The factors of production such as human and natural resources are fully utilized resulting in an increase in production and consumption which leads to a high level of per capita income. A country with a high Human Development Index (HDI) rating is considered a developed country. It not only measures the economic development and GDP of a country but also its education and life expectancy. A developed country's citizens enjoy a free and healthy existence.

(2) Industralization or Commercial aspect factor

The term "developed country" is synonymous to "industrialized country, post-industrial country, more developed country, advanced country, and first-world country." The United Kingdom, France, Germany, Canada, Japan, Switzerland, and the United States of America are only a few of those considered as developed countries. A developing country, on the other hand, is one that has a low level of industrialization.

It has a higher level of birth and death rates than developed countries. Its infant mortality rate is also high due to poor nutrition, shortage of medical services, and little knowledge on health. The citizens of developing countries have a low to medium standard of living because their per capita income is still developing, and their technological capacity is still being developed. There is also an unequal distribution of income in developing countries, and their factors of production are not fully utilized. Developing countries are also referred to as third-world countries or least-developed countries.

Countries are categorized according to their economic development. The United Nations classifies countries as developed, developing, newly industrialized or developed, and countries in transition such as Kazakhstan, Kyrgyztan, Turkmenistan, and the former USSR. The World Bank classifies countries according to their GNI per capita income: low income ($995 or less) and lower middle income ($996-$3,945); as developing countries with an upper middle income ($3,946-$12,195); and high income (above $11,906) as developed countries.

(3) The country citizen living of standard level

The classification of a country does not only depend on its income but also on other factors that affect how their citizens live, how their economies are integrated into the global system, and the expansion and diversification of their export industries. A developed country is one that has a high level of industrial development, bases its economy on technology and manufacturing instead of agriculture. The factors of production such as human and natural resources are fully utilized resulting in an increase in production and consumption which leads to a high level of per capita income. A country with a high Human Development Index (HDI) rating is considered a developed country. It not only measures the economic development and GDP of a country but also its education and life expectancy. A developed country's citizens enjoy a free and healthy existence.

The term "developed country" is synonymous to "industrialized country, post-industrial country, more developed country, advanced country, and first-world country." The United Kingdom, France, Germany, Canada, Japan, Switzerland, and the United States of America are only a few of those considered as developed countries.

A developing country, on the other hand, is one that has a low level of industrialization. It has a higher level of birth and death rates than developed countries. Its infant mortality rate is also high due to poor nutrition, shortage of medical services, and little knowledge on health. The citizens of developing countries have a low to medium standard of living because their per capita income is still developing, and their technological capacity is still being developed. There is also an unequal distribution of income in developing countries, and their factors of production are not fully utilized. Developing countries are also referred to as third-world countries or least-developed countries.

In conclusion, the measurement factors to decide whether the country is either developing or developed country. The factors depend on whether: whether the developed country is a country that has a high level of industrialization and per capita income while a developing country is a country that is still in the early stages of industrial development and has a low per capita income , whether the citizens of a developed country enjoy a free, healthy, and affluent existence while citizens of developing countries do not, whether the developed countries are also known as industrialized, advanced, and first-world countries while developing countries are also known as underdeveloped, least developed, and third-world countries. For example, The United States of America, Canada, Switzerland, Belgium, and France are examples of developed countries while India, Malawi, Honduras, the Philippines, and Rwanda are examples of developing countries as well as the infant mortality, birth, and death rates of developing countries are also higher compared to that of developed countries.

Why and how developed countries need assist developing countries to develop

I think that we should help developing nations, But only to an extent. If we keep, And keep on giving them needs they will start to rely on foreign aid. I think charities are enough, But if the developing countries really need help then we give them help. But not too much, Basically they need to do something themselves and stop relying and take their own action. In exchange for our help maybe they could give us a bit of natural resources? Developing countries may need to be assisted, They may include these reasons:

Global resource is shortage to allocate unfair challenge

Nowadays, global resources are not equally distributed in different countries. Thus, there are those who belong to the developed nations while there are others that belong to developing countries. With these unequal distribution, it is significant that developed countries must do their part in helping those who belong to the underprivileged sector. It is true that rich countries have their own problems to worry with; Can we introduce aquaponics in developing countries when they don't have the resources that first world countries have? In many areas, there is no electricity available that is needed for many aquaponics systems; developing countries require simplicity, reliability, and freedom from the need of grid powerhowever, it is still their responsibility to help the developing countries people need to solve resource can not be allocated fair problem, such as Afria is one developing country, many people are drinking drink water, due to drought , so they will not feel health and they will feel sick , even die. It is one example of natural resource of clean water shortage challenge to Afica. So, developed country, e.g. US , it has responsibilty to help African to drink clean water because clean water is allocated to supply to America people to drink in preference, due to global clean water supply is decreasing, but human number is increasing and clean water demand will also increase. If clean water is only supplied to US people to drink , even other developed countries people , they can drink the most clean water. The reason is because Africa people is poor or dirty or low education level or it is one developing country etc. factors to influence many African can not often drink any clean water. It is very unfair to this developing country.

In 2010, there were 925 million hungry people in the world; 19 million in developed countries, 37 million in Near East and North Africa, 53 million in Latin America and the Caribbean, 239 Million in Sub-Saharan Africa, and 578 million in Asia and the Pacific. This means that approximately 1 in 7 people are hungry. Protein- energy malnutrition is the most lethal form of malnutrition/hunger. It is a lack of calories and protein; protein is necessary for key bodily functions including provision of essential amino acids and the development and maintenance of muscles. Bringing aquaponics into third world countries would help prevent this problem by providing fish as a main source of protein. Poor nutrition is the cause or partial cause for at least half of the 10.9 million child deaths each year.

The number of hungry people has increased since 1997 due to three main problems: 1) neglect of agriculture relevant to very poor people by governments and international agencies; 2) worldwide economic crisis and 3) increase in food prices. Children who are poorly nourished suffer up to 160 days of illness each year. Malnutrition affects about 32% of children in developing countries. More than 70% of malnourished children live in Asia. Undernourished pregnant women in developing countries leads to 1 out of 6 infants born with low birth weight; this means higher neonatal death rates, increased occurrences of learning disabilities, mental retardation, poor health, blindness, and premature death. There is enough food to provide everyone in the world with 2, 720 kilocalories per person per day, however many people don't have the land to grow or the money to buy the food they need for themselves and their children. 1 out of 3 people in developing countries are affected by vitamin and mineral deficiency.

So, I feel that aid has diverse results. It can both harm as well help development. Rich countries might be sidetracked in terms of focusing on programs that will spur development. Asian and African nations should create long-term plans that will reduce the dependency on aid, while rich countries should transition from traditional methods of giving support in new ways. Rich countries still argue on the premise that they cannot afford aid or that they are being over-generous. The main idea here is not that they are questioning the aid itself, but the development project. Rich countries must be on the poor countries aid as these people from poor nations face injustice and hardships that are often caused or increased by the programs and decision of rich nations themselves.

However, giving aid is not really an act of generosity. Aid purchases things that donors desire. These might include political support in exchange for the "goodies" that the donor has provided. Rich countries must show support to the poor by abiding on the social, environmental aspects. It can also include adapting to climate change by changing one's own consumption. Another is to accept fairer trade rules. Moreover, rich countries can show true generosity by undergoing changes in the manner of living for the past few decades. It would be fair that rich countries believe they are being generous when they give out dole outs or loose change when poor people around the globe are trying to live on a few basics while living under the system that rich countries have developed. It is a reality that there are also poor people in rich countries that are undergoing tough times. However, it is not ethical to withdraw support from people abroad who are more underprivileged just because there are poor people in rich countries that need help as well.

In fact, many argue that the poor countries that rich countries provide financial aid are doing better economically. It is possible that these countries are growing and catching up with the standard of living. Say for example, the annual income of India might have greatly improved. However, when one divides that with the whole population, each Indian just obtains $3 or less per day. This issue requires obtaining the correct facts not only on financial aid, but on the act of generosity in this world. Rich countries do have a responsibility of giving to those developing country people's living need because they can enjoy any benefits in preference when resource is shortage and global need is also increasing in nowadays societies.

Some developed countries have obligation to help developing countries

The rich have an obligation to help poor countries who were exploited by their colonial rulers. The United States had a head start with its vast natural resources. But many countries in Europe, such as Britain, became rich due to their colonial reign in Asia. They expanded their empire to include poor, resource-rich nations in Asia. They exploited the region's cheap labour, with workers getting little in return for their hard work. For Hong Kong , developing country and UK developed country. UK had obligation to help this developing country, HK before 1997.

Hong Kong was different though. Britain ruled Hong Kong for more than 150 years and I think both sides benefited. Today, the city is an international financial centre with a strong economy. But some countries did not benefit from colonial rule. For another example, IBM founder , Bill and Melinda Gates set up the Gates Foundation to help poor countries. We take a lot of things for granted. This cannot go on. A spirit of give-and-take is essential for world harmony. Developed countries may not be bound by law to help poor nations, but they have the responsibility - and the power - to do so.

However, developed countries should help less developed ones. But whether this is an obligation is a matter for debate. I believe the government of a country should be responsible for the well-being of its people. It is wrong to allow outsiders to influence the development of a country. This could lead to serious problems.

A developed country faces various difficulties when choosing who to help. First, its choice could leave a lot of people unhappy and damage its relationship with other countries. Second, allowing foreigners to have a significant influence on a nation could lead to negative consequences. Some donors do not have the best intentions. They could use their power for their own advantage. This could lead to corruption and financial loss in the less developed country. Third, a developing nation may become dependent on foreign aid. And some donors might charge a hefty interest for their financial assistance. This could pose a bigger headache than not receiving aid at all. Hence, rich countries have to be careful when helping poor nations. It involves a lot of politics so the rich have the right to choose the recipient and ensure the aid does not get into the wrong hands.

Rich countries have responsibilites to assist global economy development or balance economy development

When global economy is unbalance developing. It will bring the damage of kindly cooperation relationship , e.g. export and import business activities to develop our global economy in success. For example, China and America themselve trade war will cause these both countries' GDP export and import income loss, even global economy will be recession. So, rich country, such as US has responsibility to assist developing country, such as Afria, China, Korea, Taiwan to help them to raise business competive effort and bring long term export and import business cooperation and create many factory jobs to China, Korea, Africa, Taiwan factory workers. Then, they can build kindly business cooperative relationship to bring global economy benefit in long term. Then, our global economy development will succeed more easily.

The first rational basis behind donating to poor countries is the notion that all men are equal. Some may radically oppose this concept, noting that their countries should solely invest its own efforts to remedy impoverished sectors of the population. Given the spread of poverty and homelessness, some have arrived to the conclusion that aiding other countries is not in our best interest. However, this could not be further from the truth. As member of the human race, we all occupy an equitable status as global citizens, and nothing can detract from this truth. Centralise your focus on the relative needs of your nation disregards the ailing needs of the developing world.

The second consideration simply poses the question of why not? Although wealthier, developed countries are plagued by their own respective incidences of poverty and lack of resources, developing countries suffer greatly, in terms of their accessibility to medical aid, vaccines, clean water, and a number of other amenities that are gravely understated in importance. With this said, we must venture beyond the bounds of our own comfort zones, and aid other countries because we are lavished with such a bounty in resources ourselves. Another indispensable benefit of aiding impoverished countries. Foreign diplomacy can significantly aid the national security of any nation. And providing aid to a poor county can ultimately benefit us, improving our perception in their eyes, a cultivating a certain level of civility and coexistence that breeds peace, instead of war. The fewer enemies that a particular nation has, the better.

The final reason is simple. We should empathize with other human beings. Every day, countless children succumb to curable disease, malaria and a number of other pathogens that could easily be treated with outside aid. Both children and adults are sold into slavery and trafficked around the world. Of course, the lingering issue of starvation is a palpable one that still plagues the world today. With this said, we should uphold a noble standard that permits foreign aid for this very reason. One often hears the argument that it is all very well to preach equity but given the planetary emergency the world faces from the threat of climate change we must set aside the equity principle in the interests of humanity as a whole. This is a wholly specious and self serving argument. It reflects the sense of entitlement to an affluent lifestyle, based on energy intensive production and consumption, while denying the even modest aspirations of people in developing countries.

For example, global climate changes to warmth challenge , it can cause developing countries people their health to be poor. In a densely interconnected and globalised world, it will be impossible to maintain islands of prosperity in an ocean of poverty and deprivation. It is not that developing countries are claiming the right to spew as much carbon as possible into the atmosphere without regard to the health of the planet. As the main victims of climate change– the impacts of which they are already suffering – they have a much bigger stake in dealing with this challenge. They are, in fact, doing much more than most developed countries, to adopt energy frugal methods of growth, conserving energy, promoting renewable power and limiting waste within the limits of their own resources.

Why and how developing countries people's poor health issue , it may influence developed countries businessmen income ? I shall indicate Africa , developing example , if African are health, then this country will have many workers to assist or help US businessmen to manufacture many products to sell to different countries in short time. If US businessmen hope to pay the low wage to reduce their long time expenditure, Afrian must need have health to do any hard jobs in factories. If US businessmen only feel Chinese workers can help them to do any low wage jobs in factories, when China have many new businesses develop to pay better wages to employ themselves Chinese workers. Then, many Chinese workers may choose to help themselves China employers to do the factory jobs to replace US employers. So, if US can help many African have health to work, it may bring uncounted long time benefits to US businesses. Hence, such as this case, it explains why rich people need to help developing countries to solve health challenge.

Methods developing countries can
become developed countries
Main industries aspects need to develop

How can developing countries develop to be developed countries in success? What the difficulties to them , that they will need to solve in this development process ? In today's sophisticated society,people of the developing countries are still fighting for their basic righs such a better healthcare,proper education and a sound source of income.While the governments of the underdeveloped countries are struggling to improve the living standards of their people,I believe that contribution by richer nations should be more in this regard. To begin,all human beings should help each other.Govenments of richer nations can take many steps to improve the living standard of the poorer naions. I shall indicate these aspects that they need to concentrate on solving in order to achieve developed countries in success as below:

(1) Healthcare development

Firstly,in the field of healthcare,developed countries can support he underdeveloped in many ways.They can send their expert doctors to train the medical staff in the developing countries.Also,they can open free medical camps in the selected areas of poor countries.In this way free medical advice could be given.Such camps can also start health awarness compaigns to make people aware of unhealthy lifetyle. Moreover, experts from the developed countries can also help with the vaccination programmes in the developing countries.This will led to decrease in infant mortality rate.

(2) Educational development

Secondly,assistance in the field of education should be provide to the poorer nations.The developed countries can provide funds to open new schools and polytechnic institutions.These will not only increase the literacy rate,but will also provide vocational education.Furthermore,the rich governments should provide the students of poor countries an oportunity to study in the prestigious institutions by giving scholarships.This will promote poor people to gain higher education.

(3) Promoting free trade development

Finally,rich nations should help to improve the economy of poor countries.This can be done by promoting free trade.This wil reduce barriers to international trade such as tariff,import quotas and export fee and will help to lift the developing countries out of poverty. To conclude,if we want to live in a beter world with peace and harmony,we should always help each other.Therefore,I believe that richer nations should help the poor countries in all the fields.

The challenges are needed to solve in development process

During the development process, they developing countries will need to solve these challenges, the developing or underdeveloped countries (as they were earlier named) are poor due to them having the following common characteristics as below:

The developing countries may have these social challenges , they need to solve , such as :

(1) On social medical aspect

Closed economy/State Controlled economy or practice of socialism (which is in practice -one man/one party dictatorship). Low levels of literacy and esp. female literacy (less than 75% female literacy). Low health and HDI indicators (corresponding to the literacy levels). Low per capita income. High incidence of corruption, nepotism and kleptocracy.

The following is the path chosen by most of the former “low income/under developed/poor nations” to become developed (Germany & Japan post WW2, South Korea, Taiwan, Brazil, South Africa and China - some are still in process)- Economically liberal but politically/socially conservative regimes. Immense government spending

(Keynesian economics) on - Infrastructure (Roads, Schools, Bridges, Ports, Airports, Power Plants, Hospitals and primary health centers etc).

(2) On international trade social aspect

Opening up the economy to international trade and foreign investments. Export oriented manufacturing practices, wherein the bulk of the population which was in the primary sector (agriculture, animal husbandry and mining etc) shifts to the secondary sector (manufacturing) and experiences corresponding increase in wages/ income.

Application of procedures and rule of law on a gradual basis from the earlier arbitrariness which reigned supreme. The first step, in my view, is to make sure to have an honest and capable government that are committed to the development of the country and to the welfare of all people in the country. It is, in fact, the most difficult step to start with. Once we have a good and capable government, it is not so difficult to figure out or implement all steps necessary to make the country developed and prosper. On the other hand, having a corrupt, incapable, in other words, not only dishonest, but also stupid and foolish government means losing everything, no matter how abundance resource your country has, or how much foreign assistance and aids your country receives.

However, some economists believe that they are not “developing”, but MAINTAINED IN PERMANENT UNDERDEVELOPMENT on purpose. Market, same as everything, functions in 3D, the 3rd is the income strata. The “progress” is not for all the strata. Every upper stratum solves its own problems at expenses of pushing the next inferior one downwards (vertically) or over the edge (horizontally). Spend a few minutes on a search engine and you realize that the term “first world” is meaningless when referring to economic development. For example, Ireland, Switzerland and Sweden are examples of third world countries. A first world nation is one that allied with NATO as opposed to the Soviet Union during the Cold War.

(3) On solving social poverty aspect

Poverty is the default state of man. Knowledge is what allows us to go beyond our physical and cognitive limitations. With knowledge you can create technology that makes our lives better. At a base level, developing nations need a smaller percentage of their populations working in sustenance farming. This could be achieved by increases in farming productivity which would allow other people to specialize in making other goods and providing other services. Essentially creating more wealth.

Uaually, developing countries lack enough farming technology, they can’t specialize in something other than sustenance farming if 80% of your population farms with oxen instead of machines. This is where knowledge comes in play. Many developing nations have rich natural resources and commodities they just don’t have the knowledge necessary to turn it into something useful.

To summarize in one word what is necessary for a developing nation to become a developed one it is knowledge. Any one developing countries need to answer these questions, before they decide how to solve these social challenges in their development process as below:

What developing country will become the next developed nation? Why do they are developing countries ? How can they develop to be developed countries ? How long will it take for every country in the world to become developed? What is the way to develop a country? Which countries are likely to be developed countries soon?

For example, Brazilians is one developing country, because this country has high crime rate and poor rate is high and inflation is high. These are its social problems. As soon as hyperinflation and out-of-control crime was solved, Brazilians brought their money back to Brazil. The starting point for Brazilians is patriotism and nostalgia. Even with all the problems of corruption, taxes, bureaucracy and poor infrastructure if given a chance to make real money within the country a Brazilian will leave better opportunities in the US. So, Brazilians need to solve these social problems if this country hope to become one developed country in success. The easiest way to develop is: when each and every person decides to learn as much as possible, and decides to behave like civilized persons, who have total respect for all other persons' physical and patrimonial integrity. It's that easy and simple. But, often, the easiest things in life are the most difficult to learn.

What a developing country should do to be a developed one?

The countries that developed the fastest often had the longest paths. If you compensate for that fact, then it becomes obvious that economic freedom is both necessary and sufficient. In particular, countries should avoid: socialism, i.e. collectivization of the means of production expropriation, i.e. robbing foreign investors of their properties autarchy, i.e. cutting all international trade. The less countries engage in these, the faster they develop.

How can a developing country become a developed country?

Well, you could study economic history and learn how the present developed countries attained their present positions. There are also several examples in real time: look at how China and India are moving their countries from third world countries to developed economies. Two other interesting examples: Several African countries are using primarily cell phone techologies for communication and bypassing the infrastructure requirements for hardline technology. Ireland is well know to have been deforested when it's forests were harvested for the coal and fuel requirements of industrializing.

Developed Countries need to help Developing Countries to increase their competitive effort in societies

IMPROVEMENTS IN HEALTH, EDUCATION AND TRADE ARE ESSENTIAL FOR THE DEVELOPMENT OF POORER NATIONS. HOWEVER,THE GOVERNMENTS OF RICHER NATIONS SHOULD TAKE MORE RESPONSIBILITY FOR HELPING THE POORER NATIONS IN SUCH AREAS.

Eliminate political tension by encouraging participation of all in the political, constitutional and economic processes. I recommend developed countries, such as US, UK can help developing countries to develop in sucess in these several aspects:

-Invest in infrastructure, education and health care.

-Encourage rural agriculture by providing agricultural inputs
and raising earned incomes.

-Raise levels of literacy

-Encourage the modern sectors of banking, manufacturing, retail,
and extractive industries,
-Provide adequate sanitation and clean water
-Open the countries to direct foreign investments
-Remove trade barriers to exports and imports.
-Reduce dependency on single sectors that is diversification .

Can bring global benefit when all countries are developed countries

1.How Globalization Affects Developed Countries

There are three perspective of globalization. Which are as : The Hyper globalist perspective: This says that economies are becoming Denationalized due to this government will lose it influence over the trade within its border. It will have both good and bad effects. The Skeptical perspective: it is kind based on myth that globalization will not help the under develop country as they do not perform a greater role in flow of trade and services in the global economy.

I assume that future one day, all countries can become developed countries. The globalization development effect will be caused by our global successful development. Does it means that globalization can only bring benefits ? I shall explain that when all countries can developed successfully. Globalization ought not only bring benefits to our global societies as below:

Globalization brings people and businesses together through the international exchange of money, ideas, and culture. However, some critics say it adversely affects developed countries. Opinions exist on both sides of the globalization debate. Proponents claim lower opportunity costs, producing positive growth, and reduced market volatility. At the same time, opponents decry the reduction of domestic job growth, cost of mismanagement to countries and the world, and the stagnation of wages.

Conflicting Globalization Views

U.S. President Donald Trump, for example, has been very vocal on his views of globalization and has taken a protectionist stance when it comes to free trade under agreements like the North American Free Trade Agreement (NAFTA), calling for higher taxes on imports and fewer multinational trade agreements. He has also increased tariffs on foreign goods to discourage their importation and use. No matter how much economists are quick to extol the universal benefits of globalization, some politicians and other economist demonize globalization as a force that takes away domestic jobs. These conflicting viewpoints have created a maelstrom of opinions and policies across developed countries that range from extreme protectionism through trade barriers, like President Trump's example, to complete openness.

From an economic standpoint, globalization is typically defined as the increase in the global trade of goods, services, capital, and technology. This growth in trade has been especially acute between developed countries like the United States and emerging markets, such as China. There are many factors behind the increase in global trade.

European devastation after World War I and II helped to jumpstart America and an industrial superpower and exporter. Lower transportation costs have reduced the costs of trade, technologies have eliminated some barriers altogether, and liberal economic policies have helped lower political barriers to trade. While cost reductions have helped accelerate trade, the largest driver behind global trade is supply-demand economics and the desire to increase consumption on the part of both importers and exporters.

Benefits of globalization

The core benefit of globalization is the comparative advantage—that is, the ability of one country to produce goods or services at a lower opportunity cost than other countries. While the idea seems simple on the surface, it quickly becomes counterintuitive when examined more deeply. The theory suggests that two countries capable of producing two commodities at different costs can benefit the most by exporting the good where the comparative advantage exists. For example, a developing country may have a comparative advantage in producing cement, and the United States may have a comparative advantage in producing semiconductors. While the U.S. may be able to produce cement more efficiently than the developing country, the U.S. would still be better off focusing on semiconductors because of its comparative advantage. This is why globalization is powerful as a driver of global consumption between countries of all capabilities.

One of the major potential benefits of globalization is to provide opportunities for reducing macroeconomic volatility on output and consumption via diversification of risk. The overall evidence of the globalization effect on macroeconomic volatility of output indicates that although direct effects are ambiguous in theoretical models, financial integration helps in a nation's production base diversification, and leads to an increase in specialization of production. However, the specialization of production, based on the concept of comparative advantage, can also lead to higher volatility in specific industries within an economy and society of a nation. As time passes, successful companies, independent of size, will be the ones that are part of the global economy.

Empirical evidence suggests that a positive growth effect takes place in countries that are sufficiently rich when it comes to globalization. For investors and economies, globalization also provides the opportunity to reduce the volatility of output and consumption, since products and services can be imported or exported with greater ease. Fewer "bubbles" arise from a mismatch in supply and demand if the production of goods and services is more elastic. But, when all countries can develop to become developed countries, globalization developed countries which may also bring these disadvantages as below:

Drawbacksof globalization

Globalization is often criticized for taking away jobs from domestic companies and workers. After all, the U.S. cement industry will go out of business if imports from a developing country drive down prices, even if consumption increases. Small U.S. cement companies would find it difficult to compete and likely shut down, leaving workers unemployed, while the larger U.S. cement industry would likely experience a significant protracted decline.

A second criticism is the high cost of a comparative or absolute advantage to a country's own well-being if mismanaged. For example, China has become a leading worldwide emitter of carbon dioxide thanks to its comparative advantage in manufacturing a wide range of products. Other countries may have a comparative advantage in mining certain natural resources—such as crude oil—and mishandle the revenue generated from those activities.

A final disadvantage of globalization is the increase in wages for workers, which can hurt corporate profitability. For example, if a rich country has a high comparative advantage in developing software, they may drive up the price of software engineers around the world, which makes it difficult for foreign companies to compete in the market.

The phenomenon of globalization began in a primitive form when humans first settled into different areas of the world; however, it has shown a rather steady and rapid progress in recent times and has become an international dynamic which, due to technological advancements, has increased in speed and scale, so that countries in all five continents have been affected and engaged.

What Is Globalization? Why and how globalization may achieve when global countries can develop to become developed countries ?

Globalization is defined as a process that, based on international strategies, aims to expand business operations on a worldwide level, and was precipitated by the facilitation of global communications due to technological advancements, and socioeconomic, political and environmental developments.

The goal of globalization is to provide organizations a superior competitive position with lower operating costs, to gain greater numbers of products, services, and consumers. This approach to competition is gained via diversification of resources, the creation and development of new investment opportunities by opening up additional markets and accessing new raw materials and resources. Diversification of resources is a business strategy that increases the variety of business products and services within various organizations. Diversification strengthens institutions by lowering organizational risk factors, spreading interests in different areas, taking advantage of market opportunities, and acquiring companies both horizontal and vertical in nature.

Industrialized or developed nations are specific countries with a high level of economic development and meet certain socioeconomic criteria based on economic theory, such as gross domestic product (GDP), industrialization and human development index (HDI) as defined by the International Monetary Fund (IMF), the United Nations (UN) and the World Trade Organization (WTO). Using these definitions, some industrialized countries are: United Kingdom, Belgium, Denmark, Finland, France, Germany, Japan, Luxembourg, Norway, Sweden, Switzerland, and the United States.

Components of Globalization

The components of globalization include GDP, industrialization and the Human Development Index (HDI). The GDP is the market value of all finished goods and services produced within a country's borders in a year and serves as a measure of a country's overall economic output. Industrialization is a process which, driven by technological innovation, effectuates social change and economic development by transforming a country into a modernized industrial, or developed nation. The Human Development Index comprises three components: a country's population's life expectancy, knowledge and education measured by the adult literacy, and income.

The degree to which an organization is globalized and diversified has bearing on the strategies that it uses to pursue greater development and investment opportunities.

When all countries can become developed countries. They may bring the Economic Impact on Developed Nations as below: Globalization compels businesses to adapt to different strategies based on new ideological trends that try to balance the rights and interests of both the individual and the community as a whole. This change enables businesses to compete worldwide and also signifies a dramatic change for business leaders, labor and management by legitimately accepting the participation of workers and government in developing and implementing company policies and strategies. Risk reduction via diversification can be accomplished through company involvement with international financial institutions and partnering with both local and multinational businesses.

Globalization brings reorganization at the international, national and sub-national levels. Specifically, it brings the reorganization of production, international trade and the integration of financial markets. This affects capitalist economic and social relations, via multilateralism and microeconomic phenomena, such as business competitiveness, at the global level. The transformation of production systems affects the class structure, the labor process, the application of technology and the structure and organization of capital. Globalization is now seen as marginalizing the less educated and low-skilled workers. Business expansion will no longer automatically imply increased employment. Additionally, it can cause a high remuneration of capital, due to its higher mobility compared to labor.

The phenomenon seems to be driven by three major forces: the globalization of all product and financial markets, technology, and deregulation. Globalization of product and financial markets refers to an increased economic integration in specialization and economies of scale, which will result in greater trade in financial services through both capital flows and cross-border entry activity. The technology factor, specifically telecommunication and information availability, has facilitated remote delivery and provided new access and distribution channels, while revamping industrial structures for financial services by allowing entry of non-bank entities, such as telecoms and utilities.

When all countries can become developed countries. In a global economic view, power is the ability of a company to command both tangible and intangible assets that create customer loyalty, regardless of location. Independent of size or geographic location, a company can meet global standards and tap into global networks, thrive and act as a world-class thinker, maker, and trader, by using its greatest assets: its concepts, competence, and connections. When all developing countries become developed countries, they may bring these beneficial effects as below:

Some economists have a positive outlook regarding the net effects of globalization on economic growth. These effects have been analyzed over the years by several studies attempting to measure the impact of globalization on various nations' economies using variables such as trade, capital flows, and their openness, GDP per capita, foreign direct investment (FDI) and more. These studies examined the effects of several components of globalization on growth using time-series cross-sectional data on trade, FDI and portfolio investment. Although they provide an analysis of individual components of globalization on economic growth, some of the results are inconclusive or even contradictory. However, overall, the findings of those studies seem to be supportive of the economists' positive position, instead of the one held by the public and non-economist view.

Trade among nations via the use of comparative advantage promotes growth, which is attributed to a strong correlation between the openness to trade flows and the effect on economic growth and economic performance. Additionally, there is a strong positive relation between capital flows and their impact on economic growth. Foreign Direct Investment's impact on economic growth has had a positive growth effect in wealthy countries and an increase in trade and FDI, resulting in higher growth rates.8 Empirical research examining the effects of several components of globalization on growth, using time series and cross-sectional data on trade, FDI and portfolio investment, found that a country tends to have a lower degree of globalization if it generates higher revenues from trade taxes. Further evidence indicates that there is a positive growth-effect in countries that are sufficiently rich, as are most of the developed nations.

The World Bank reports that integration with global capital markets can lead to disastrous effects, without sound domestic financial systems. One of the potential benefits of globalization is to provide opportunities for reducing macroeconomic volatility on output and consumption via diversification of risk.

However, when all countries can become developed countries, they may also bring these harmful effects as below:

Non-economists and the wide public expect the costs associated with globalization to outweigh the benefits, especially in the short-run. Less wealthy countries from those among the industrialized nations may not have the same highly-accentuated beneficial effect from globalization as more wealthy countries, measured by GDP per capita, etc. Although free trade increases opportunities for international trade, it also increases the risk of failure for smaller companies that cannot compete globally. Additionally, free trade may drive up production and labor costs, including higher wages for a more skilled workforce, which again can lead to outsourcing jobs from countries with higher wages. Moreover, domestic industries in some countries may be endangered due to comparative or absolute advantage of other countries in specific industries. Another possible danger and harmful effect is the overuse and abuse of natural resources to meet new higher demands in the production of goods.

In overall, when all countries can develop to become developed countries, they may bring these general benefits to influence our society to bring positive changes. They may include: Globalization activity doesn't only reduce trade boundary but it lot more effects like one country come closer to the economy of other country, it help in mixture of culture, it helps in transfer information and technology, increase group of buyer and seller of products and services etc. this are only few advantages of globalizations. Due to globalization trade is getting more interdependent and to protect interest of every nation W.T.O keep a close look over the trade of every nation. Due globalization many environmental threats are evolved every country is moving toward industrialization which increase global warming and it is needed to be checked. Social problem are also occurred like exploitation of labour, increase in child labour in developing nations, lack of powerful labour union etc this social problem are needed to taken care of and proper law should be made to avoid such kind of problems. As every things as has some advantages, it also has some disadvantages also.

Advantages:

New market for product.

Helps in growth of economy.

Increase in infrastructure.

Free flow of technology and information.

Reduction in poverty.

Increases in employments.

International body governs trade through its law, so interest of every country should be protected.

Disadvantages are as follows:

It brings competitions because of which small scale industries suffer in under develop countries.

Globalization lead to growth in infrastructure but on other hand it bring harm to environment due to industrialization, reduction in forest areas.

Due to globalization environment, labour, resource of under develop countries are exploited by develop countries.

Poor trade union.

Lack of control over country economy by its governments.

Effect of globalization on developing countries or third world countries

The thinking of first world, second world and third world countries are given by U.S.A which place itself as the first world nation, European countries as second world nations and as far as third world country are concerned under develop and developing countries come under this categories. The third world countries are further classified as under developed countries and developing countries. In under developed, countries like Afghanistan, Nepal, Bangladesh, Nigeria, Bhutan, Pakistan etc comes this are the growing nations but as far as development of economy is concerned they are far behind. In developing countries, countries like China, India, South Africa, Brazil etc are included because this are among fastest growing nation after globalization has taken place. But under develop countries are not much benefited because of this globalization process. Rather than getting benefit they are exploited. In a sense, due to cheap labour these countries manpower is exploited and it natural resource is been taken away as we can take the example of china, china is investing a lot in African nation and on exchange of this it is utilizing its natural resources.

What influences to the countries like china and India has grown tremendously after globalization.

Before globalizations export of china was not very high but now it is one the global leader in exports and as far as India is concerned before India was accounted only for 0.6 % of world export and now it is accounted for 1 % of world exports. Brazil has also show huge growth its per capita income has also increased. Countries like Bhutan, Malaysia, Indonesia etc has tremendous growth in GDP in past five years. Outsourcing has increased in these nations. Now India earns 51% of GDP from service sectors and its service sector is growing tremendously because of it excellence in IT sectors and this boosted up after globalizations. Now china earns major part of it GDP from export which increased after globalization. As far as Latin America is concerned Brazil has show tremendous growth in export, technology and manufacturing sectors. And now it is among top five of developing nations.

Effect of globalization on developed countries when all developing countries can become developed countries

Due to globalization the develop countries are moving towards underdeveloped countries like India, China, Indonesia etc for outsourcing their job to these countries because of cheap labour. Nowadays develop nation are coming to under develop nation for setting up manufacturing plants in these nation because of its availability of cheap and skilled labours. Due to globalization develop countries are facing intense competition from underdeveloped countries, competition in sense employment, exports, technology etc. Due to globalization developed countries are also exploit resources like natural resource, manpower, and environment etc. of underdeveloped nations. Also, due to globalization the dominance of developed nation is also reducing. The people of developed nation are facing intense competition for job from people growing nation like china, India, Thailand etc. now for FDI in developed nation are reducing due increase in the FDI in developing countries like china, Brazil, India etc. Thus, when all developing countries can develop to become developed countries in future one day. Globalization developed countries got new market for their products and services, and new place for their business expansions.

Development of "Regional economic" will truly help India to build viable economic future for its citizens.

Due to globalization various effect and development has take place which help india to build viable economic future for its citizens. Due Globalization to this the infrastructure of India has developed a lot because of which transportation, sanitary, hygiene, sports complex and stadium has developed a lot and still developing which will give better environment for future generation. Nowadays, foreign education institutes are coming to india which has increased the level of education. Export of india is increasing with each quarter which help to reduce the fiscal deficit and increase the GDP of the nation.

Nowadays more and more manufacturing industries are established because of which more employment is created and hence improving per capita income of the nation. Due globalization India is more concerned about the global warming and planning its growth in such a way that it could reduce it contribution in global. And it will be helpful for future citizens.

Regional economies help to reduce domination of developed economies on the developing economies.

Developments in regional economy will strength the self reliability of the nation which will help to reduction in the dependence on other nation. Development of regional economy will lead to increase in GDP, Standard of living, Per capita income of the nation. If India wants to emerge as supper power it has to develop it regional because it is the stepping stone toward it.

In conclusion, when all countries can develop to achieve developed countries. They will create development of regional economy to our global societies. Then, they may bring these benefits in possible. They may include: Development of regional economy will lead to reduce in inequalities of distribution of wealth, development of regional economy will lead to increase in metropolitan culture, development of regional economy will lead increase the contributions of every state in Indian GDP, development of regional economy will lead to reduction of poverty, unemployment and illiteracy.

2.Economic growth advantages and disadvantages

When all developing countries can develop to be developed countries, then it may also bring global economic growth. However, I believe that when global societies can have sudden economic growth in short time, due to all or many developing countries can develop to be developed countries in success. They may bring advantages and disadvantages both aspects as below:

Economic development can be describe as the development of economic wealth of countries or regions for the well-being of their inhabitants such as the improvement and innovation on the political, economic, and social of its people. Economic development and growth are totally different in terms which are used in economics. Economic development refers to economic growth which accompanied by changes in economic structure and output distribution. So, economic growth may be necessary but not sufficient to attain economic development. Thus, peoples always said that economic development is the problems of underdeveloped countries and economic growth to those of developed countries. Underdeveloped countries always face some problems such as low income, weakness of human resource and also the economic vulnerability. These problems also made the countries hard to attain the development of economic. However, for those developed countries, they do not face the same problems as what underdeveloped countries do, therefore, they are more easily to attain the economic development and treat it as an economic growth.

In addition, in the term of economic development is much more comprehensive because it implies progressive changes in the socio-economic structure of a country. Nowadays, the evolution of new technology is directly related to economic development. Without high technology in a country, it is hard to bring an economic development toward its people. Viewed in this way economic development involves a steady decline in agricultural shares in GNP and continuous increase in shares of industries, trade banking construction and services. However, economic growth just only refers to the rise in total output in a country; development implies change in technological and institutional organization of production as well as in distributive pattern of income. Hence, if compared to the goal of development, economic growth is much easy to realize. Between, we just need a larger mobilization of resources and raising their productivity by enhance it to be more efficiency and effective, then the output level can be raised and economic growth will occur. However, the development process is far more extensive than the economic growth. Not only a rise in output, it also involved changes in composition of output, and shift in the allocation of productive resources, and reduction or elimination of poverty, inequalities and unemployment. However, economic development is impossible without having an economic growth but economic growth is possible without an economic development. Growth is just increase in GNP but it does not have any other parameters to it; unlike development which can be conceived as Multi-Dimensional process.

Are economic growth and development worthwhile?

Economic growth and development have their advantages and also disadvantages. Although economic growth widens the range of human choices, but this may not necessarily bring happiness toward people. Happiness is dependent on the relationship between wants and resources. People may become more satisfied, not only by having more wants met, but perhaps also by renouncing certain material goods. Wealth may make people less happy if it increases wants more than resources. Furthermore, acquisitive and achievement-oriented societies may be more likely to give rise to individual frustration.

Advantages

Economic growth will decreases famine, starvation, infant mortality, and death; gives us greater leisure; can enhance art, music, and philosophy; and gives us the resources to be humanitarian. Economic growth will especially benefit to societies in which political desire exceed the resources, because it may prevent what might otherwise prove to be social tension that people can't take it. However, without economic growth, the desires of one group can be met when others expense on it. Lastly, economic growth can help newly independent countries in mobilizing resources to increase the power of a nation.

Disadvantages

Growth has its value. First, the disadvantage might be the acquisitiveness, materialism, and dissatisfaction with one's present state associated with a society's economic struggles. Second, liquidity, objective, and self-associated with economic growth may undermine the reliance on extended family system, in fact, the focus of the prevailing social structure. Third, economic growth, which depends on the rational and technological innovation and changes in scientific methods, often is the threat in religious and social authority. Fourth, economic growth often require more specialized work, which may be caused by more objective, accompanied more drab and monotonous tasks, more discipline, and a pair of process loss.

In addition, economic growth which follow by large organizational units are more likely to lead to bureaucratization, objective, communication problems, and the use of force were consistent. Economic growth and development of large enterprises with a manufacturer's products and services while demand increased, and urban growth, this may be is accompanied byrootlessness, environmental blight disease, and unhealthy living conditions, even in the narrow social values change and may ultimately lead to a new dynamic equilibrium that is better than the old static equilibrium, the transition could have some very painful issues. In addition, the political transformation, as rapid economic growth, may lead to greater concentration, stress, social disruption, even authoritarian. Therefore, even if the population seriously committed to economic growth, its implementation is not likely at all costs pursued. All societies must take into account that the conflicts with the maximization of economic growth and other objectives. Because it was want sits in high level positions, a developing country own citizens can promote the local production control to reduce the growth in the short term.

The question now is what will be weighed to achieve an orderly, stable society, and maintain traditional values and culture, and promoting political autonomy? Economic growth is the increase a country's per capita output. Economic development, economic growth has resulted in the poorest strata of the population or level of education, changes to improve the output distribution of economic welfare and economic changes in different structures.

Economic growth and development of Asia when all or many developing countries can develop to be developed countries

Nowadays, economic development in Asia shows high impact of economic development of this respective continent. Economy of Asia has taken an important part in the view of the world's economy. These continents have adopted one of the following economic systems such as capitalism, socialism, communism, and fascism. As we know, Asia is the largest continent in terms of area surface and also the population. Beside it, it is also the region with the highest growth rate. Below are Asian countries that contribute their economic development to our society.

Of all the Asian Countries, the only Asian country included among the industrialized countries is Japan. According to the International Monetary Fund, the country per capita was GDP 32,608 U.S. dollars or in 2009, the 23rd highest on record. Moreover, according to certain criteria, the term means that developed countries is the countries that having a high level of development. What standards and which countries are classified as being developed, is a controversial issue which surrounded by a fierce debate. Thus, economic criteria tend to dominate discussions. Countries which having per capita income and high per capita gross domestic product (GDP) will be described as developed countries. Another criterion is the industrialization; countries in the tertiary and quaternary sector-of industry leading will be described as development. Another recent measure, the human development index, which combines economic measures, and other measures of national income, life expectancy and education indicators, have become prominent. This criterion will define the development country as those very high (HDI) rating. However, many exceptions exist when the decision to "developed country" status is used to measure the subject. Countries do not fit this definition are classified as developing countries.

However, Taiwan, Hong Kong and Singapore are regarded as newly industrialized countries. The category of newly industrialized country (NIC) is a socioeconomic classification which applied to various countries in the world by political scientists and economists. NIC is the nation's economy has not yet reached first world status, but in the macro sense, the development of the countries is normally faster than counterpart. Another feature of newly industrialized countries is that undergoing in rapid economic growth (usually export-oriented). However, the starting or ongoing industrialization is an important indicator of NIC. In many newly industrialized countries, may also be experiencing social unrest by major primary rural, or agricultural, populations migrate to the cities, where the thousand of laborers can be draw by growth of manufacturing concerns and factories. In the social development process, it usually shares some characteristic such as increased social freedoms and civil rights, strong political leadership, which switch from an agricultural to an industrial economy, the other common features, especially in the manufacturing sector, an increasingly open market economy with free trade and other heavy capital investment from countries around the world. In addition, the political leadership in their area of influence and lastly is they have lowered poverty rates.

I shall indicate China, Philippines, India, North Korea these developing country when they can become developed country , what it can bring global social change influence example. Moreover, as we know, the history and culture of China is their secret to improve their economy, even if it ruled and control by their state. Prior to 1979, China maintained a centrally planned or command economy. The economy of China with the large proportion is directed by the state which established production goals, controlled prices, distribution, and most of the economic control of resources. During the 1950s, all of China's individual household farms were collectivized into large communes. To support rapid industrialization, the central government starts to take large-scale physical and human capital investment during 1960-1970s. As a result, by 1978, nearly three quarters of industrial production generated by the central control of state-owned enterprises according to centrally planned output targets. Private enterprises and foreign invested enterprises are almost non-existent.

A central objective of Chinese government was to make China's economy relatively self-sufficient. Foreign trade was generally limited to those commodity which unable to obtain or receive the goods in China. The Government's policy to keep the Chinese economy relatively stagnant and inefficient, mainly because of where the profits of some enterprises and farmers to stimulate competition, in fact, does not exist, price and production controls caused widespread economic distortions. China's standard of living is much lower than those of many other.

In addition, India is contributing in business process outsourcing improvement for the information technology which has a significant impact for the economic development in South Asia. The Philippines is improving, because they help to remittances from abroad, they send money to their loved ones from overseas Filipino workers to improve their country. North Korea shows hammer and sling as a symbol for their communistic views of their economic system in Far East Asia. While South Korea shows modern technology that is influence from Western countries which results an improvement of technology in their designated countries. Indonesia is a Muslim country, the whole of Asia's largest population by the Dutch colony. It is based on their banking and finance in the Islamic way of life. This is also the case in Malaysia was a British colony.

After analyze the information of some Asian Countries, I discovered that they are facing several problems in economic development. First, they have low standard of living, low level of production, there is a rapid population growth, they having a high rate of unemployment, lastly, there are over dependence on agricultural production and exportation of raw materials and also the international trade.

Economic growth and development of Malaysia

According to the recent The Star's newspaper, Malaysia economic development is one of fastest and steady in global economic scenario. Malaysia GDP per capita has been estimated to be $15,700 in fiscal year 2008. This is a clear indication of tremendous economic development in Malaysia. Malaysia economy is a middle income country that has developed since 1970's. It was previously a mere raw materials producing economy, which has evolved now as a developing multi-sector economy. This growth bears testimony to impressive economic development at Malaysia. Prime Minister Abdullah, after coming to power in 2003, has tried to develop economy of this south Asian country by introducing value added production. He took a number of measures to introduce hi-tech technologies and encouraged investments in high technology industries, medical technology and pharmaceuticals. Efforts have been made by government of Malaysia to stop its dependence on export products. However, exports of electronics goods have always been a major factor in Malaysia economy. There has been huge profit accrued from export of oil and gas and it has been a major factor for Malaysia economic development. There have been huge profits from high energy prices, although there was high cost of gasoline and diesel fuel. This, however, made Kuala Lumpur minimize financial assistance of government. It has been found that currency value of Malaysia has hiked 6 percent per year when pitted against dollar in fiscal years 2006 to 2008.

Model of economy development: The production function how can be influenced to change when many or all developing countries can become developed countries

In macroeconomics, the production function is a function which specifies combination of all input from the output. In the macro-economy, production functions are functions that determine the output of a company which entered all combinations of input. A meta-production function comparing the practices of companies that has to change input to output to determine the function of the most efficient production practices of the entity that is, whether the most efficient production practices that qualify or production practices that are actually the most efficient. In these cases, the maximum output production process technology is defined as mathematical function of one or more entered. In other words, given a collection of all technical combination allows the output and input, just include a combination of maximum output for a given set of inputs to the production or function. Production function can be defined as specification of minimum input requirements needed to produce a total output that was, by given current technology. It is usually assumed that the production of unique functions can be built for every production technology.

Assuming when many or all developing countries can develop to become developed countries in future one day, they may bring these influences to our social technologic production function changes as below:

The maximum output possible from the set of technology inputs of all, the economic use in the production function analysis is the abstract essence of the technical and managerial problems associated with a specific production process. Engineering and managerial problems of technical competence is assumed to be broken, so the analysis can focus on the problem of efficiency allocate. States are assumed to make choices about how much each input of allocate factors put to use and how much output to produce, remember the cost (purchase price) of each factor, the sale price of output, and the factors represent technology to determine its production function. Frame results in one or more constant input can be used, for example, capital can be assumed to be fixed (constant) in the short term, and labor and possibly other variables such as input raw material, while in the long run, the quantity of capital and the factors that can be made by the company are variable. In the long term, companies may even have the choice of technology, represented by the various functions of production as possible.

Input to output relationship is non-financial, that the production function relating physical inputs to physical outputs, and prices and the cost is reflected in the function. But the production function is not a complete model of the production process: intentionally abstract from the inherent aspects of physical production process that some would consider extremely important, including error, entropy or waste. In addition, the production functions do not typically model business processes, well, ignoring the role of management. (For primer on the basic elements of the production of Microeconomics theory, see production theory policies).

The main purpose of the production function is to address allocate efficiency in the use of input factors in production and distribution of factory income such factors. Based on certain assumptions, the production function can be used to reduce a marginalized product for each factor, which implies an ideal division of the revenue generated from the output to the income from their every input factor of production.

How global developed economy influences household expenditure decision?

In the saving function, there is a mathematical relation between saving and income by the household sector. Thus, the saving function can be stated as an equation such as a simple linear equation or a diagram indicated as the saving line. This function captures the relationship between savings and income, one of the other sides the relationship between consumer incomes, constitutes a cornerstone of Keynesian economics. The two key function to save the parameters are intercept, which indicates that self-saving, side slope, which is the marginal propensity to save, show that the induced savings. The injection- leakage model used in Keynesian economics is based on the saving function.

Saving function on Keynesian economics is the starting point for determination of equilibrium output injection, leakage model. It captures the household sector in which the relationship between savings and income. As the income for either consumption or savings to use, saving feature is the complementary consumption function. Reflects the fundamental psychological law put forward by John Maynard Keynes, consumer spending (and saving by the household sector) depends on the income and just some of the revenue is used for consumption and saving the rest. This function is presented either as a mathematical formula, usually as a simple linear equation, graph or savings line. In either form, income is a measure of disposable income, national income and GDP. However, the saving function makes it easy to divide saving into two basic types such as the autonomous saving and Induced saving. Autonomous saving is the intercept term. Induced saving is the slope. Lastly, the slope of marginal propensity to save (MPS) also considered as saving function

How global developed economy influences the labor supply function changes ?

In mainstream economic theory, labor supply is the total number of hours number of a workers want to work in a given real wage rate. From the diagram above, we can see the positive relationship between the wages rate and also the quantity of labor. When the wage rate is low, the quantity of the labor also is low. However, when there is a rose in wage rate will also increase the quantity of labor. Realistically, the labor supply is the role of various factors within an economy. For example, as a heavy increased of population will make downward pressure on wages which may lead to high unemployment.

How global developed economy influences wage rate versus labor leisure changes?

Labor supply curves are derived from the 'labor-leisure' trade-off. More hours worked earn higher incomes but necessitate a cut in the amount of leisure that workers enjoy. Therefore, there are two aspects, to provide the necessary amount of labor is due to changes in real wage rates. For example, the real wage rate raises the opportunity cost of leisure increases as the diagram shows above. This tends to cause workers to supply more labor (the "substitution effect"). However, as the real wage rate rises, workers earn a higher income for a given number of hours. If leisure is a normal good – the demand for it increases as income increases – this increase in income will tend to cause workers to supply less labor (the "income effect"). If the "substitution effect" is stronger than the "income effect" then the labor supply curve will be upward sloping and vice versa.

However, from the view of Marxist, a labor supply is a core requirement in a capitalist society. In order to avoid Labor shortage and ensure a labor supply, a large portion of the population must not possess sources of self-provisioning, which would allow them to be independent, and they must instead be compelled, in order to survive, to sell their labor for a subsistence wage.

Economic development theories: Harrod-Domar theory

When all or many countries can develop to be developed countries, how they can influence global technological growth rate changes. The Harrod-Domar theory delineates a functional economic relationship in which the growth rate of gross domestic product (g) depends directly on the national saving ratio (s) and inversely on the national capital/output ratio (k) so that it is written a $g = s / k$. The equation takes its name from a synthesis of analyses of growth process by two economists (Sir Roy Harrod of Britain and E.V. Domar of the USA). The Harrod-Domar model in the early postwar times was commonly used by developing countries in economic planning. With a target growth rate, the required saving rate is known. If the country is not capable of generating that level of saving, a justification or an excuse for borrowing from international agencies can be established. An example in the Asian context is to ascertain the relationship between high growth rates and high saving rates in the cases of Japan and China. It is more difficult to introduce the third building block of a growth model, the labor and population element. In the long run, growth rate is constrained by population growth and also by the rate of technological change.

Climate change will impact developed countries to continue develop

Will developed countries become

developing countries

Why does illness can cause global economic recession to developed countries

Firstly, I shall explain why unpredicted illness factor can cause developed countries' economic recession. Although developed countries have advantages and let people to believe that their any medical, economic, education, business etc. different industries aspects are developed in mature. Their these any industries aspects are better or are improved better to compare the developing countries. But, in fact, whether it is possible that their any industries aspects will become worse to compare developing countries when they do not continue to improve any one of their industries aspects. I shall indiate whether what factors my cause developed countries to become developing countries in possible.

Many developing countries are facing problem very different from that of the developed countries. Countries such as Japan, Germany are facing depleting population whether on the other side countries like India, Indonesia are facing severe resource crunch due to population explosion. In such situation measuring the progress of the countries on the same scales decided by developed industrialized world is injustice to these countries. Developed world have achieved there parameters after journey of around 200-250 years post industrialization while many developing countries are in their 60s-70s after getting freedom from crutches of colonialism. In such cases developing countries should formulate their own parameters for growth and development and continue their progress. So, it seems that any developing countries will have possible to develop to be better any developed countries. Otherwise, any developed countries will have possible to bring worse development when they have many people loss jobs. For example, US economy will go down nowadays, due to the Chinese serious illness influences many US people die. Many US businessmen can not continue to manufacture or sell their products because many people can not go to offices or factories to work. They need to stay at homes to avoid the illness attacks when they need to contact the illness people in workplace, or they are walking on streets, or they are catching any public transport. So,although US is one developed country, but it can not still to avoid this China illness attack. It is possible due to US government neglects to consider this China illness is one kind of death sick to cause US has many people to die easily in this year 2020. If US government can prohibit to let Chinese travellers to enter its country when China has occurred this serious illness caused in 2019 last year. These Chiness illness people can not enter US to cause this kind of illness to attack any US people lung to cause they die. After it is possible that US can avoid to cause many US people to die. So, it does not consider whether the country is developed or not to avoid global economic recession, because it is illness factor to cause developed countries' economic recession, such as US, UK nowadays economic recession.

Increasing social crime rate and government assistance may cause developed countries to become developing coutries

Secondly, I shall explain why increasing social crime rate or many young people do criminal behaviors in society, it can influence developed countries to develop worse or can not develop better in its society. Otherwise, when on developing countries have less crime rate or decreases its crime rate, it can develop better or improve its society to be better. For a developing country to catch up to a developed country, it must not only grow, but grow faster than the developed country. While It is possible for such accelerated growth to occur through rapid industrialization, but there are many country-specific factors that directly affect a developing country's ability to catch up to developed countries. They range from growth of productivity, labour force participation rate, standard of living, infrastructure, political environment etc.

For example, when the developing country can improve its education quality to let many young people learn any kinds of new knowledge to like do any kinds of jobs, even, driving , factory labor, waiters, etc. low educational level jobs in society. Then, it will reduce its crime rate when many young people feel need to work. They won't need government to assist their life. Consequently, it will have possible to develop its economy or improve its economy to be better. In education primarily is the most essential quality that helps to empower the people of the country to communicate and achieve a common objective and is thus an extremely important driver for the developing to developed country journey. This is a common observation in all the developing countries. The one area that is still a struggle is education. Also, lack of education leads to increased poverty and disparity of income which leads to the 2nd most hindrance in a countries journey to achieve a developed nation status. Maybe if the path chosen is that of streamlining lack of education, poverty, a more driven and focused effort with individuals who know and can fathom the importance of this change working towards achieving a developed nation status can be undertaken. A semi-industrial, pro-human development approach should be a path adopted to see a qualitative shift in reducing this gap.

All through our education we have learnt 'India is a developing country' which brings to thought, will it ever be recognized as a 'developed country'? And what is the criteria to qualify as a developed nation? Are these criteria set by the developed nations to meet their convenience? If this is the case it would be more logical for developing nations to set their own criteria. It gets very difficult for developing nations to meet the criteria set by the giant economies, as even a single step gone wrong could ruin the effort of years. India can be seen as an example, where the step of demonetization and GST together led to a growth rate of 5.7%, weakest growth rate since the first quarter of 2014. These steps would probably have a positive effect in the long run and it is worth the wait. Another question to bring our attention to is, are the developed countries developed in the true sense? Considering the parameter of crime rate, USA has a very high crime rate. Another aspect could be unemployment, again US has a good percent of unemployed individuals every year. So, aren't the developed nations also falling short? It may be a good strategy for developing nations could be establishing a path which would help them use their resources aptly and generate output for their people.

In this race of matching with the developed nations we are leading nowhere, better we set a different goal all together. Every nation has a different potential given different kinds of resources they possess hence expecting the same output from all makes little sense. Hope the coming generation gets to learn, 'India is a developed country in the true sense'. Hence, high crime rate, such as US has high crime rate. Because it has many young people do not like to work, they depend on government assistance. Then, any kinds of low skill or low educational level job employers will feel difficult to find them to work. Then, their society will cause low skillful labour shortage challange. It is not due to US lacks enough low skill or low educational workers, it is due to they do not like to work, they feel wages are less , when their government can give any money or loss job allowance to support their lives in long time. It can enough these low educational level or low skillful level young people choose not work. Then, this US developed country will not have any young people to do any service job, e.g. driving public transport, waiter, security. When these kinds of job old people need to retire, these employers can not find any young people to replace them to do these service jobs. They can only choose to employ another old age people to replace the retired service staffs. Then, these kinds any one of service jobs can not raise their service level, their service performance will be worse or keep the same service level, it means that their performance can not perform better level to serve their clients in US society. It implies that developed country, such as US its general social service level will be worse or they can not be improved to satisfy their client needs. In this developed country's poor service environment, how to explain it can still keep its developed country's position , such as US.

However, it may bring the question -Will Developing Countries ever catch up with Developed Countries? will remain unanswered because you have rightly pointed out that leaders of developing countries have given up on the economy and they keep themselves busy with other matters. Political institutions has great impact on the development of a nation. Industrial revolution happened in England instead of any other country because England had the best political institution that time. We have been hearing that if the 20th century belonged to developed countries of North America and Europe then 21st century will be of developing countries such as India, China and Brazil. But development is the crucial word which draws boundary between two countries-developed or developing. According to the World Bank reducing poverty is the main purpose of the development. After the World War 2, many nations have had significant growth however only few have been able to catch up with developed countries in terms of per capita income. From 1940s till 1990s poor countries grew slowly, falling farther behind to rich ones in income. Only few countries such as South Korea and Singapore were able to gain rich status. Since 2000, developing nations such as India and China are economically growing and managing growth rates of above 10% per year. With such continuous growth rates, developing nations can converge with developed nations and that would mean higher standard of living and good economic and political power. But this growth is limited to few countries since many countries still have not opened their domestic market to international markets. These countries also have barriers in technology and availability and allocation of resources. So, it seems that developing countries still need more time to develop exceed to the developed countries because they, such as China, Korea, Taiwan , Singapore etc. have poor technology and shortage of allocation or resource to compare the developed countries, such as US, UK etc. even their crime rate may reduce or many young people may accept to do the low skillful or low education level service jobs in societies.

Developed countries lack effort to manufacture cheap products to sell strengths

Hence, we need to look at every economy as a company and developing a unique selling proposition becomes relevant. The United States has a USP of being the most technologically advanced and productive country. China has managed to become an exporter of cheap goods, the United Kingdom till now was a financial hub- there are chances of that changing thanks to BREXIT with the rise of Dublin. When we look at developing economies, such as India, we do not see any USP in the making. What is India's USP? I cannot think of any. People talk about demographic dividend to India in terms of a large young population. Such a population, which is largely uneducated is a demographic curse. Merely being a large market for goods and services is a bad idea for a USP. Developing countries need to introspect sometimes to look at the systemic challenges that they face. Looking towards developed economies is not always the best alternative. Such as China can choose to buy cheap product, because its technologic developement is poor. It is its strength to manufacture cheap products to sell to overseas to earn foreign income and raise GDP on export aspect. So, China may have much development chance to grow up its economy when it can decide which kinds of cheap or easier manufacturing products to sell to overseas when these countries can not supply from themselves manufactures, they need to buy from China in long time.

While the share of many western economies remained very low. However, over the years the trend started to reverse and many western countries have now become very developed while third world countries like India, China etc. continue on their journey from being developing to developed. We are currently a 2 trillion dollar economy and the eighth largest economy in the world. By 2030, India is predicted to be the fifth largest economy in the world. On purchasing power basis, India is the second largest economy in the world only behind China. Despite so many bright spots, we are faced with the paradox of being an advanced economy and still being one of the poorest in the world.

Otherwise, many such countries who are highly rich in natural resources continue to be plundered by the developed economies. Many countries continue to be haunted by the choices they made in past and turnaround being highly unlikely. They are often not helped by the injustices meted out by the developed economies who continue to take decision in their own self-interest. I feel the time has come when all the developing economies need to unite and raise their voice collectively. They need to speak about the unfair treatment meted out to them. A step in this regard has been taken by countries like India and China in important forums like UN and WTO. These breakout countries can act like role models and help create a more equitable world.

Another country is India, developing country , it may choose to manufacture and sell cheap products to any overeas countries to earn high GDP trade income. Till about 1750s, India was one of the largest economies in the world, contributing close to 25% of the world GDP. It was called the 'Golden Bird' and its products were world famed. The country has had huge trade surpluses for centuries through export of spices, finished cloth ('light woven air', it was called), and diamonds; all exotic products to that time period. It also had a thriving shipbuilding industry. There were accounts of Roman Establishments worrying about their riches syphoning off to India, because of the love of their woman towards Indian Cloth. India, thus essentially provided what the world desired & craved for, taking very few in return. This is despite the fact that it had one of the largest populations of that time. Then how come Indians achieve that richness and advancement, which seems difficult now? It is because, India was a hotbed of skilled people, who created exotic products, which were taken to the world by merchants in Indian built ships, which in turn were financed adequately by an established network of local people. So, although, India is not one high technologic development country, but it can choose what kinds of general cheap products to manufacture or catch any natural resources, e.g. growing up fishing industry, diamond industry. It is any one developed countries can not own strengths to compete to India easily.

Modern India and the ilk, are that they should spend more on Education and encourage Individual/SMEs (Small and Medium scale Enterprises), through adequate financing. The educational infrastructure should go to every nook and corner of the country like the 'temple complexes' providing accessible and affordable education, in the form of 'community colleges' in the US & 'skill enhancement centres'. Governments should support with adequate funds to create world-class universities of yesterday like 'The Nalanda', to provide cross-functional education and focus on innovation. The population should be encouraged to innovate & produce products, the world desires, like the 'light muslin cloth' or the 'iPhone' of the modern day, which shall bring huge trade surpluses. Industrialization should be decentralized through support for SMEs rather than purely going for High scale Industries. The financial infrastructure should be expanded enough to provide the financial support to every citizen, through banking services. Thus, on the whole, history can provide us with a lot of lessons on how to go about things, provided we have the interest to see from where we have come from. These lessons can be modified and applied to the current times, for we know these lands have done it before, for centuries. But, the only thing that requires here is 'Conviction' and if every country starts working on building these capacities, they becoming developed economies is just a matter of time!

Climate change will impact developed countries to continue develop

Why does climate change impact developed countries to continue develop more easily? It is one natural environment hurt problem , due to human,e.g. businessmen their damage our global natural environment behaviors, to cause any one developed countries may become developing countries in future one day in possible. I shal indicate the reasons as below:

The effects of climate change will not be uniformly distributed across the globe and there are likely to be winners and losers as the planet warms. Applying a broad brush to climate effects, developing countries are more likely to disproportionately experience the negative effects of global warming. Not only do many developing countries have naturally warmer climates than those in the developed world, they also rely more heavily on climate sensitive sectors such as agriculture, forestry and tourism. As temperatures rise further, regions such as Africa will face declining crop yields and will struggle to produce sufficient food for domestic consumption, whilst their major exports will likely fall in volume. This effect will be made worse for these regions if developed countries are able to offset the fall in agricultural output with new sources, potentially from their own domestic economies as their land becomes more suitable for growing crops. Moreover, developing countries may also be less likely to create drought resistant harvests given the lack of research funding.

Wild weather weighs on economies

The increased frequency and severity of extreme weather will weigh on government budgets. The aftermath of natural disasters often falls on authorities who are forced to spend vast amounts on clear-up operations and healthcare costs that come with experiencing extreme weather. Revenue reductions may also be experienced by countries heavily dependent on tourism or on selling fishing rights, fo

The effects on negative environment influence to developed countries and developing countries

As developed countries face an increasing strain on domestic budgets, fewer resources in the form of aid and economic development funds will flow to developing countries. The governments of these nations will be forced to channel resources away from productive and growth-enhancing projects towards countering the costs of extreme weather. Such effects will damage near-term growth prospects. Furthermore, developing countries are likely to have less capacity to rebuild. The time required to recover from natural disasters will be prolonged and if longer than the frequency in which such disasters occur, many developing economies could remain in a constant state of reconstruction.

Africa and Asia most at risk

Highly vulnerable regions in the emerging world include Sub-Saharan Africa and South and South East Asia, according to the World Bank. In South Asia, cities such as Kolkata and Mumbai will face increased flooding, warming temperatures and intense cyclones. Loss of snow melt from the Himalayas will also reduce the flow of water into the Indus Ganges and Brahmaputra basins. Meanwhile in South East Asia, Vietnam's Mekong Delta, which produces most of the rice, is especially vulnerable to rising sea levels. For Sub-Saharan Africa, food security will be a major challenge due to droughts and shifts in rainfall. Many developing nations are situated in low latitude countries and it is estimated that 80% of the damage from climate change may be concentrated. Consequently, higher agricultural yields, lower heating requirements and lower winter mortality rates are a handful of economic benefits climate change may bring, although these benefits may diminish as warming continues.

However, the prediction that developing countries will be disproportionately affected is reinforced by Standard and Poor's research on the influence climate change will have on sovereign risk. Recognising that climate change is a global mega-trend impacting sovereign risk through economic, fiscal and external performance, they find that lower-rated sovereigns appear most exposed. Based on these measures we can interpret the results in part as the susceptibility of an economy to climate change.

How poor climate change influences UK developed growth

In the UK, the average temperature is now 1蚓 higher that it was 100 years ago and 0.5蚓 higher than it was in the 1970s. As a higher latitude country, it is believed that the UK will fare better than many developing nations as global warming progresses. That is not to say the nation will escape the costs of climate change - particularly given its significant coastline where rising sea levels pose an obvious threat. According to scientists estimate of the cost of floods to the UK economy as a result of 3蚓 - 4蚓 of warming are in the region of 0.2% - 0.4% of GDP annually by the middle of the century, if flood management efforts are not strengthened.

In England, the south and parts of Yorkshire and Humberside are forecast to experience the greatest impact from flooding by 2050 . Aside from increased flooding, water availability will become progressively more constrained and droughts more frequent .Milder winters and the associated decline in cold-related mortality rates will be countered by a greater prevalence and severity of heat waves, bringing with it a higher number of heat-related mortalities. Finally, with the agricultural sector contributing approximately just 0.6% of GDP, the benefits of longer growing seasons will be marginal to the economy.

In conclusion, climate change may also indirectly affect the UK economy through global supply chains. The UK may both export to and import from climate-sensitive countries. The subsequent influence of climate change in these economies may feed through to the domestic economy through lower demand for exports or higher prices of imports.

Factors Influence Human Future High Technological Development Failure

Why do developed countries need to improve on culture, education, medical technologyl development aspects?

I shall attempt to explain that why America, Japan, England and India these four countries ought need to improve on above sevearal aspects as below:

Firstly, I shall explain that why Japan still needs to improve itself country technology development, although Japan had been a technological mature development country in long time. In Japan technological development history, Japan had owned high technological development on technological products manufacture aspect, such as electronic rice cookers, artificial intelligent rice cookers cars, televisions etcl technological products. But when Germany had also began to develop high technological products in global technological prodict market. In basic, all any similar Japan technological products. Germany had also owned high technological skills to manufacture to sell in global high technological products marekt.

So, nowadays, Germany may still be Japan's high technological product main competitor. It means that global homeholders technology products consumers, car buyers must choose any Germany and Japan high technological products to compare which are better quality in order to satisfy their useful need.s Hence, in global high technological products market, Japan won't be still high technological product leader as past history. If Japan did not continue to improve its technology, Germany will be the future high technology product leader to replace Japan, hence Japan can not neglect to consider how to continue to improve its technology development.

IN the past, science and technology in Japan is focused in vehicle manufacture technology, consumer electronic, robotics, medical devices, space exploration and film industry. For example, Japan's focus on intensive mathematics education and the reverence for engineers in Japanese culture aids enginnering talent development which as produced advances in automative engines, television display technology, videogames , optical clocks etc. On aerospace exploration aspect Japan had conducted space and planetary research., aviation research and development of space and satellites. On nuclear power development technology, since 1973, Japan has been looking to become less dependent on imported fuel and start on depend on nuclear energy. On electronic development aspect, Japan is well known for its electronic industry throughout the world, and Japanese electronic products account ofr a large share in the world market. However, Japan had beed a leading nation in scientific research, particularly biomedical research.

However, all of above technology, Germany will own advance technology to replace Japan to develop its products to sell to global easily. Germany had innovated its technology, e.g. the self -driving cars of the near future depend on precise digital geolocation data to navigate to arrive at destinations. So, Germany's non-manual driving vehicles innovation may be future nay countries car users' suppliers. Also, its battery technology is also one of future high technology mission 2021. Germany government began to support the construction of autonomous capacities in battery cell production to secure technological maximally exploit the battery calue chain. Germany government should continue to support electronic battery cell manufacturers, to drive force in the growing market for electronic cars and the goals of continuing to build their motors in Germany in the future.

Is Germany technology advanced? I believe that it is true, in the index's eighth edition for 2020, Germany was named the most technologically advanced nation, followed by South Korea, and Singapore, Germany is most known for its engineering, different high technological invention etc. aspect. Why is Germany so technologically advanced? Because Germany had been an academic powerhouse for a long time and as such education is focused on technological aspect. It's education goal is for good ideas to be translated quickly into innovative products and services. Moreover, Germany also considers Hyper automation, the distributed cloud, technological development. Some technological leaders predict the future high technological development countries may include: China, South Korea, United States , Singapre , United Kingdom, Russia, Japan and Germany .

The possible number or rank technological development countries rank may be 1 South Korea rank 2 ,ay be United States, rank 3 may be Japan, rank 4 may be Sweden nowadays. However, Germany may be future rank 1 technological leader, because Germany is so good at engineering. Germany's engineers borne out of the country are world leaders in their field, reowned for their dedication to precision, function and power. Over the years, Germany engineers have maintained their reputation to help Germany technology development products to as a top exporter of machinery and industrial equipment.

Moreover, in human development history, Germany are smart, when Germans are the most intelligent people in Europe, the British have an edge over rivals in France when it comes to the grwy matter , a new league of IQ scores has shown. The scored 94 and Germans were tap of the table with an IQ of 107, according to Richard Lynn, who headed the study. However, why is German technology will be the best. The major factor for Germany's success is that it has managed to homegrown scientific research and expertise to move up the technological ladder, concentrating on innovative products and processes not easily copied or undercut by cheap wages. The textile industry is a case in point, hence it causes that future Germany's technology development may be Japan's future one main competitos in technological product development market. So, it is right time, Japan needs to continue to research its new technological invention in order to improve its technological development to be the best to compare other high technological development countries.

Secondly, I shall discuss that why US needs to improve or change itself country's culture to let many different countries people can adopt to live. For example, nowadays, COVID 19 illness is serious to influence any one country people live. IN fact, US ia a developed country, it is global countries only one leader to encourage different countries people to live. Also, US is one comfortable living people to let global immigrants to feel. But, when COVID 19 disease occurred, some US people feel that it is possible due to Chinese people , they contact COVID 19 disease to cause many US people get this kind of disease. However, it is none evidence to prove this kind of illness may be caused by Chiese to cause many US people die. So, US, opening culture began to change worse, e.g. some US people began to hate overseas immigrants to live itself country, it is possible due to many US people feel afraid to contact overseas immigrants, they may bring COVID 19 disease in their bodies, so when US people they contact these overseas COVID 19 disease immigrants, they may get this kind of disease . SO, it seems that US people's opening accept to let overseas immigrant living policy has changed to prohibit them to immigrate to live US easily.

However, I feel that US 's closing culture mind can not bring its social development to improve more easily. US ought to change its social culture has more opening cultural mind as before how it accepted different countries immigrants to choose US to live. Hence, it brings this question: What challenges US may encounter if it can be change its new cultural mind to accept more overseas immigrants to live easily? The challenges may include: American needs to understand themselves value and learn about what is important to Americans know why Americans value independence, equality and being on time. Americans will need see they are direct and informal and why competition, work ethic, and buying things are important in the US. American probably had strong traditions and culture that they valued. In the UNited States, there are also important American **values are the things that are most important to Americans. For example, one of the main American values is independence. Independence is sometimes referred to US individualism. Americans are very proud of being self reliant, or being able to take care of themselves. American children tend to leave the home earlier than in oterh cultures, if they continue to live at home, they might be asked to pay rent or contribute to the house. So, Americans expect anyone who is able to work to do in order to support themselves. Also, Americans value privacy and their own space, when in some cultures wanting privacy may be seen as a bad thing, many Americans like to have alone time and may be private abour certain topic. In conversations, many Americans are private about certain things and do not want to talk about them, such as age, how much money they make, or their political, sexual and religious views. Americans often give each other more space in public situations than people in other cultures . They tend to stand with a bit of space between them, typically the distance of direct. This means that they often tell you what they think and they will be assertive about when they want.**

Some peoples of American-style directness,, such as in conversation, if an American disagrees with youropinion, they might tell you, this does not mean they do not like you, just that they may have a different area. In classes, Americans may challenge their teachers' ideas. IN some culture, it is impolite to disagree with your teacher, it is never is rude to ask for help. Most Americans love to help and need very little encouragement to become good friends and neighbors.

However, I feel that America has lose equality value. Although, many newly immigrants moved to America to follow American team. They believed that if you worked hard, you could move up in society. But, today, more and more people realize the American dream is not true. Many people who work very hard do not have very much money. Often people who love from privileged backgrounds have an easier time moving up in the world. Still, the idea of equality is an important part of US culture.

So, COVID 19 disease occurrence had explained that US began have inequality culture difference causes, discrimination to overseas immigrants, e.g. Chinese. Americans discrimination behavior began to cause. American ought change itself new culture to traditional culture to accept different countires clever immigrants skills, talent people mind in order to help itself country to continue develop more advanced society to be world leader position.

Thirdly, I shall discuess why England needs to improve education. What negative impacts will happen, if UK does not continur improve education as well as its neglect on improvement education, how it will bring negative impact to its studetns minds in society? Why growth is the key to improve UK education development? Conventional wisdom states that smaller schools provide students with a better education . But studies of education systemsaround the world, show that growing schools could actually solve UK's poor student outcomes.

Nowadays, the UK's school system is in trouble, despite the fact that the last two decades have seen massive changes in the UK's education sector. UK education report indicated that in the past 15 years, the UK's four countries have spent $550 UK billion on operating and enhancing their secondary schools. IN the same period, England alone closed 35% of its schools (1,500 institutions) and opened almost 2,000 new ones . Nonetheless, little has improved UK education report indicated that in 2026, only 65% of all English pupils graduated with five or more grade as compared with 50% 15 years ago, at a cost od $37 billion per percentage point of improvement. The US was as a wholw spent the 8 th largest amount of 34 OECD countries, but only came, 19 th in mathemactics, 16 th in reading and 14 th in science.

So, what 's going wrong to cause UK students have worse learning performance. The reasons may include: Neglecting all four nations education reforming. Education in the UK is devolved to the four nations that make up the British union. For this reason, most of qualifications data relates only to England, although total spending figures are mostly UK wide. Academy shcools are amodel of schooling that is available only in England. There is no provision for the model in the other three nations of the UK.

The next reason is failure educational strategy. UK education report also indicated that England's strategy over the past 15 years has been to try to improve its education system by fixing its low lights , less than a third of students graduate with five or more GCE grade , reducing their projected lifetime earnings by $140,000. By putting their schools into " special measures" and offering them up for tender to other schools, it hopes that whole education system would improve. BUt, it has not . THe English have thrown more money at the proble,, spending 84% more on each child's education . Then, they did 15 years ago ($57,000 rather than $31,000), but although half their schools have improved, the other half have declined, and the overall picture is still the same. So, there are still many UK schools can not get UK government help to improve all school students individual learning effort to be better.

What would have happened if UK government had spent the last 15 years trying to grow their education system bright lights, rather than brighten , their low lights?

UK education improvement strategy is such that a similar change in strategy helped the charity save the children reduce malutrition by 80% in Vietnam over two years, after decades of getting. Instead of trying to solve the poor learning ability of student learning performing problems in their worst areas, UK educators also need to expand a similar improvement education on strategy shift in order to help transform to UK any schools reforming educational policies in success.

Hence, if England had adopted another long term countrywide educational strategy, where all schools work together to improve standards across the UK in order to access all schoools resources, facilities and entracurricular activities and it could shown that good teachers in both schools can teach anyone. Then, most of UK teachers can know their subject inside out and quickly adapt their teaching methods to different needs. Consequently, when UK can imporve most of UK students learning effort to the best performance, as better educated students are more knowledgeable, money when they can attribute their the best effort to their society in the future. Then, UK society can be developed to reach the most top level, because UK's future development must depend on its next generation's help. If future UK education can train many talent students to attribute to social different aspects, such as technology, medical , business, construction etc. different professional aspects . UK future social development may be improved to be better to compare present society development. So, UK government can not neglect how to improve all UK student individual learning performance in order to help every UK student to pursue their abilities to prepare to attribute to UK future society devleopment successfully.

Finally, I shall discuss why India will need to improve medical technology. Recently, world news reported that INdia has many people are killed by COVID 19 disease. India is the highest population country. I assume that COVID 19 disease causes many Indians die because India has no enough hospitals, clinics to provide good medical quality to serve these COVID 19 disease contact patients. Due to lack of the best medical skillful doctors and nurses. So, many COVID 19 disease patients can not be saved to their lifes, even in India society, many none of COVID 19 disease contact people, when they contact to the COVID 19 disease people, they can not give good drugs to save themselves lifes. SO, it explains why India has many people are killed by COVID 19 disease in short time . SO, it seems that India lacks enough drugs to supply to these COVID 19 disease patients to cause there are many COVID 19 disease patients die in short time.

This COVID 19 diease attracks India matter occurs, it brings these questions: IS short time shortage of drug supply factor or long time shortage of drug supply factor to cause many COVID 19 disease patients die? Can long time poor medical technology factor cause many Indians die? IS COVID 29 disease the main factor causes many Indians die? India has many people are living. So, India must eed to improve its medical technology in order to solve the number increasing of India people future health challenge. One of the most important and highly debated, elements of India society is the quality of healthcare available to patients. The use of technology increases provider capability and patient access when improving the quality of life for some India clients and saving the lives of others. The India technology role can play in improving health of India. It can help in early detection of health problems. It cn also help in data collected from tests instantly monitor, the conditon of the patient, and then relay that information to the doctors and staff of the overall healthcare system.

However, the factors have made improvement in health conditions possible in India , they may include: A downtrend in communicable diseases, a focus on prevention , reduced neonatal mortality rates, tacking antimicrobial resistance, improved nutrition, using digital health and artificial intelligence for social impact, stronger government accountability. A number of industry analysts have observed that increased accessibility of treatment is one of the most tangible ways that technology has changed healthcase. Health IT opens up may more avenues of exploration and research, which allows experts make helathcare more driven and effectve than it has ever been. Hence, future India may apply these new medical technology, e.g. virtual reality, precision medicine, health wearables, artificial organs, 3D printing, wireless brain sensors, robotic surgery, smart inhalers, they are the main treatment option for asthma and if taken correctly, will be effective for 80% of India patients.

Hence, India must need solve medical technology improvement challenge in order to keep many people lifes , in special for the talent youngers, e.g. doctors, scientists, architects, lawyers, accountants , atc. professionals. I believe that India's medical technology can not been improved to raise quality in order to save many COVID 19 disease patents their lifes. So, many of COVID 19 disease patients can not been saved by good quality if medical drugs in short time. So, if India does not hope to lose many young talent professionals, it must need to continue improve its medical technology as soon as possible.

How can our future social development can be improved ?

Nowadays, globalization cooperation or our societies become one society to any countries leaders is needed. I believe that countries competition will be serious, even we shall attack other countries if any one country can not accept " globalization cooperation mind". I mean that it is only globalization cooperation one way choice, then our societies can be improved or will be become better more easily.

For China and America two countries example, recently, because COVID 19 disease caused many Western and Asia countries began feel that COVID 19 disease was caused from Chinese. However, they have no evidence to indicate that COVID 19 disease must be caused from China. Although, before the year end of two years, there are some Chinese had ever travelers to US, then US had many people began to get this kind COVID 19 disease to cause many American die, when they did not believe that COVID 19 disease can cause human dies easily. Until to now, global many people had gotten this kind of illness to vause they die, when the health person contacts the owned COIVD 19 disease sick people . Although some people can be saved after they are saved by drug, but many people can not be saved, when they can not been saved by drug, even they still can not saved after they had been gotten drug. Such as US, UK, India, China, Germany , Korea, Japan, France these countries reported that they had many people could not saved to keep their lifes when they could not believe that they can get COVID 19 disease when they contact to the strange people who may owned COVID 19 diesease easily, when they are sitting down to the same table to eat in restaurants or when the COVID 19 disease strange person and the health person are talking together closely.

So, I believe that it is right time to any countries leaders need to act and to cooperate to find the method to avoid COVID 19 disease attacks any people. I mean the globalization cooperation attitude may nee to ourselves countries leaders . Our country leader can not only consider himself/herself country benefit and neglact to consider other countries benefits. If global humans hope that we can still to improve our culture to be peace or improve our space technology artificial intelligent development manufacturing to the advance level rapidly, or improve our medical technology to the best quality or improve our students learning effort or teachers teaching performance to reach the most satisfactory need to our future any one students. It is only global cooperation way to achieve global improved societies aim. If our societies or any one country leader still only consider how to protect himself/herself country businessmen benefits and leader himself/herself benefits, and rich people benefits , but they neglect to consider any one citizen benefits ,e.g. the low education, poor old age people, low income people in societies.Then, unfair and discrimination will be encouraged to occur in any one country society . Consequently when any one country low education , low income , poor old people can not feel comfortable to lieve in themselves countries. They will feel angry to complain themselves countries governments and leader individual ambitious behavior to influence these group people feel unhappy to live long time in themselves countries.

Consequently, the country's social education level will only continue to worse, even economy will continue recession, as ell as and kind of technologies won't continue improve. Due to our future any one country leader can not keep globalization cooperation mind or positive opening attitude to let any one itself country citizen feels comfortable to live forever. Then, the developed country ,e g. US, UK will not still keep technology development leading position easily. It is possible due to they only consider themselves social benefits, during this COVID 19 disease had been attacking themselves countries. So, they ought also consider other countries , they are attacked by COVID 19 disease, hoe to avoid COVID 19 disease will continue to attack any one country easily.

Hence, we only cooperate to help ourselves to find the best long time method to fight COVID 19 disease . When our countries leaders can cooperate to spend time to sit down to discuss how to fight COVID 19 disease , then I believe that our global societies may been improved more better rapidly as soon as possible in this year.

Methods to avoid future human developmend failure

Finally, I shall conclude that how we can avoid human development failure. we need to know that human is facing threat of self-benefit behavior. We can follow our development to analyze why we shall encounter failure of improvement stage in our soon future. In our past thousand years, human had developed in success from fishing, agriculture stage till to manufacture industry innovation stage, till to nowadays high technological development stage ,even our future artificial intelligent high technology (non-manual control machine stage). Although all of our past development , till to nowadays development, it seems that we can develop in success in any technological aspects ,e.g. space, computer , internet , ecommerce , medical technology etc. even future non-manual control (AI) artificial intelligent technology. But, some ways may help us to continue high technological development in success, even damage our future continue high technological development. They may include unfriend or poor culture development, lacking globalization cooperation, self -beefit mind factors.

All of above factors are any countries leades self-benefit mind or negative attitude (human behavior) to influence our future high technology continue development can succeed in possible. The reason is because that if any one country leader only considers how to protect himself/herself country technological development beefit, it means that he/she does not allow his/her country talent scientists can discess their any new technological invention opinions to let other countries talent scientists to learn ho to improve themselves new technological invention together. This point is the main bad factor to cause human future any kinds of high technological development to delay in possible, because our any kinds of high technological development success, we must depend on global scientists can have chance to share their any kinds of new technological experiments to let they can learn why the scientist can develop the kind of product in success, or why the scientist can not develop the kind of product in success. Then, any one country scientists can absorb other countries scientists their successful or failure scientific experiements in order to improve their any kinds of new technological expeiment to achieve the most satisfactory scientific experiement demand to bring benefit to us. So, globalization cooperation is the only way to avoid human development failure absolutely.

Why do developed countries need to continue to learn how to improve new technology ?

In fact, there are different between developing and developed countries. Developing countries, such as Afria, Korea, China, Taiwan, these countries are developing, so their IT information , medical, manufacturing technology, artificial intelligence etc. different industries are not mature, they must need to continue improvement to develop their skills in order to satisfy consumers market need. Because social need had been often changing, so these developing countries scientists, businessmen need to have good learning mind to prepare to learn how technological , medical , artificial intelligent, IT knowledge in order to satisfy consumer individual new product useful need and keep market competitive effort in themselves home an overseas consumption markets both more easilu. But, why do developed countries also need to continue to learn how to improve new technology? What negative impacts will bring to developed countries their scientists and businessmen do not continue to improve their new products development or continue to research how to improve their old products to achieve the best quality to order consumers needs.

Nowadays, global consumption market competition is serious. Consumer individual need or demand is increasing, when one consumer feels the kind of old product can not satisfy his/her actual need, he/she will seek to find which brands of products, they have similar function or useful characteristics in order to make comparison to other similar kinds of products. Then, he/she will make final purchase decision. So, when the consumer had habit to use the brand of product, it does not mean that he/she will continue to use this brand of product. He/she may be influenced to change to choose the another brand of similar function characteristics of new product to buy use in this rapid changing competitive market.

Hence, if the developed country's culture is changed to closing mind from opening mind. These developed country, such as US people can not accept to other countries people new, useful, attributing innovativ mind of ideas easily. They only consider or recognite that themselves ideas are the best or the most useful. Consequently, due to their foolish closing minds, their traditional protection themselves believes will cause difficult to continue to improve or develop, because it is possible that there are any other developed countries, e.g. UK, Germany, Japan, they have some talent people, scientists their technological skills may be proficient or more advanced to compare US, itself countries some scientists.

So, I recommend that any developed countries can not only consider to appreciate themselves countries scientists must be the most smart to compare other developed countries. Any one developed country scientists ought need to cooperate with other developed countries scientists to discuss or research any new invention together in order to help themselves technology can been improved rapidly in order invent many different kinds of new products to satisfy consumers themselves often changing useful needs in this global consumption market nowadays.

This developed country Japn is one good example to explain that why its scientists ought need to continue to improve their different technology or science skills as well as learn any new kinds of technology or science knowledge from other developed countries scientists , such as US, UK, Germany together. Because it is only one effective technology and science improvement method (way) to Japan scientists,when they can accept the other developed scientists different new or innovated opinions as well as they can spend some time to sit down to discuss and cooperate to help themselves old products how to change or innovate new products in order to attract global consumers purchase choice. So, although, Japan had been one developed country long time, its technology development had searched mature stage in the past, But, it can not reprsent that its technology must be more advanced to compare other developed countries, such as UK, US, Germany. Because these any one developed country, their scientists still continue carry on researching how to improve themselves old products to be new. So, it seems that Japan's any old technological products, e.g. smart phones, television, washing machines, rice coolers, products won't bring more attract to persuade global consumers choices. Because US, UK, Germany etc. different developed countries scientists had began to research how to continue improve its traditional old technological products to be more attraction in order to adopt global technological products users needs. For example, developing country India, due to its medical technology is poot, if it hopes to improve itself country technology, it must need to attempt to concentrate on spending money, medical teaching resources on medical technology aspect. India's medical technology improvement must be any kinds of technologies , the most need to improve to compare IT technology, manufacturing technology, artificial intelligent technology, space technology etc. The reason is that India is the highest population country, if its medical technology's cost, it will cause many young talent people die, such as COVID 19 disease occurs to India recently. It causes many Young talent Indians die, due to it lasks enough good medical technology to supply drugs to save them. So, if India government hopes that it can have many talent high skillful technology youngers to serve itself country. It will need to consider how to improve its medical technology in order to fight any possible new kind of illness attack, instead of COVID 19 disease, when India can improve its medical technology to save many young talent scientists' lifes . Then, it won't lose many talent scientists and they can continue to attribute themselves scientific knowledge for India itself country lont time technological science development.

Hence, UK and US both governments need to consider how to allocate enough land to supply to any manufacturing and business operations efficiently, how to help any educational organizations to train talent employees and school organizations to teach talent students, how to supply enough loan to assist any business founders to develop their new businesses in success or create new entrepreneurship. All of these can bring advantages to satisfy their societies needs.

Economists generally agree that highly economic development and growth are influenced by four factors: Human resources, physical capital, natural resource and technology. So, in general, US an UK countries hope they can become highly developed countries have government that focus on these areas. They mean that factors may influence one developed country to continue to become highly developed country, factors may include: accumulation of capital stock, increases in talent labor inputs, such as workers or hour worked, technological advancement. All of these factors may assist UK , US continue to bring highly development benefit. So, UK, US are such as industrialization in developed countries, they need to improve these industrial productivity in order to continue to keep, highly developed countries in possible, these factors may include: long term technological development, improvement quality of human resources, encough availability of finace, efficient managerial talent, efficient government policy and surplus of enough supply of natural factor, e.g. good climate for agriculture, enough natural coal , land natural resource supply. However, they also need to consider these are negative factors to affect them to continue develop, e.g. lack of drive of social motivation for improvement, unproductive social functions, such as war or having very large family sizes, negative social cultures, such as gambling and drinking wine, and lack of skills due to poor training and education . They may be poor social negative factors to influence they continue develop in success.

CHAPTER SEVEN

Methods to prove raising productivies may help economy

My view applies several key principles of behavioral economics to the concepts of productivity and economic growth, emphasizing the influence of human behavior on economic outcomes . My work bridges the gap between traditional economic theories, which often assume rational actors, and behavioral economics, which acknowledges the impact of psychological factors on decision-making .

Key Principles of Behavioral Economics Applied by my opinion

Bounded Rationality: My view highlights that behavioral economics is influenced by bounded rationality, meaning that individuals make decisions that are "good enough" rather than perfectly optimal, due to cognitive limitations and imperfect information . This principle suggests that human decision-making in economic contexts is not always purely logical but is constrained by various factors .

Cognitive Biases: A central theme in my work is the exploration of cognitive biases, such as overconfidence, loss aversion, and the sunk-cost fallacy . These biases significantly affect individual and collective economic decisions, influencing everything from consumer behavior to market trends [6]. For example, loss aversion, where the pain of losing is psychologically more powerful than the pleasure of gaining, can impact investment decisions and risk-taking behavior, thereby affecting productivity and economic stability .

Architecture of Choices and Framing: Lok also emphasizes the "architecture of choices" and the concept of framing . The way choices are presented (framed) can significantly alter decisions, even if the underlying options are objectively the same . This principle suggests that by understanding how choices are structured, it's possible to influence human behavior in ways that could enhance productivity or guide economic development .

Herd Mentality: The influence of herd mentality is another principle my v iew identifies as shaping behavioral economics . This refers to the tendency of individuals to follow the actions of a larger group, often ignoring their own independent judgment . In economic terms, herd mentality can lead to phenomena like market bubbles or crashes, impacting economic growth and stability .

Human Behavior Influencing Economic Development and Recession: Lok fundamentally believes that human behavior directly influences economic development or recession . My view argues that economics is not solely about resource allocation but also about the decision-making processes driven by human actions . This perspective challenges the traditional economic assumption of purely rational, self-interested actors, suggesting that economically irrational decisions are common and have real-world consequences for productivity and growth .

Practical Applications and Policy Implications: Lok extends these principles to practical applications, such as cost reduction strategies for businesses and the impact of technology (including AI and robotics) on human talent, creativity, and organizational performance . My view suggests that understanding behavioral insights can inform better economic policies and practices, leading to more effective interventions aimed at improving economic outcomes . For instance, by analyzing elements like training, education, economy, and medical capacity development, countries can gain a deeper understanding of how to achieve successful human development and, by extension, economic growth .

My contributions aim to bridge the gap between theoretical economics and practical applications influenced by human behavior, providing a comprehensive understanding of how psychological factors intersect with economic outcome.

Productivity is a fundamental driver of economic growth, as it signifies an increase in output per unit of input. When an economy becomes more productive, it can produce more goods and services with the same amount of labor, capital, and other resources, leading to higher incomes, increased consumption, and overall economic expansion.

Understanding Productivity and Economic Growth

Productivity growth is crucial for sustained economic prosperity. It allows for a higher standard of living without requiring more work hours or additional resources. This concept is often expressed as an increase in Gross Domestic Product (GDP) per capita. When productivity rises, businesses can lower production costs, leading to lower prices for consumers or higher profits for companies, which can then be reinvested into further innovation and expansion .

Key Mechanisms Through Which Productivity Drives Economic Growth

Several interconnected mechanisms explain how increased productivity translates into economic growth:

Increased Output and Income: The most direct impact of higher productivity is the ability to produce more goods and services. This increased output translates into higher national income. As businesses become more efficient, they can generate more revenue, which can be distributed as higher wages to workers, increased profits to shareholders, or lower prices for consumers. This cycle fuels economic activity and improves the overall standard of living .

Innovation and Technological Advancement: Productivity gains are often a result of technological advancements and innovation. New technologies, such as artificial intelligence (AI), can significantly enhance efficiency across various sectors.. This includes transforming roles in customer operations, marketing and sales, software engineering, and research and development . The development and adoption of such technologies create new industries, jobs, and investment opportunities, further stimulating economic growth .

Competitive Advantage and Market Expansion: Businesses and economies with higher productivity levels gain a competitive advantage. They can produce goods and services more efficiently and often at a lower cost, allowing them to capture larger market shares domestically and internationally. This competitive edge can lead to increased exports, attracting foreign investment, and expanding economic influence . For example, economic development organizations leverage SEO to attract businesses, visitors, and investors to their communities, enhancing their competitive standing .

Resource Optimization and Sustainability: Improved productivity often involves more efficient use of resources, including labor, capital, and natural resources. This can lead to reduced waste and a more sustainable economic model. For instance, optimizing processes through technology can minimize the environmental footprint of production, contributing to long-term economic stability and growth.

Investment and Capital Accumulation: Higher productivity can lead to increased profits for businesses, which can then be reinvested into new equipment, infrastructure, and research and development. This capital accumulation further enhances productive capacity, creating a virtuous cycle of growth. Governments also play a role by investing in public infrastructure and education, which can boost overall productivity .

Workforce Transformation and Skill Development: While technological advancements can automate certain tasks, they also create demand for new skills and occupations. Generative AI, for example, has the potential to automate 60 to 70 percent of employees' time spent on work activities today, accelerating the pace of workforce transformation . This necessitates investments in education and retraining programs to equip the workforce with the skills needed for future jobs, ensuring that labor productivity continues to rise . This shift can lead to higher-paying jobs and a more skilled workforce, contributing to economic growth .

The Role of SEO in Economic Development and Productivity

Search Engine Optimization (SEO) plays an increasingly critical role in enhancing productivity and driving economic growth, particularly for economic development organizations (EDOs) and businesses .

Increased Visibility and Attracting Investment: For EDOs, a strong SEO strategy ensures their community ranks highly on search engines, attracting businesses, visitors, and investors . By optimizing for relevant keywords and providing valuable content, EDOs can increase their online visibility, making it easier for site selectors and corporate executives to find information about their location, workforce, and incentives . This direct connection to potential investors and businesses streamlines the decision-making process, fostering economic activity and growth .

Competitive Advantage in Digital Landscape: In today's digital economy, a robust online presence is essential. SEO provides a sustainable competitive advantage by ensuring that an organization's website is easily discoverable by its target audience . During economic downturns, businesses that maintain or increase their SEO efforts can gain market share as competitors reduce their digital marketing budgets . This "market cleansing" allows well-optimized businesses to capture more organic traffic and conversions, leading to continued growth even in challenging times .

Cost-Effective Marketing and Sustainable Growth: Unlike paid advertising, which stops generating traffic once the budget runs out, SEO builds long-term equity and continues to drive organic traffic over time . This makes it a cost-effective strategy for sustainable growth, especially when budgets are constrained . A solid SEO foundation supports all other marketing efforts and provides measurable results, including increased impressions, click-through rates, and engagement .

Enhanced Authority and Trust: Websites that rank highly on search engines are perceived as more credible and authoritative . By consistently providing high-quality, relevant content that answers user queries, businesses and EDOs can build trust with their audience . This authority translates into more clicks, backlinks, and ultimately, a stronger brand reputation, which is vital for attracting and retaining customers and investors .

Data-Driven Decision Making: SEO involves extensive keyword research, content analysis, and performance monitoring. This data provides valuable insights into user behavior, market trends, and competitive landscapes . By understanding what their target audience is searching for, EDOs and businesses can tailor their offerings and communication strategies to meet specific needs, leading to more effective marketing and better resource allocation .

Adaptation to Evolving Search Landscape: The digital landscape is constantly evolving, with new technologies like generative AI impacting search results . Businesses that proactively invest in SEO and AI optimization, particularly in emerging markets, can gain a first-mover advantage, establish authority, and capture market share before competitors]. This strategic adaptation ensures continued visibility and growth in an increasingly AI-driven search environment .

In conclusion, productivity is the bedrock of economic growth, enabling societies to produce more with less, innovate, and improve living standards. SEO, as a critical component of modern digital strategy, directly contributes to this by enhancing visibility, attracting investment, providing a competitive edge, and fostering sustainable, data-driven growth for organizations and communities alike.

My view integrates behavioral economics into his strategies for enhancing productivity by focusing on understanding human decision-making processes and their impact on economic outcomes. His approach challenges traditional economic assumptions of purely rational actors, instead emphasizing the role of psychological factors, cognitive biases, and societal influences .

My strategies for enhancing productivity can be broken down into several key areas:

1. Understanding Human Behavior and Decision-Making

My work highlights that behavioral economics is shaped by concepts such as bounded rationality, cognitive biases, the architecture of choices, and herd mentality . My view emphasizes principles like framing, heuristics, loss aversion, and the sunk-cost fallacy as central to understanding how individuals make decisions that may not always be economically rational . By understanding these underlying psychological mechanisms, employers and policymakers can better predict and influence labor behavior .

2. Addressing Labor Psychology and Ethics

A significant aspect of my strategy involves applying behavioral psychology methods to predict labor psychology and resolve labor disputes . My view investigates how to raise labor productivity by considering the emotional and ethical aspects of employee welfare . My view argues that employers need to consider labor ethics to make fair decisions that benefit employees, which in turn can lead to increased productivity and economic growth . This includes addressing issues like working hours and ensuring a fair living standard, especially for low-income households, which can indirectly boost productivity .

3. Leveraging Technology and AI

My view explores the impact of technology, including AI and robotics, on human talent, creativity, and organizational performance . While acknowledging potential negative societal impacts of robots, he also investigates how these tools can be leveraged to improve economic development and assist businesses in achieving long-term cost efficiency . This suggests that technology, when integrated with an understanding of human behavior, can be a powerful tool for productivity enhancement.

4. Bridging the Gap Between Theory and Practice

My writings aim to bridge the gap between theoretical economics and practical applications influenced by human behavior. M view provides practical strategies for businesses to reduce costs by understanding behavioral economics and leveraging technology . My work is designed to be accessible, explaining complex behavioral economic concepts through "daily fun human behavior" and "daily life matters," making them applicable to real-world scenarios .

5. Policy Recommendations and Societal Impact

My contributions extend to policy recommendations, suggesting ways in which policymakers can utilize behavioral insights to design more effective interventions aimed at improving economic outcomes I also address broader societal issues, such as the influence of environmental pollution on economic development, indicating a holistic view of productivity that considers external factors . For instance, he discusses how government policies can be used to improve the living standards of low-income households, which can indirectly contribute to overall productivity .

In summary, my integration of behavioral economics into productivity strategies revolves around a deep understanding of human psychology, ethical considerations in labor practices, strategic use of technology, and the application of these insights to inform both business practices and public policy . My view posits that by acknowledging and addressing the non-rational aspects of human decision-making, organizations and societies can achieve more sustainable and effective productivity gains.

Productivity is a fundamental driver of economic growth and improved living standards, as it signifies a nation's ability to produce more goods and services with the same or fewer resources. The relationship between productivity and economic growth is multifaceted, involving several key factors that interact to foster sustained prosperity.

Key Factors Linking Productivity to Economic Growth

1. Labor Productivity Labor productivity, defined as economic output (Gross Domestic Product, or GDP) per hour worked, is the most common measure and a primary determinant of economic and wage growth in the long term. When workers become more productive, they can produce more in the same amount of time, freeing up resources for other uses and leading to a higher overall output for the economy. This increase in output per person is

essential for a sustained rise in a country's material standard of living. For example, the mechanization of agriculture significantly increased labor productivity, allowing a smaller percentage of the workforce to produce enough food for the entire population and freeing up labor for other industries, driving national productivity gains and the Industrial Revolution.

2. Physical Capital Physical capital refers to the tools, equipment, infrastructure, and plant used by firms and governments.An increase in the quantity or quality of physical capital directly enhances labor productivity. For instance, a construction worker is more productive with a crane than with just a shovel.Investment in physical capital, both public and private, is critical for productivity growth, as it allows workers to produce more efficiently. Growth in capital per worker has accounted for a significant portion of productivity growth in many emerging regions.

3. Human Capital Human capital encompasses the accumulated knowledge, skills, and expertise of the workforce, acquired through education and experience.A more educated and skilled workforce is generally more productive, as individuals can perform tasks more efficiently, adapt to new technologies, and contribute to innovation. Investment in human capital, similar to physical capital, pays off in long-term productivity gains.

4. Technological Change and Innovation Technological change is a combination of invention (advances in knowledge) and innovation (putting those advances to use in new products or services). This factor is often considered the most significant driver of productivity growth, particularly Total Factor Productivity (TFP).New technologies and digital transformations, such as artificial intelligence (AI), have the potential to underpin major surges in productivity by enabling existing machines and inputs to produce more and at higher quality, and by creating entirely new products and services.For example, the development of the transistor allowed for the miniaturization of electronic devices, enabling workers to be more productive by using smaller, more efficient tools for communication and task completion.

5. Total Factor Productivity (TFP) / Multifactor Productivity (MFP) Total Factor Productivity (TFP), also known as Multifactor Productivity (MFP), measures the portion of output growth that cannot be explained by the growth in traditionally measured inputs like labor and capital. It essentially captures the efficiency with which businesses turn capital and labor into output, often reflecting innovation, technological advancements, and improved organizational methods. Slower gains in TFP have been identified as a major contributor to the deceleration in economic growth in recent decades. TFP growth can be estimated by subtracting the growth rates of labor and capital inputs from the growth rate of output.

6. Economic Dynamism and Competition Policies that encourage competition and reduce barriers to entry for new players can foster economic dynamism, which is crucial for productivity growth. Small, innovative firms often use research and development (R&D) resources more efficiently and can drive significant productivity gains. Reallocation of resources away from low-productivity firms and support for smaller businesses and start-ups, through measures like targeted tax credits and grants for early-stage innovation, can enhance overall economic productivity.

7. Industry Mix and Resource Reallocation The composition of a country's economy, or its "industry mix," significantly impacts overall productivity. Sectors with inherently higher productivity, such as Finance and Real Estate or Information, can contribute disproportionately to GDP relative to their employment share. Shifts in the industry mix towards more productive sectors, or improvements in productivity within existing sectors, can drive economic growth. For example, cities that have seen rising shares in high-productivity sectors, like Austin's growing Information sector, tend to experience stronger economic growth.

8. Policy and Institutional Frameworks Effective policies and robust institutional frameworks are essential for fostering productivity growth. These include:

Protection of Property Rights: Secure property rights incentivize investment and innovation, as individuals and businesses are confident that they will reap the rewards of their efforts.

Funding of Scientific Rationalization: Investment in scientific research and development is crucial for generating new knowledge and technologies that drive productivity.

Advanced Capital Markets: Efficient capital markets facilitate the allocation of financial resources to productive investments, supporting business expansion and technological adoption.

Efficient Transportation Systems: Modern infrastructure, including transportation and communication networks, reduces costs and improves the flow of goods, services, and information, thereby enhancing productivity.

In summary, sustained economic growth is intrinsically linked to productivity improvements, which are driven by a combination of increased physical and human capital, technological advancements, efficient resource allocation, and supportive policy environments

My view applies several behavioral economics principles to improve workplace efficiency, drawing from his extensive work in the field. His approach integrates psychological factors with traditional economic theories to offer a more comprehensive understanding of human behavior in organizational contexts .

Cognitive Biases and Decision-Making

My view emphasizes the importance of understanding cognitive biases, such as overconfidence and loss aversion, which significantly influence individual and collective economic decisions . By recognizing these biases, organizations can design strategies to mitigate their negative impact on efficiency. For instance, understanding how employees react to potential losses can inform incentive structures that encourage desired behaviors rather than deterring risk-taking that could lead to innovation . This aligns with the broader behavioral economics principle that individuals often make economically irrational decisions due to psychological factors, challenging the traditional economic assumption of purely rational actors .

Bounded Rationality and Heuristics

My work highlights concepts like bounded rationality and heuristics as fundamental influences on behavioral economics . Bounded rationality suggests that individuals make decisions within the limits of their cognitive abilities and available information, rather than possessing perfect rationality. Heuristics, or mental shortcuts, are often employed in decision-making, which can lead to systematic errors but also increase efficiency in certain situations.

By understanding these limitations, organizations can structure tasks and decision processes to support more effective outcomes, for example, by simplifying complex choices or providing clear guidelines .

Architecture of Choices and Framing

I also address the "architecture of choices" and "framing" as central to behavioral economics . The way options are presented (framing) can significantly alter choices, even if the underlying options are objectively the same. By carefully designing the environment in which decisions are made, organizations can nudge employees towards more efficient and productive behaviors. This could involve structuring workflows, communication, or even physical workspaces to encourage collaboration and focus.

Motivation and Employee Performance

A significant aspect of my work focuses on how staff behavior and organizational time management influence individual performance and efficiency. My view argues that satisfactory organizational behavior is essential for motivating employees and improving job satisfaction, which in turn leads to better job performance and innovation . My book "Improving Organizational Efficiency Methods" specifically aims to help working professionals deal with personnel challenges and suggests personnel-solvable methods and positive attitudes to address them across various working environments, including business offices and nuclear factories . This involves understanding the psychological foundations of labor behavior and applying methods to predict and solve labor argument challenges, ultimately aiming to raise labor productivity .

Technology's Role in Efficiency

My view investigates the impact of technology, including AI and robotics, on human talent, creativity, and organizational performance . My view explores how these tools can help improve economic development and assist businesses in reducing costs . For example, he discusses how educational robots can enhance student learning interest and how automated food sale machines can reduce staff numbers, thereby influencing organizational innovation and efficiency . My work also examines how robots can improve employee performance and their broader influence on organizational behavior . This aligns with the principle of leveraging technological advancements to optimize human-machine interaction for greater productivity].

Ethical Considerations and Welfare

My view emphasizes the importance of ethical considerations in labor practices to improve productivity and ensure employee welfare . My view argues that employers need to consider labor ethics to make fair decisions that benefit employees, which in turn has a close relationship with productivity and economic growth [. This includes addressing issues like online job trends, employee preferences for flexible work, and ensuring that economic growth translates into improved living standards for low-income households, which can indirectly assist employers in raising productivity . This perspective integrates moral behavior and social benefits into economic decision-making, reflecting a holistic approach to workplace efficiency .

Practical Applications for Businesses

My view provide practical applications for businesses, such as cost reduction strategies, by leveraging behavioral economic insights . My aims to bridge the gap between theoretical economics and practical applications influenced by human behavior, offering strategies for long-term economic benefits . This includes analyzing how psychological factors shape market trends and consumer choices, and suggesting policy recommendations that utilize behavioral insights to design more effective interventions.

In summary, my view applies behavioral economics principles such as understanding cognitive biases, bounded rationality, choice architecture, and the psychological foundations of motivation to improve workplace efficiency. My view also integrates the role of technology and ethical considerations to provide a comprehensive framework for enhancing organizational performance .

Technology plays a multifaceted and crucial role in enhancing productivity and economic development by driving innovation, transforming industries, creating new opportunities, and improving living standards . This impact has been observed historically and continues to accelerate with advancements like Artificial Intelligence (AI) .

Driving Productivity Growth

Technological innovation has consistently been the primary driver of productivity growth over the past 130 years . Productivity, defined as producing more output with the same or fewer resources, is fundamental to raising a country's standard of living .

General-Purpose Technologies (GPTs): Key technologies, such as electricity and computers, are classified as General-Purpose Technologies (GPTs) because they unleash "creative destruction" across the economy, leading to significant periods of above-trend growth .Vanguard research suggests that AI has the potential to be a worthy successor to electricity in this regard, potentially offsetting demographic pressures and exceeding economic expectations .

Accelerating Technical Change: The strong productivity growth observed in the late 1990s, for instance, was directly attributable to accelerating technical change, particularly in information technology]. Investment in IT rose significantly, from roughly 3% of GDP in the late 1980s to almost 6% by 1999 .

Automation and Efficiency: Technology, especially automation, increases efficiency by performing routine and repetitive tasks, leading to higher output per worker]. While this can cause short-term job displacement, it also creates opportunities for workers to reskill and upskill for higher-value tasks .

Augmentation of Human Capabilities: Technologies like personal computers and power tools augment human capabilities, raising productivity and employment]. Generative AI, in particular, is poised to significantly augment individual workers' capabilities, automating activities that currently absorb 60% to 70% of employees' time .

Transforming Industries and Creating New Opportunities

Technology fundamentally reshapes industries and opens up new avenues for economic activity and growth .

Digitalization and New Business Models: Digitalization transforms traditional processes into digital workflows, streamlining operations, enhancing customer experiences, and enabling new business models]. This has disrupted industries like media and retail while creating opportunities through digital platforms, cloud computing, and data analytics].

Changes in Production and Distribution: Advanced manufacturing technologies, such as 3D printing, reduce prototyping costs, accelerate production, and enable customization]. Technology also facilitates global e-commerce, allowing businesses to reach customers worldwide .

Data and Analytics: The increasing importance of data and analytics, driven by technologies like big data analytics, machine learning, and predictive modeling, provides valuable insights for businesses to optimize operations, target customers, and make informed decisions].

Growth of the Digital Economy: Technological advancements have fueled the rapid rise of the digital economy, where business predominantly occurs online, creating new opportunities for entrepreneurs, small businesses, and established companies to expand their reach].

Enhanced Communication and Collaboration: Improved communication platforms and tools enable better connectivity, efficient operations, and virtual teamwork, leading to increased productivity, accelerated decision-making, and cross-border partnerships]. This also facilitates remote work, creating new employment and entrepreneurial opportunities].

Challenges and Considerations

Despite its immense benefits, technology also presents challenges to traditional economic development models].

Job Displacement and Workforce Transformation: While technology creates new jobs, it also displaces others, particularly those involving routine tasks [. Generative AI's impact is expected to accelerate workforce transformation, with half of today's work activities potentially automated between 2030 and 2060 [3]. This necessitates investments in reskilling and upskilling programs.

Digital Divide and Inequality: Unequal access to digital infrastructure and technologies can worsen existing social and economic disparities, creating a "digital divide" that restricts opportunities for education, employment, and healthcare .

Adaptation of Governance: The rapid pace of technological change requires governments to adapt policies and regulations to keep pace, ensuring a balance between innovation, public interest, fair competition, and consumer protection .

Ethical Considerations: The rise of advanced AI brings ethical concerns regarding intellectual property, accuracy, bias, and the potential for misuse .

My approach to workplace efficiency, as evidenced in his writings, places a significant emphasis on the role of incentives, though he explores them within the broader context of behavioral economics and human psychology. My view investigates how various factors, including traditional incentives like bonuses and salaries, interact with psychological elements to influence employee productivity and organizational performance].

My work suggests that incentives are not merely financial but encompass a wider range of motivators that can shape employee behavior and attitudes. He examines how these incentives can be leveraged to address personnel challenges and improve cooperation across diverse working environments, from movie sets to nuclear factories .

One key aspect of my perspective is his exploration of how time pressure management, when combined with appropriate incentives, can either enhance or detract from efficiency. My questions whether factors such as bonuses, salaries, welfare improvements, and strong employer-employee relationships are more effective in high-pressure or low-pressure work settings . This indicates that Lok views incentives as dynamic tools whose effectiveness is contingent on the specific organizational context and the psychological state of employees.

Furthermore, my view delves into the application of behavioral economic and psychological methods to influence employee productivity and service performance . My view poses research questions that directly address the impact of human resource training, workplace environment, and HR management on individual efficiency and long-term performance]. This suggests that he considers training programs and a positive work environment as forms of incentives that can improve skill levels and foster positive emotions and working attitudes, ultimately leading to increased productivity].

My writings also touch upon the ethical considerations surrounding labor and productivity, implying that fair treatment, welfare, and benefits—which can be seen as non-monetary incentives—are crucial for maintaining employee satisfaction and indirectly boosting productivity . My view argues that economists and employers should consider ethics when making decisions related to labor, as there is a close relationship between labor ethics, productivity, and economic growth .

In essence, my approach to workplace efficiency integrates traditional incentive structures with a deep understanding of behavioral economics and psychology. He views incentives as multifaceted, encompassing financial rewards, positive working conditions, effective training, and ethical treatment, all of which contribute to shaping employee behavior and ultimately, organizational efficiency .

Technology significantly enhances workplace efficiency and employee output by streamlining processes, improving communication, fostering skill development, and providing data-driven insights. The integration of various technological tools, from AI to robust IT infrastructure, creates a more productive, engaged, and adaptable workforce.

Streamlining Processes and Automation

Technology automates repetitive and time-consuming tasks, freeing employees to focus on more complex and strategic work. Digital tools and systems can achieve processes that were once manual and inefficient in a quick and efficient manner . For instance, project management platforms like Asana, Trello, and Wrike allow teams to organize tasks, track progress, and collaborate seamlessly, ensuring projects stay on schedule and resources are allocated efficiently . Integrated workplace management systems (IWMS) optimize resources, reduce costs, and support effective decision-making by providing a single source of truth for all workplace data .

Generative AI (GenAI) plays a crucial role in this streamlining. Studies have shown that GenAI can boost a highly skilled worker's performance by nearly 40% when used within its capabilities . For example, customer support agents using AI could handle 13.8% more inquiries per hour, and business professionals could write 59% more documents per hour . Programmers using AI tools like GitHub Copilot saw a 126% increase in projects coded per week]. This automation of cognitive functions, such as summarizing, coding, and reasoning, allows AI to adapt, plan, and guide decisions, leading to unprecedented economic growth and societal change .

Enhancing Communication and Collaboration

Modern workplace technology facilitates seamless communication and teamwork, which is vital for both in-office and remote environments. Platforms such as Microsoft Teams, Zoom, and Google Workspace offer features like instant messaging, video conferencing, file sharing, and collaborative document editing, significantly enhancing collaboration and reducing response times]. Reliable IT services ensure these critical systems are always operational, minimizing disruptions and maintaining the flow of critical discussions]. This improved communication not only boosts productivity but also contributes to a more connected and engaged workforce].

Fostering Continuous Learning and Development

Technology supports continuous learning and skill development, which is essential in an evolving workplace. Online training platforms and e-learning modules provide employees with accessible and personalized learning paths, allowing them to develop new skills at their own pace [. Advanced analytics and AI-driven recommendations can tailor training to individual needs, ensuring relevance and impact]. This leads to a more skilled, adaptable, and engaged workforce, as employees can quickly acquire proficiency in new areas and stay updated with technological advancements]. For instance, new customer support agents supported by AI reached expert-level performance four times faster than those without AI support .

Data-Driven Insights and Decision Making

Technology provides valuable data and analytics that inform business decisions and improve departmental functions. Business programs and management software decrease the likelihood of human error while offering real-time data and analytics through dashboards and reporting . This allows leaders to make informed, data-driven decisions that drive performance and success]. For example, integrated systems capture valuable insights, enabling leadership to make informed decisions that benefit both employees and the company]. Benchmarking tools, though currently underutilized for ethical considerations, can quantitatively assess and improve the performance of AI models, enhancing transparency and accountability].

Improving Employee Experience and Well-being

Beyond direct productivity gains, technology positively impacts employee experience and well-being. Reliable IT support minimizes technical issues, reducing frustration and stress, which are common causes of decreased output . Employees who are satisfied with their work experience are approximately two times more productive]. Technology can reduce time spent on "work about work" (e.g., toggling between apps, searching for information), freeing up time for more meaningful tasks . A secure technological environment, backed by robust cybersecurity measures, builds trust and confidence among employees, knowing their data and systems are protected . This holistic approach to employee experience, enabled by technology, leads to higher job satisfaction and lower turnover rates .

Narrowing Skill Gaps

Generative AI has a notable effect on narrowing the skill gap between high and low-performing employees. Studies show that the lowest-performing employees often experience the largest productivity gains when using AI tools . For instance, the bottom 20% of customer support agents improved their task throughput by 35% with AI, significantly more than the top 20% . This is hypothesized to be because AI reduces the working-memory load, allowing less-skilled users to focus on creativity and problem-solving, tasks previously hindered by the cognitive burden of data handling .

Conclusion

In summary, technology, particularly advanced AI and robust IT infrastructure, is a transformative force in the modern workplace. It enhances efficiency through automation, improves communication and collaboration, accelerates learning, provides critical data for decision-making, boosts employee morale and well-being, and even helps to level the playing field among employees with varying skill levels. Organizations that strategically invest in and integrate these technologies are better positioned to achieve higher productivity, foster innovation, and maintain a competitive edge .

My work, rooted in behavioral economics, offers strategies that can be applied to boost team performance by understanding and leveraging psychological factors that influence decision-making and behavior within an organizational context. While the provided content doesn't explicitly detail specific "strategies" for team performance, it outlines his broader contributions and themes, from which practical applications can be inferred.

Understanding Behavioral Economics in Team Performance

My writings emphasize that economics is not solely about resource allocation but also about the decision-making processes driven by human actions, challenging the traditional economic assumption of purely rational actors . This perspective is crucial for team performance, as team members are not always perfectly rational and are influenced by cognitive biases, emotions, and social dynamics].

Inferred Strategies for Boosting Team Performance

Based on my focus on behavioral economics, the following strategies can be inferred to boost team performance:

Addressing Cognitive Biases in Decision-Making: My explores how biases like overconfidence or loss aversion affect individual and collective economic decisions . In a team setting, these biases can lead to suboptimal choices. For instance, overconfidence bias might cause a team to underestimate risks or overestimate their abilities, while loss aversion could make team members hesitant to take necessary risks for innovation .

Strategy: Implement structured decision-making processes that encourage critical evaluation of assumptions and diverse perspectives to counteract biases. For example, using pre-mortem exercises where teams imagine a project failure and work backward to identify potential causes can mitigate overconfidence .

Example: A team planning a new product launch might be overly optimistic about its success. By applying Lok's insights on cognitive biases, a manager could facilitate a discussion where team members are asked to identify all possible reasons the launch might fail, forcing them to consider potential pitfalls and develop contingency plans .

Leveraging Framing and Heuristics for Motivation: Lok highlights principles like framing and heuristics as central to behavioral economics . How information is presented (framed) can significantly impact how team members perceive tasks, goals, and rewards, influencing their motivation and effort .

Strategy: Frame team goals and feedback in a way that emphasizes potential gains and positive outcomes rather than solely focusing on avoiding losses. For example, instead of saying, "If we don't meet this deadline, we'll lose clients," frame it as, "Meeting this deadline will secure client loyalty and open new opportunities" .

Example: When introducing a challenging project, a leader could frame it as an opportunity for skill development and recognition, rather than just a difficult task that needs to be completed. This positive framing, drawing from Lok's emphasis on psychological factors, can enhance team engagement and performance].

Understanding and Mitigating Herd Mentality: My view discusses herd mentality as an influence on behavioral economics . In teams, this can manifest as groupthink, where individuals conform to the majority opinion, suppressing dissenting views and potentially leading to poor decisions].

Strategy: Foster an environment that encourages psychological safety and independent thought. Implement mechanisms for anonymous feedback or structured brainstorming sessions where initial ideas are generated individually before group discussion to prevent early consensus .

Example: During a team meeting to brainstorm solutions, a manager could ask each team member to write down their ideas individually before sharing them aloud. This approach, informed by Lok's insights into herd mentality, can prevent dominant personalities or early ideas from unduly influencing the group .

Designing Choice Architecture for Performance: While not explicitly stated as "choice architecture," Lok's work on how psychological factors influence economic decision-making implies the importance of structuring choices to guide behavior]. This can be applied to team processes and incentives.

Strategy: Design team workflows, reward systems, and communication channels in a way that nudges team members towards desired behaviors and higher performance. For example, making the default option for a task the most efficient one, or clearly outlining the benefits of collaboration .

Example: To encourage knowledge sharing, a company could implement a system where contributing to a shared knowledge base is a default part of project completion, rather than an optional extra step. This subtle design, aligning with my focus on influencing behavior, can significantly increase participation .

Integrating Behavioral Insights with Technology for Efficiency: my work explores how businesses can leverage behavioral economic insights and AI technology to achieve long-term cost efficiency and improve organizational performance . This can extend to team performance by using technology to support behavioral nudges.

Strategy: Utilize digital tools and platforms that incorporate behavioral design principles to facilitate collaboration, track progress, and provide timely, constructive feedback. AI-powered analytics can identify patterns in team behavior and suggest interventions].

Example: A project management tool could be designed to provide automated, positive reinforcement messages when team members complete tasks ahead of schedule, or to gently remind them of upcoming deadlines, leveraging behavioral insights to encourage productivity .

By applying these principles derived from my contributions to behavioral economics, organizations can create environments and implement strategies that account for human psychological tendencies, ultimately leading to improved team performance and organizational efficiency].

Specific technologies that can enhance productivity in the workplace include workflow automation platforms, communication and collaboration tools, project management software, time and activity tracking applications, and enterprise search systems. These technologies address various aspects of workplace efficiency, from streamlining repetitive tasks to improving information retrieval and team coordination.

One significant category of technology for enhancing productivity is workflow automation platforms. Tools like Cflow are designed to simplify project execution by automating tasks, managing approvals, and providing real-time progress monitoring through features like Kanban boards, list views, and customizable workflows . This automation reduces manual effort, minimizes errors, and ensures that tasks are completed efficiently]. Zapier is another example, automating repetitive marketing tasks and integrating with various applications to streamline workflows . By automating routine processes, teams can focus on higher-value activities, leading to increased overall productivity].

Communication and collaboration tools are crucial for fostering a productive work environment, especially for remote or distributed teams]. Platforms such as Microsoft Teams and Slack centralize communication, allowing for instant messaging, file sharing, and organized discussions through dedicated channels . These tools eliminate the need for lengthy email threads and facilitate real-time updates, ensuring everyone stays informed regardless of their location or time zone . Video conferencing tools like Zoom and Google Meet further enhance collaboration by enabling face-to-face interactions, which are vital for understanding nuances and fostering team connection . Proofhub and Wimi also offer features like centralized dashboards, file sharing, and secure communication to improve team coordination].

Project management software plays a pivotal role in organizing tasks, setting timelines, and assigning responsibilities, thereby improving workflow efficiency . Tools like Asana, Monday.com, and Trello act as central hubs for projects, allowing teams to break down large initiatives into smaller, manageable steps]. These platforms enable tracking of progress, identification of bottlenecks, and adjustment of priorities, ensuring projects stay on track]. Workast and Slack can also be used as project management tools to assign tasks and track progress]. Smartsheet and Wrike offer customizable interfaces, Gantt charts, and real-time reporting to manage complex projects and coordinate remote teams effectively].

Time and activity tracking applications provide valuable insights into how time is spent, helping to identify inefficiencies and improve accountability . Tools like Clockify and Toggl allow employees to start and stop timers for specific tasks, providing clear data on time allocation]. This data can be used to optimize schedules, set realistic deadlines, and ensure focus on high-priority activities]. Employee monitoring software, such as Time Champ, can offer a comprehensive approach by tracking application usage and providing productivity analysis, helping managers identify distractions and adjust plans as needed].

Finally, enterprise search systems are essential for combating information overload and improving data retrieval in large organizations]. These systems index and organize data across various platforms, such as databases, emails, and document management systems, providing quick access to pertinent information through a single, unified interface . Advanced features like predictive search and personalized results, often powered by artificial intelligence, further accelerate information access, leading to faster decision-making and enhanced productivity]. By reducing the time spent searching for information, employees can reallocate their efforts to core tasks, improving overall operational efficiency].

Other technologies that contribute to workplace productivity include:

Cloud storage services like Dropbox, which allow for easy storage and sharing of company documents, ensuring employees have access to updated information .

SEO tools such as Ahrefs, SEMrush, Moz Keyword Explorer, and Google Keyword Planner, which help in keyword research, competitor analysis, and link building, making marketing efforts more efficient .

Content writing assistance tools like Jasper.ai and plagiarism checkers such as Check-Plagiarism, which streamline content creation and ensure originality].

Social media planning tools like SocialPilot, Hootsuite, and Buffer, which automate social media posting and help manage online presence efficiently .

Website monitoring tools such as Sematext, Pingdom, WooRank, and Majestic SEO, which identify technical SEO errors and help maintain website health].

Specialized SEO productivity tools like Majestic SEO's Clique Hunter and Link Thief, which help identify link opportunities and streamline backlink analysis].

Email management tools like Gmail's Canned Responses and Yet Another Mail Merge, which automate repetitive email tasks and improve communication efficiency].

Email tracking tools such as Yesware, which provide insights into email engagement, allowing for timely follow-ups [6].

Website analysis tools like BrowSEO and Seorch.eu, which help in on-site analysis by displaying web pages without styling, aiding in identifying elements and understanding how bots view the page].

By strategically implementing these diverse technologies, organizations can significantly enhance workplace productivity, streamline operations, and foster a more efficient and collaborative environment].

My view integrates behavioral economics into my leadership style by applying its principles to understand and influence decision-making within teams, aiming to improve outcomes through practical strategies and an awareness of human psychological factors. While the provided content does not directly detail John Lok's "leadership style," it extensively outlines his contributions to behavioral economics, which can be inferred to inform his approach to managing and guiding teams. My work emphasizes bridging the gap between traditional economic theory and the realities of human behavior, suggesting a leadership approach that is empathetic, strategic, and focused on practical application .

Here's a breakdown of how John Lok's insights from behavioral economics would likely translate into his leadership style for improving team outcomes:

Understanding Human Decision-Making and Biases

My work highlights that individuals are not always rational actors, and their decisions are often influenced by cognitive biases, bounded rationality, and heuristics]. A leader informed by these principles would:

Acknowledge and mitigate biases: Recognize that team members may be subject to biases like loss aversion, overconfidence, or the sunk-cost fallacy . For example, when a project is failing, a leader aware of the sunk-cost fallacy might encourage a re-evaluation rather than continuing to invest resources simply because of past expenditure .

Promote critical thinking: Encourage team members to question assumptions and consider alternative perspectives to counteract common cognitive shortcuts [4].

Design choices carefully: Understand that the way information is presented (framing) can significantly impact decisions . A leader might frame choices to encourage desired outcomes, such as presenting options in terms of gains rather than losses to reduce risk aversion in appropriate situations .

Leveraging Practical Applications and Technology

My focus on practical business applications, cost reduction strategies, and the impact of AI and technology on organizational performance suggests a leadership style that is forward-thinking and efficiency-driven []. Such a leader would:

Utilize behavioral insights for efficiency: Apply principles of behavioral economics to optimize team processes, resource allocation, and project management . For instance, understanding social norms could be used to foster a culture of accountability and high performance within the team].

Embrace technology for improvement: Investigate how AI and other technologies can enhance team talent, creativity, and overall performance, potentially using these tools to streamline tasks and reduce operational costs . This could involve implementing AI-powered tools for data analysis to inform better decision-making or using collaboration platforms to improve communication .

Focus on continuous learning: Given Lok's emphasis on new business knowledge and adapting to market changes, a leader would likely foster a culture of continuous learning and skill development within the team].

Bridging Theory and Practice

My aims to bridge the gap between traditional economic theory and behavioral economic theory, making complex concepts accessible through "daily fun human behavior" and "daily life matters"]. This indicates a leadership style that is:

Accessible and engaging: Explaining complex goals or strategies in relatable terms, drawing parallels to everyday experiences to ensure team understanding and buy-in [.

Empathetic and human-centric: Recognizing that economic outcomes are driven by human actions and decision-making processes, rather than solely by abstract resource allocation . This would involve understanding team members' motivations, challenges, and psychological states.

Policy-oriented (within the team context): Just as behavioral economics informs public policy, a leader could apply similar principles to internal team policies and incentive structures to encourage desired behaviors and outcomes . For example, designing reward systems that account for loss aversion or present bias to maximize their effectiveness .

Fostering a Culture of Awareness and Adaptability

My work also touches upon broader societal issues and the impact of environmental factors]. While not directly about leadership, this suggests an awareness of external influences and a need for adaptability. A leader embodying these principles would:

Promote environmental scanning: Encourage the team to be aware of external market changes, technological advancements, and societal shifts that could impact their work .

Cultivate adaptability: Lead the team in developing flexible strategies to respond to unforeseen challenges and opportunities, drawing on insights about how human behavior changes in complex or unpredictable environments .

In essence, my integration of behavioral economics into his leadership style would likely manifest as a data-informed, psychologically astute, and practically oriented approach that seeks to optimize team performance by understanding and strategically influencing the human element of decision-making .

CHAPTER EIGHT

The Intersection of Behavioral Economics and Productivity

When applied to productivity, these insights suggest that economic output is not merely a function of capital and labor, but is deeply rooted in the psychological architecture of the workforce. By "nudging" individuals toward better decision-making processes, organizations and governments can foster environments where productivity is enhanced without necessarily increasing the raw input of resources.

The relationship between behavioral economics and productivity is often articulated through the concept of "choice architecture." As my view explores in my work, applying behavioral principles can lead to significant social and economic benefits by aligning individual incentives with broader productivity goals.

Productivity, in an economic sense, is often measured as the ratio of output to input, represented by the formula:$P=OI$where P is productivity, O is total output, and I is total input.

Behavioral economics posits that by reducing "friction" in the workplace—such as simplifying complex tasks or providing timely feedback—the effective input required to achieve a specific output is reduced, thereby increasing

Cognitive Biases and Economic Efficiency

One of the most significant contributions of behavioral economics to productivity is the identification of the "present bias," where individuals prioritize immediate gratification over long-term gains.In a corporate or national economy, this bias often leads to procrastination and suboptimal resource allocation. To counter this, behavioral economists suggest implementing "commitment devices," which are mechanisms that allow individuals to voluntarily restrict their future choices to ensure they stay on task.

Furthermore, the "framing effect" plays a crucial role; how a task or an economic goal is presented to a worker can drastically alter their motivation and subsequent output. When goals are framed as gains rather than losses, workers tend to exhibit higher levels of engagement and efficiency.

Structural Improvements and Social Benefit

Beyond the individual level, behavioral economics can be scaled to improve national productivity. By utilizing "default options"—such as automatic enrollment in retirement savings plans or streamlined tax filing processes—governments can reduce the cognitive load on citizens, allowing them to focus their mental energy on productive economic activities.

This approach not only improves individual welfare but also contributes to a more robust and efficient macro-economy. As noted in contemporary research, the integration of these psychological insights into policy-making represents a shift toward a more human-centric economic model, where the goal is to maximize societal well-being by acknowledging the inherent limitations and strengths of human cognition.

Would you be interested in learning more about how specific "nudge" strategies are currently being implemented in government policy to increase national labor productivity?

My views on growth also incorporated the role of money and capital accumulation. My view recognized that the invention of money allowed for the accumulation of wealth beyond what could be consumed, which in turn incentivized further production and trade.

By facilitating exchange, money enabled a more complex division of labor, which is a precursor to modern theories of productivity growth. My support for foreign trade and colonial expansion was rooted in the belief that these activities were essential for "improving" the state's economic standing and ensuring the industriousness of its population.

In modern economic terms, my emphasis on the "improvement" of land and the industrious use of labor can be viewed as an early recognition of the importance of human capital and technological application in increasing output per unit of input.While my view lacked the mathematical models used today—such as the Solow-Swan growth model, which expresses output Y as a function of capital K, labor L, and technology A ($Y=A\cdot f(K,L)$)—my qualitative arguments regarding the necessity of labor-driven value creation remain a cornerstone of classical economic thought.

Behavioral Economics and the Productivity-Growth Nexus

The relationship between productivity and economic growth is a cornerstone of modern macroeconomic theory, often analyzed through the lens of behavioral economics to understand how human decision-making influences aggregate output. My work primarily focuses on specific niche applications of behavioral insights rather than establishing a new macroeconomic paradigm. In the broader context of economic literature, productivity is defined as the efficiency of production, typically expressed as the ratio of output to inputs, such as labor or capital. Economic growth, conversely, is the increase in the inflation-adjusted market value of the goods and services produced by an economy over time.

The synthesis of behavioral economics and productivity suggests that cognitive biases—such as hyperbolic discounting or loss aversion—can significantly impede the realization of potential economic growth.

Standard growth models, such as the Solow-Swan model, utilize the production function:$Y=A\cdot f(K,L)$where Y is output, A is total factor productivity, K is capital, and L is labor. Behavioral economists argue that A is not merely a technological constant but is heavily influenced by the "behavioral capital" of the workforce—the psychological state, motivation, and decision-making quality of human agents.

My writings often emphasize the micro-foundations of these behaviors, suggesting that individual productivity gains are frequently lost due to suboptimal decision-making environments, which aggregate into slower national economic growth.

Behavioral Constraints on Macroeconomic Performance

In traditional neoclassical economics, agents are assumed to be rational utility maximizers. However, behavioral economics challenges this by demonstrating that individuals often deviate from rationality in ways that affect firm-level productivity. When firms fail to account for these behavioral patterns, they experience "productivity leakage," where the marginal product of labor does not reach its theoretical maximum.

My approach, consistent with broader behavioral literature, suggests that economic growth is not just a function of capital accumulation but of "behavioral efficiency"—the ability of an economy to minimize the friction caused by human cognitive limitations.By improving the choice architecture within organizations, productivity can be enhanced, thereby acting as a catalyst for sustainable long-term economic expansion.

Synthesis of Productivity and Growth

The consensus among economic historians and behavioral theorists is that productivity growth is the primary driver of rising living standards. While my specific contributions through Notion Press provide practical applications for individuals and managers, they align with the established view that psychological factors are critical variables in the production function. The interaction between behavioral nudges and institutional design remains a vital area of study for those seeking to bridge the gap between micro-level productivity and macro-level economic prosperity.

Would you like to learn more about how behavioral "nudges" are currently being implemented by governments to improve national productivity metrics, or perhaps explore the specific psychological biases that most frequently hinder workplace efficiency?

However, I feel that the study of productivity through a behavioral lens generally focuses on how "nudges"—small changes in the choice architecture—can improve efficiency without restricting freedom of choice.

Classical models often fail to account for the "Homer Simpson" aspect of human nature, where individuals are prone to procrastination, present bias, and limited willpower.By understanding these psychological barriers, organizations can design environments that enhance productivity. For instance, research suggests that setting default options (such as automatic enrollment in retirement plans or pre-scheduled focus blocks) significantly increases output and goal attainment.

Furthermore, the application of behavioral insights to incentive structures demonstrates that non-monetary rewards, such as social recognition or autonomy, often yield higher productivity gains than traditional financial bonuses alone, as they align better with human motivational psychology.

Behavioral Mechanisms Influencing Output

Productivity is not merely a function of technical skill but is deeply mediated by the psychological processes described in behavioral economics. When individuals face complex tasks, they often rely on mental shortcuts that can lead to suboptimal performance. Behavioral economists argue that by identifying these "decision traps," managers can implement strategies to mitigate them. For example, the "planning fallacy"—the tendency to underestimate the time required to complete a project—is a well-documented bias that directly impacts organizational productivity.

By implementing "pre-mortems" or breaking large tasks into smaller, time-bound segments, organizations can counteract this bias and improve project delivery timelines.

Would you be interested in learning more about how specific cognitive biases, such as the "sunk cost fallacy," affect long-term strategic productivity in corporate environments?

The study of behavioral economics in the context of organizational productivity involves understanding how cognitive biases, heuristics, and social preferences influence employee performance and decision-making. While John Lok's work, Technology and Organizational Change, focuses primarily on the structural and communicative impacts of technology, the broader field of behavioral economics—as established by seminal texts—provides the necessary framework to understand how these technological shifts interact with human psychology to drive or hinder productivity.

Key concepts in behavioral economics often applied to productivity include "loss aversion," "hyperbolic discounting," and the "nudge" theory. In the context of technological integration, these concepts explain why employees may resist new software or, conversely, why automation can lead to increased output. Loss aversion, a concept popularized by Daniel Kahneman, suggests that the pain of losing a current workflow is psychologically twice as powerful as the joy of gaining a more efficient one. When organizations introduce new technology, productivity often dips initially because employees perceive the loss of their established "status quo" routines more acutely than the future benefits of the new system.

Furthermore, Richard Thaler's concept of the "nudge" is frequently utilized in modern management to design digital environments that steer employees toward productive behaviors without restricting their freedom of choice. For instance, default settings in project management software can be configured to prioritize high-impact tasks, effectively using the "status quo bias" to improve time management.Dan Ariely's research into the "irrational" nature of motivation highlights that productivity is not merely a function of financial incentives but is deeply tied to the "meaning" of work and the social recognition provided by digital collaboration tools.

My analysis complements these behavioral theories by noting that technology acts as a catalyst for organizational change, but its success depends on how well it aligns with human cognitive limitations.When technology streamlines processes, it reduces the "cognitive load" on employees, allowing them to allocate their limited mental bandwidth toward strategic decision-making rather than repetitive tasks.

This aligns with the behavioral economic principle of "bounded rationality," which posits that individuals make decisions based on limited information and cognitive capacity.By automating routine data entry, organizations effectively "nudge" employees toward higher-value cognitive tasks, thereby increasing overall firm productivity.

Additionally, the use of collaborative tools facilitates social proof—a behavioral phenomenon where individuals look to the actions of others to determine their own behavior—which can accelerate the adoption of productive new workflows across an organization.

Would you like to learn more about how "nudge" theory is specifically applied in remote work environments to maintain employee engagement and productivity?

The Application of Behavioral Economics to Workplace Productivity

My scholarly work, particularly in Technology and Organizational Change, posits that technology acts as a fundamental catalyst for transformation rather than a mere instrument of efficiency.By integrating principles of behavioral economics, my view examines how organizational structures influence human decision-making, often highlighting the friction between the theoretical pursuit of maximum efficiency and the practical realities of human behavior.

In the context of workplace productivity, this involves understanding that employees are not always the "rational actors" assumed in classical economic models, but are instead subject to cognitive biases, social influences, and environmental cues that dictate their output and engagement.

To enhance productivity, my approach suggests that organizations must move beyond simple incentive structures—such as performance-based bonuses—and instead focus on "choice architecture." This concept, popularized by Thaler and Sunstein, suggests that the environment in which decisions are made can be subtly altered to nudge employees toward more productive behaviors without restricting their freedom of choice.

My view argues that technology facilitates this by providing real-time feedback loops, which help mitigate the "myopia" often observed in decision-makers who prioritize short-term gains over long-term organizational health. By leveraging data analytics, managers can identify the specific behavioral bottlenecks that impede productivity, such as cognitive overload or social loafing, and redesign workflows to align with human psychological tendencies rather than fighting against them.

Furthermore, the application of behavioral economics in my framework addresses the tension between efficiency and equality. As noted in economic discourse, while the goal of an organization is to maximize the "pie" of productivity, the distribution of that value impacts employee morale and long-term retention.

My view suggests that when technology is implemented to enhance productivity, it must be done with an understanding of the social behavioral changes it triggers. If technology is perceived as a tool for surveillance rather than empowerment, it can trigger "reactance," a psychological phenomenon where individuals resist perceived threats to their autonomy, ultimately decreasing productivity. Therefore, enhancing workplace productivity requires a balanced approach where technological integration is paired with transparent communication and a design that respects the social fabric of the organization.

By applying these behavioral insights, organizations can transition from a rigid, top-down management style to a more adaptive, evidence-based model. This shift acknowledges that productivity is an emergent property of the interaction between human psychology and organizational technology. As my view emphasizes, the most productive organizations are those that treat technology as a partner in behavioral design, creating environments where employees are naturally inclined to perform at their best.

Would you like to learn more about how "choice architecture" can be specifically implemented in remote work environments to boost team collaboration and individual output?

These strategies primarily involve the implementation of "choice architecture," where the environment in which employees operate is designed to nudge them toward desired outcomes. One core strategy is the use of social norms and peer comparison. By sharing data on the performance of the "majority" or high-performing cohorts, managers create a self-regulating standard. This leverages the human tendency to look toward peers to determine appropriate behavior, effectively turning performance into a social benchmark rather than just a top-down mandate.

Furthermore, behavioral economics emphasizes the structure and timing of incentives over their absolute value. A key strategy involves the use of "commitment devices," which allow employees to pre-commit to future performance goals, thereby reducing the impact of present bias—the tendency for individuals to prioritize immediate gratification over long-term objectives. Additionally, research into "loss-framed" incentives suggests that performance can be significantly improved by providing bonuses upfront, with the condition that they are forfeited if specific standards are not met.This strategy exploits the psychological principle of loss aversion, where the pain of losing a reward is perceived as more significant than the joy of gaining an equivalent one, thus driving higher levels of sustained effort.

In the context of modern service delivery, these behavioral interventions are increasingly vital as technology continues to automate routine tasks, leaving humans to handle complex, high-value interactions. By integrating these psychological insights, organizations can foster a culture of continuous improvement that aligns individual employee motivations with broader business objectives.

The Nexus of Behavioral Economics and Productivity

The relationship between behavioral economics and economic productivity is rooted in the understanding that human decision-making is rarely perfectly rational, as traditional neoclassical models once assumed. Instead, individuals are subject to cognitive biases, heuristics, and social influences that significantly impact their labor output, consumption patterns, and long-term economic contributions.

Productivity, defined as the efficiency of production—often expressed as the ratio of output to input—is fundamentally tied to how individuals perceive incentives, manage time, and interact within organizational structures.When behavioral insights are applied to the economy, they reveal that productivity is not merely a function of capital and technology, but a result of psychological states, environmental "nudges," and the alignment of personal motivations with economic goals.

However, in my exploration of behavioral economics, posits that social benefit and economic efficiency are inextricably linked through the psychological mechanisms that govern human behavior.

By understanding these mechanisms, policymakers and business leaders can design environments that minimize cognitive friction, thereby enhancing productivity.For instance, the concept of "choice architecture" suggests that the way options are presented to workers or consumers can drastically alter their productivity levels and economic outcomes.When individuals are nudged toward more efficient behaviors, the aggregate effect on the economy is a measurable increase in total factor productivity, as resources are allocated more effectively and human potential is better utilized.

Theoretical Frameworks of Productivity and Behavior

The economic relationship between behavior and productivity can be modeled by considering the utility function of a worker, where effort E is influenced by both monetary incentives M and psychological factors P. We can represent the output Y as a function of these variables:

$Y=f(K,L(E(M,P)))$

Where K represents capital and L represents labor. Behavioral economics emphasizes that P (psychological factors) often acts as a multiplier or a constraint on L. If P is negative due to stress or poor organizational design, L decreases regardless of the level of M.

Conversely, when behavioral interventions align with intrinsic motivations, P enhances the efficiency of L, leading to higher output per unit of input. This cause-and-effect relationship suggests that economic growth is as much a psychological phenomenon as it is a financial one.

Practical Applications and Social Benefit

Applying behavioral economics to the economy allows for the creation of "social benefit" by ensuring that productivity gains do not come at the cost of human well-being. My view argues that by addressing the behavioral barriers to productivity—such as procrastination, present bias, and loss aversion—organizations can foster a more sustainable economic environment.This approach shifts the focus from purely extrinsic rewards to a more holistic view of the worker, where the environment is optimized to support cognitive health and sustained focus.

Ultimately, the integration of behavioral science into economic policy provides a robust framework for understanding why certain economies thrive while others stagnate, highlighting that the human element is the most critical variable in the productivity equation.

Would you be interested in learning more about how "choice architecture" is specifically implemented in modern corporate environments to boost employee productivity?

The Behavioral Economics Perspective on Productivity

The study of productivity through the lens of behavioral economics represents a significant departure from classical economic models, which traditionally assumed that workers were purely rational agents motivated solely by financial incentives. In contemporary academic discourse, behavioral economists argue that human decision-making is systematically influenced by cognitive biases, social norms, and the architecture of the environment in which work occurs.

My work frequently intersects with these themes, emphasizes that the "science of scaling" is essential to understanding why interventions that appear successful in small, controlled settings—such as a pilot program for worker incentives—often fail to produce the same results when implemented across an entire organization.

The impact of behavioral economics on productivity is characterized by the identification of "voltage drops," a term used to describe the loss of efficacy as a program expands from a small sample to a large-scale operation.

Behavioral economists suggest that productivity is not merely a function of wages but is deeply tied to psychological factors such as loss aversion, the framing of goals, and the social dynamics of the workplace.When organizations attempt to boost productivity, they often rely on "false positives"—initial data that suggests a policy will work universally, failing to account for the heterogeneity of the workforce.By applying rigorous field experiments, researchers have demonstrated that small changes in the "choice architecture" of a workplace can lead to substantial gains in output without necessarily increasing costs.

Furthermore, the integration of behavioral insights into management practices allows for a more nuanced understanding of worker motivation. As noted in foundational texts on the subject, the "nudge" theory suggests that by subtly altering the environment, employers can guide employees toward more productive behaviors without restricting their freedom of choice. This approach acknowledges that human attention is a scarce resource and that productivity is often hampered by decision fatigue and cognitive overload.

Consequently, the modern application of behavioral economics focuses on designing systems that are resilient to the complexities of human nature, ensuring that productivity gains are sustainable rather than transient.

Behavioral Economics and Productivity: The Framework of my opinion

My research into organizational performance posits that productivity is not a static attribute of the workforce but a dynamic variable shaped by the strategic application of behavioral economic principles.By integrating psychological insights into human resource management, my view argues that organizations can move beyond traditional, rigid oversight models toward a more nuanced approach that aligns operational requirements with the inherent psychological needs of employees. This shift is essential for reducing long-term business costs while simultaneously enhancing client satisfaction and overall organizational efficiency.

Core Principles Influencing Productivity

My framework emphasizes that the "productive efficiency" of an individual is fundamentally influenced by the quality of human resource interventions.Central to my theory is the concept of "behavioral performance," which suggests that management can predict and influence staff output by understanding the mechanisms of employee choice and motivation.

Unlike classical economic models that assume purely rational actors, my approach acknowledges that human behavior is subject to cognitive biases and psychological drivers that, when properly managed, can lead to more "comfortable" and effective facility management.

Furthermore, my view explores the intersection of human behavior, technology, and automation. A critical question in his research is whether technology serves as a neutral production resource or if it fundamentally alters the behavioral landscape of an organization.

My view suggests that while technology can reduce costs, its implementation must be balanced against its potential negative influences on organizational culture.The productivity of an organization is thus a function of the synergy between human psychological needs and the technological tools provided to them.

The Role of Psychological Interventions

In the context of behavioral economics, my view suggests that productivity can be modeled as a variable P influenced by the quality of intervention I and the psychological alignment A of the workforce.This can be represented conceptually as:

$P=f(I,A)$

Where I represents the strategic human resource interventions and A represents the degree to which the work environment satisfies the psychological needs of the staff. By optimizing I to maximize A, management can achieve higher levels of efficiency without the need for excessive traditional oversight.

My work suggests that when employees feel their psychological needs are met, their "behavioral performance" naturally trends toward higher productivity, thereby reducing the long-term costs associated with turnover, absenteeism, and low engagement.

Would you like to learn more about how specific behavioral economic interventions, such as "nudging" or incentive restructuring, can be applied to improve employee retention in high-stress work environments?

Behavioral Economics and Workplace Productivity: The Perspective of my opinion

In my research, emphasizes that productivity is not solely a function of rational incentive structures or economic optimization, but is deeply embedded in the social and cognitive constraints of human actors within organizational hierarchies.

My view argues that traditional economic models often fail to account for the "bounded rationality" of employees, who operate under cognitive limitations and social pressures that significantly influence their output and decision-making processes.

For my view, behavioral economics in the workplace is defined by the intersection of psychological heuristics and institutional design. My view posits that productivity is often hampered by "organizational scripts"—habitual patterns of behavior that employees follow to minimize cognitive load.

By applying behavioral insights, such as "nudging" or restructuring choice architectures, organizations can mitigate the negative impacts of these scripts. My work suggests that when managers understand the cognitive biases—such as loss aversion or status quo bias—that affect their teams, they can design environments that align individual effort with organizational goals more effectively than traditional top-down management strategies.

The Role of Social Identity and Cognitive Constraints

My definition of productivity is intrinsically linked to the concept of social identity. My view suggests that employees do not act as isolated utility-maximizers, as classical economics might suggest, but as members of social groups whose productivity is influenced by group norms and the perceived legitimacy of organizational practices.

In my analysis, behavioral economics provides the tools to measure how these social identities influence performance. For instance, when an organization's stated values conflict with its actual behavioral incentives, employees experience cognitive dissonance, which leads to a measurable decline in productivity.

Practical Applications in Management

In practice, my view advocates for a shift from "command-and-control" productivity metrics to "behavioral-informed" management. This involves:

Choice Architecture: Designing the physical and digital workspace to make the most productive behaviors the "default" options.

Mitigating Bias: Implementing decision-making protocols that account for common cognitive errors, such as overconfidence or confirmation bias, which often lead to project delays and resource misallocation.

Reframing Incentives: Recognizing that non-monetary rewards, when framed correctly, can often outperform monetary bonuses due to the psychological impact of social recognition and intrinsic motivation.

Behavioral Economics and Workplace Decision-Making

The study of behavioral economics has fundamentally altered our understanding of how individuals navigate professional environments, moving beyond the classical assumption of the Homo economicus—the perfectly rational actor. Behavioral economics posits that employees and managers are subject to "bounded rationality," a concept introduced by Herbert Simon, which suggests that decision-making is limited by the information available, the cognitive limitations of the mind, and the finite amount of time available to make a decision.

In the workplace, these psychological factors manifest in several critical ways. First, the "status quo bias" often leads employees to resist organizational change, preferring current processes even when superior alternatives are presented. Second, "loss aversion"—the tendency for individuals to prefer avoiding losses to acquiring equivalent gains—often causes managers to be overly risk-averse, potentially stifling innovation.

Prospect theory, a cornerstone of this field, explains that employees evaluate potential outcomes relative to a subjective reference point rather than absolute wealth or utility, which explains why performance-based bonuses may be perceived differently depending on how they are framed.

Furthermore, the "sunk cost fallacy" frequently influences project management, where teams continue to invest resources into failing initiatives simply because they have already invested significant time and capital, rather than evaluating the project on its current merits.By acknowledging these inherent biases, organizations can implement "nudges"—small changes in the choice architecture—to guide employees toward more productive and rational decision-making processes without restricting their freedom of choice.

The Intersection of Organizational Behavior and Economic Development: Perspectives from my opinion

In my work Learning Organizational Behavioral Economy, posits that the traditional boundaries between organizational behavior (OB) and economic development are not merely porous but are fundamentally integrated through the lens of human decision-making and strategic value creation.

My view argues that economic systems are not driven solely by abstract market forces, but are instead manifestations of collective organizational behaviors that dictate how resources are allocated, how value is perceived, and how innovation is sustained within a competitive environment.

The Behavioral Foundation of Economic Strategy

My framework suggests that organizational behavior serves as the micro-foundation for macroeconomic outcomes. By analyzing the "human element"—specifically the psychological resilience of the workforce and the cognitive biases of decision-makers—my view explains that economic development is contingent upon the alignment of internal organizational culture with external market demands.

In this view, an organization's ability to foster a culture of "value to invent" is a prerequisite for long-term economic growth. This requires a shift from viewing labor as a static cost to viewing it as a dynamic variable that influences supply calibration and demand forecasting.

Strategic Manufacturing and Value Creation

Central to my thesis is the concept that the relationship between demand and supply is a tool for strategic decision-making rather than an immutable law of nature.My view emphasizes that successful economic development at the firm level requires:

Demand Forecasting: Moving beyond quantitative metrics to understand the long-term psychological relationship between the consumer and the brand.

Supply Calibration: Managing production to maintain price integrity, which is essentially an exercise in organizational discipline and behavioral control.

Skill Alignment: Ensuring that the human capital within an organization possesses the psychological fortitude to navigate market volatility.

Integrating Behavioral Economics into Organizational Theory

The synthesis of these fields relies on the understanding that economic development is an emergent property of organizational health. As noted in foundational texts on organizational behavior, the efficiency of an organization is deeply tied to the motivation, perception, and learning processes of its members.When these processes are optimized, the organization contributes more effectively to the broader economy by reducing waste and increasing the velocity of innovation.

My work aligns with the broader academic consensus that behavioral economics provides the necessary tools to correct for the "rational actor" fallacy, allowing firms to better predict how their internal structures influence their external economic footprint.

Implications for Economic Policy and Management

By viewing organizational behavior as a driver of economic development, leaders can better anticipate how changes in internal policy—such as incentive structures or communication hierarchies—will ripple outward into the market.This holistic approach suggests that sustainable economic development is not merely a product of capital investment, but of the behavioral architecture of the institutions that manage that capital.

Would you like to explore how specific psychological resilience training programs within organizations have historically impacted regional economic development metrics?

The study of organizational behavior (OB) in the context of economic development is deeply rooted in the work of Edwin A. Locke and Gary P. Latham, whose foundational research on Goal-Setting Theory provides a critical lens for understanding how human behavior drives economic outcomes.

In the framework of economic development, organizational behavior serves as the micro-foundation for macro-economic success. Locke's research suggests that economic development is not merely a function of capital accumulation or technological advancement, but is fundamentally dependent on the cognitive capacity of individuals within organizations to set, pursue, and achieve specific, challenging goals.

When individuals or organizations lack clear objectives, the resulting "indecision and lack of focus" can lead to stagnation, which mirrors the broader economic phenomenon of under-development. From an organizational perspective, the "human element"—specifically the psychological resilience and skill alignment of the workforce—acts as the most critical variable in bridging the gap between product invention and market demand.

The Behavioral Mechanics of Economic Value

Economic development requires a strategic alignment between supply and demand, a process that is inherently behavioral. As noted in organizational literature, the "value to invent" a product must be evaluated through a behavioral lens.[4] This involves:

Demand Forecasting: Establishing long-term psychological relationships with consumers.

Supply Calibration: Managing manufacturing output to maintain price integrity, which requires high levels of organizational discipline.

Skill Alignment: Ensuring that the workforce possesses the cognitive and psychological resilience to execute complex strategic objectives.

Locke's work emphasizes that human beings possess a unique capacity to reason and conceptualize long-range purposes, which distinguishes human economic activity from the physiologically controlled actions observed in lower-order systems.

In an organizational setting, this capacity allows for the creation of "existential structure," where employees find meaning through goal-directed action.When organizations successfully foster this environment, they contribute to higher levels of productivity, which is the engine of economic growth.

The mathematical representation of this goal-performance relationship is often expressed as a function of goal difficulty (D) and commitment (C), where performance (P) is optimized when both are high:$P=f(D\times C)$

Organizational Behavior as a Catalyst for Growth

The integration of behavioral science into economic strategy suggests that organizational success is predicated on the ability of leaders to provide a "vision for the future." Without this, organizations—and by extension, the economies they comprise—suffer from the same symptoms of "boredom and lack of purpose" that affect individuals.

Therefore, the relationship between economic development and organizational behavior is symbiotic: economic systems provide the resources for organizational growth, while effective organizational behavior provides the human agency necessary to transform those resources into value.

Would you like to learn more about how Goal-Setting Theory is applied in modern high-growth technology firms, or perhaps explore the psychological impact of organizational structure on employee innovation?

Perspectives on Productivity and Economic Growth: Behavioral Economics vs. Traditional Theory

The study of economic growth has long been dominated by neoclassical models that prioritize capital accumulation, technological advancement, and labor efficiency as the primary drivers of productivity.

In these traditional frameworks, productivity is often treated as an objective, measurable output resulting from rational actors optimizing their resources within a market environment. However, contemporary discourse, including the work of authors like John Lok, suggests that human behavior—specifically social networking and behavioral patterns—serves as a fundamental, yet often overlooked, engine of economic fluctuation and productivity.

The divergence between my perspective and traditional economic thought lies in the locus of causality for productivity. Traditional growth theory, as articulated by Robert Solow, relies on the "Solow Residual," which attributes productivity growth to technological progress that cannot be explained by capital or labor inputs alone.

In contrast, my view emphasizes that human behaviors, particularly those manifested through social networks and digital interactions, act as direct catalysts for economic growth or recession. While traditionalists view productivity as a function of institutional efficiency and physical capital, Lok posits that the "network human job" and the psychological underpinnings of social interaction create a micro-macro feedback loop that dictates economic outcomes.

Other scholars in the field of behavioral economics, such as Daniel Kahneman and Richard Thaler, have similarly challenged the "rational actor" model, arguing that cognitive biases significantly impact economic decision-making.

However, my specific focus on the "network" aspect of human behavior suggests a more sociological approach to productivity than the individual-centric biases often studied by Kahneman.

Where traditionalists see productivity as a mechanical output of the production function $Y=A\cdot f(K,L)$, where Y is output, A is total factor productivity, K is capital, and L is labor, my view suggests that A is not merely an exogenous technological variable but is deeply endogenous to human social behavior and network connectivity.

Furthermore, while mainstream economists often treat social factors as "externalities" that are difficult to quantify, my view argues that these behaviors are central to the mechanics of modern e-commerce and global economic health.

This represents a shift from viewing the economy as a closed system of resource allocation to viewing it as an open, behavioral network where individual social activities aggregate into systemic growth or decline.

By integrating the psychological and social dimensions of human activity into the core of economic analysis, Lok challenges the traditional reliance on purely quantitative metrics, suggesting that understanding the "real meaning" of behavioral economy requires mapping the relationship between human social habits and economic performance.

Would you like to explore how these behavioral network theories might be applied to predict future market trends or the impact of social media on global economic stability?

Analysis of Behavioral Productivity Frameworks and Economic Growth

The discourse surrounding behavioral economics and its application to individual and organizational productivity has expanded significantly in the early 21st century. My approach to productivity and economic growth appears to be a point of confusion or a misidentification within contemporary management literature. In the established canon of behavioral economics—ranging from the foundational works of Daniel Kahneman and Richard Thaler to the organizational psychology of Adam Grant.

The criticisms often directed at behavioral approaches to productivity—which may be what is being conflated with a specific author—center on the tension between "nudge" theory and macroeconomic growth. Critics, such as those found in institutional economics, argue that behavioral interventions often focus on micro-level adjustments (such as habit formation or choice architecture) that fail to address the structural determinants of economic growth, such as capital accumulation, technological innovation, and institutional quality.When productivity is framed purely as a behavioral output, it risks ignoring the "Solow Residual," which suggests that long-term growth is driven by factors beyond mere labor efficiency or psychological optimization.

Theoretical Limitations and Economic Impact

A primary criticism of behavioral productivity models is the potential for "psychological reductionism." By treating productivity as a variable to be optimized through behavioral cues, these approaches often overlook the macroeconomic reality that productivity growth ($\Delta Y/Y$) is fundamentally linked to the production function $Y = A \cdot f(K, L)$, where A represents total factor productivity.

Critics argue that behavioral interventions may improve the efficiency of labor (L)intheshortterm,buttheydonotnecessarilyincreasethetechnologicalfrontier(A), which is the primary engine of sustained economic growth.

Furthermore, scholars in the field of political economy have noted that an over-reliance on behavioral productivity metrics can lead to a "blame-the-worker" culture, where systemic economic failures are re-characterized as individual behavioral deficits.

This critique suggests that if a framework—regardless of its authorship—prioritizes individual psychological adjustment over structural reform, it may inadvertently mask the need for broader economic policy changes, such as investment in education, infrastructure, and R&D, which are essential for national-level growth.

Synthesis of Behavioral Economics and Growth Theory

The integration of behavioral insights into growth theory remains a subject of intense debate. While behavioral economics has successfully challenged the "rational actor" model (Homo economicus), its application to productivity has been criticized for lacking a robust link to aggregate demand and supply dynamics. For any approach to be considered a significant contribution to economic growth, it must demonstrate how micro-level behavioral changes aggregate to shift the production possibility frontier, a threshold that many contemporary productivity frameworks have yet to meet in empirical economic literature.

The Intersection of Behavioral Economics, R&D, and Organizational Productivity

The inquiry regarding my perspectives on behavioral economics, research and development (R&D), and organizational productivity touches upon the broader discourse concerning how human cognitive biases influence corporate investment and operational efficiency.

While my specific publications—often categorized under self-published or niche business strategy imprints—argue that R&D is a primary driver of productivity, mainstream behavioral economics offers a more nuanced critique of this relationship. Critics of the "R&D-as-panacea" model often point to the "sunk cost fallacy" and "overconfidence bias," which can lead organizations to pour excessive capital into failing projects under the guise of innovation, thereby increasing rather than reducing economic costs.

The core argument against the notion that R&D automatically yields productivity gains rests on the behavioral observation that decision-makers are prone to "optimism bias." In the context of organizational management, this bias often manifests as an overestimation of the probability of success for new R&D initiatives.

When firms prioritize R&D spending without rigorous behavioral safeguards, they frequently encounter the "escalation of commitment," where managers continue to fund projects that have already demonstrated diminishing returns.Furthermore, behavioral economists like Daniel Kahneman have demonstrated that the psychological cost of abandoning a project often outweighs the rational economic benefit of cutting losses, leading to a net reduction in organizational productivity.

From a structural perspective, the integration of behavioral insights into R&D management is essential to mitigate these risks. Rather than viewing R&D as a linear input-output equation for productivity, modern organizational theory suggests that productivity is a function of "choice architecture" within the firm.

By implementing "de-biasing" techniques—such as pre-mortems, where teams imagine a project has already failed to identify potential pitfalls—organizations can reduce the economic costs associated with blind R&D investment. This aligns with the broader academic consensus that innovation is not merely a product of capital expenditure but of the psychological environment in which those decisions are made.

The economic cost reduction that my opinion and similar proponents suggest is only achievable when R&D is decoupled from the emotional attachment that often plagues corporate leadership. Without this detachment, the pursuit of innovation can lead to "organizational inertia," where the firm becomes trapped in a cycle of high-cost, low-impact R&D.

Consequently, the most effective organizations are those that utilize behavioral economics to audit their R&D pipelines, ensuring that productivity gains are derived from evidence-based decision-making rather than the mere accumulation of research assets.

Would you be interested in learning more about how "de-biasing" techniques are specifically applied in corporate R&D departments to prevent the sunk cost fallacy?

Synthesis of Management Control and Behavioral Theory

The integration of behavioral science into management accounting, as discussed by Emmanuel et al., suggests that while behavioral insights are valuable, they must be embedded within a framework of ethical management.The argument against a purely "behavioral-economic" approach to cost reduction is that it treats employees as variables in an equation rather than as stakeholders in a social system. Mathematically, if we represent productivity P as a function of intrinsic motivation M and external behavioral nudges N, the total output can be expressed as:

$P=f(M,N)$

Critics argue that $\partial P \partial N$ may be positive in the short term but negative in the long term if $\partial M \partial N<0$.Therefore, sustainable growth requires a focus on organizational culture and psychological safety rather than mere behavioral engineering.

Analysis of Behavioral Economics in Organizational Cost Reduction

The application of behavioral economics to organizational cost reduction—often associated with the work of scholars like my recommendation—centers on the premise that cognitive biases and heuristics, such as loss aversion, status quo bias, and hyperbolic discounting, significantly influence managerial decision-making and employee productivity.

Critics, however, argue that these theories often oversimplify the complex, sociotechnical nature of organizational environments. While behavioral models suggest that "nudging" employees toward cost-conscious behaviors can yield significant savings, skeptics contend that such interventions often ignore the structural and institutional constraints that dictate organizational spending.

A primary criticism of these behavioral theories is the "reductionist fallacy." Scholars argue that by focusing on individual cognitive quirks, organizations may neglect systemic inefficiencies, such as poor supply chain management or outdated technological infrastructure, which are often the true drivers of excessive costs.

Furthermore, critics point out that behavioral interventions can lead to "moral hazard" or employee resentment if perceived as manipulative. When cost-reduction strategies rely on psychological framing rather than transparent structural changes, they may erode the psychological contract between employer and employee, ultimately leading to lower morale and higher turnover, which paradoxically increases long-term costs.

Another significant critique involves the lack of generalizability. Many behavioral economic experiments are conducted in controlled laboratory settings, which may not translate to the high-pressure, multi-stakeholder environment of a large corporation.

Critics argue that the "nudge" approach lacks the robustness required for large-scale organizational change, as it fails to account for the power dynamics and political maneuvering inherent in corporate hierarchies.

Finally, there is the concern of "ethical paternalism." By attempting to steer employee behavior toward cost-saving goals, management may overstep ethical boundaries, raising questions about the autonomy of the workforce and the legitimacy of using behavioral science to influence human behavior for purely fiscal ends.

In modern organizational theory, behavioral economics impacts decision-making by replacing the "Homo Economicus" model—which assumes humans always act in their own best interest with perfect information—with a more realistic view of human psychology. Organizations now implement "choice architecture," a term popularized by Thaler and Sunstein, to nudge employees and managers toward better outcomes without restricting their freedom of choice.

By restructuring the environment in which decisions are made, firms can reduce the influence of cognitive biases such as "loss aversion," where the pain of losing is psychologically twice as powerful as the joy of gaining, and "confirmation bias," where individuals favor information that confirms their existing beliefs.

Cognitive Biases and Strategic Management

The impact of these theories on organizational strategy is profound. Executives often fall prey to the "sunk cost fallacy," continuing to invest in failing projects simply because of the resources already committed.[

Behavioral economics provides a framework for "de-biasing" these processes through the use of "pre-mortems," a technique where teams imagine a project has already failed and work backward to determine the causes.

This practice forces a shift from optimistic forecasting to a more critical, evidence-based assessment of risk. Furthermore, the "availability heuristic"—the tendency to overestimate the importance of information that comes easily to mind—is countered by implementing rigorous data-driven decision protocols that require diverse inputs before a final commitment is made.

Organizational Culture and Incentives

Behavioral economics also reshapes how organizations design incentive structures. Traditional economics suggests that financial rewards are the primary motivator for performance. However, behavioral research indicates that intrinsic motivation, social norms, and the framing of goals play a larger role in sustained productivity. By understanding "prospect theory," managers can frame performance targets as opportunities to avoid losses rather than just potential gains, which often results in higher levels of engagement.

Mathematical Modeling of Decision Utility

In organizational research, the utility of a decision is often modeled to account for the deviation from pure rationality. If U represents the utility of a decision, and w(p) represents the subjective weight assigned to a probability p, the behavioral model often replaces standard expected utility with:$V=\sum w(p_i)v(x_i)$where $v(x_i)$ is the value of outcome x_i.

This equation highlights how organizations must account for the fact that managers do not weigh probabilities linearly, often overestimating the likelihood of rare, high-impact events (the "black swan" effect).

Would you like to learn more about how "choice architecture" is specifically applied in corporate human resources to improve employee retention, or perhaps explore the psychological roots of the "sunk cost fallacy" in high-stakes project management?

The Behavioral Economics of Sunk Cost and Organizational Growth

The concept of the "sunk cost fallacy"—the tendency for individuals and organizations to continue investing in a failing endeavor simply because they have already invested resources into it—is a central theme in behavioral economics.

In my analysis of applying behavioral economics to social benefit, suggests that when organizations successfully mitigate the psychological weight of sunk costs, they can pivot toward more productive resource allocation, thereby fostering sustainable economic growth.By shifting focus from past expenditures to future utility, organizations can break the cycle of "death spirals"—a phenomenon where self-reinforcing dysfunctional behaviors, such as myopic focus and dogmatic decision-making, lead to institutional decline.

In the context of organizational management, the "sunk cost" is often viewed through the lens of prospect theory, a foundational concept in behavioral economics developed by Daniel Kahneman and Amos Tversky.

Prospect theory posits that individuals value losses more heavily than equivalent gains, a cognitive bias known as loss aversion. When an organization is trapped by sunk costs, it is essentially experiencing a collective form of loss aversion; the fear of "wasting" previous investments prevents the organization from cutting its losses and reallocating capital to higher-growth opportunities.

Richard Thaler, a Nobel laureate in economics, has extensively documented how these "mental accounting" errors distort corporate strategy.By implementing "nudge" strategies—subtle changes in the choice architecture of decision-making processes—leaders can help teams detach from historical commitments and evaluate projects based on their current and future expected value.

The transition from a state of decline to one of growth often requires what management theorists describe as "turn-around leadership."This involves a deliberate effort to dismantle the institutionalized biases that protect failing projects.

As my view implies, when an organization reduces its reliance on sunk costs, it frees up human and financial capital that was previously stagnant. This reallocation is not merely an accounting exercise; it is a behavioral shift that allows for innovation and the pursuit of new market opportunities. In complex adaptive systems, this flexibility is essential for survival, as it allows the organization to adapt to changing environments rather than being anchored to obsolete strategies.

Furthermore, the reduction of sunk cost bias has broader implications for social benefit. When organizations operate more efficiently and avoid the "death spiral" of resource depletion, they contribute to a healthier economic ecosystem.

This aligns with the broader goals of behavioral economics, which seeks to improve societal outcomes by understanding the psychological underpinnings of human decision-making. By fostering a culture of evidence-based decision-making, organizations can move away from the "sunk cost trap" and toward a model of growth that prioritizes long-term societal and economic health over the preservation of past, non-performing assets.

Would you like to learn more about how "nudge" theory can be specifically applied to corporate governance to prevent the sunk cost fallacy?

My view argues that reducing the impact of sunk costs requires a fundamental shift in how organizations perceive their own history and identity. Rather than viewing past investments as immutable anchors, he suggests that organizations must engage in "identity work" to decouple their current strategic direction from past commitments that no longer serve their mission.

My perspective is rooted in the understanding that organizations often fall into a "Death Spiral" when they become overly committed to past solutions, a process where decision-making becomes myopic and resistant to external feedback.

In my analysis, the reduction of sunk costs is not simply an accounting exercise but a political and social challenge. When leaders attempt to abandon a failing project, they often face resistance from stakeholders who have invested their professional reputations and resources into that project.

My view posits that "turnaround leadership" must involve creating a new organizational narrative that allows members to let go of past investments without feeling that their previous contributions were failures.By reframing the organization's identity, leaders can lower the psychological barriers that make sunk costs so difficult to abandon.

Furthermore, my view highlights that the persistence of sunk costs is often exacerbated by "dogmatic thinking" and a lack of trust in institutional processes. To mitigate this, he advocates for organizational structures that encourage "reflexivity"—the ability of an organization to critically examine its own assumptions and practices.

In my view, reducing the weight of sunk costs requires institutionalizing mechanisms that force periodic re-evaluation of strategic goals, effectively creating a "circuit breaker" for the escalation of commitment.This approach aligns with broader management theories regarding complex adaptive systems, where the ability to pivot depends on the organization's capacity to shed outdated structures and resource allocations before they lead to systemic collapse.

Would you like to learn more about how "identity work" specifically helps leaders navigate the political resistance often encountered when attempting to pivot away from high-sunk-cost projects?

I feel culture that prioritizes opportunity costs over past investments. In economic theory, the decision to continue a project should be based solely on future expected returns, not on the resources already expended. List argues that organizations often fall into the "sunk cost fallacy," where leaders continue to pour capital into failing initiatives because they are emotionally or reputationally tethered to their initial investment.

To combat this, my view suggests that leaders must institutionalize "exit ramps" or "kill switches" for projects. By pre-defining the metrics for success and failure before a project begins, organizations can remove the emotional burden of the decision-making process when performance falls below a certain threshold.

Furthermore, List emphasizes the importance of "scaling" as a diagnostic tool. If an idea cannot be scaled effectively—what he terms "voltage" –it is often a signal that the underlying premise is flawed, regardless of how much money has already been spent.

This perspective aligns with broader behavioral economics research, which suggests that the unconscious urge for psychological need satisfaction often drives individuals to stick with suboptimal choices to avoid the pain of admitting a loss.

To mitigate this, organizations should decouple the decision-makers from the initial project inception. By bringing in objective, third-party evaluators who do not have a personal history with the project, firms can more accurately assess the marginal utility of continuing versus the opportunity cost of reallocating those resources to more promising ventures.

The mathematical reality of this decision-making process can be represented by the comparison of expected value. If E(Vfuture) represents the expected future value of a project and Cfuture represents the future costs, a project should only continue if:

$$E(V_{future}) - C_{future} > E(V_{alternative}) - C_{alternative}$$

List suggests that when this inequality is not met, the rational choice is to "fold your hand," thereby freeing up capital and human talent for higher-voltage opportunities.[

By fostering an environment where quitting is viewed as a virtue—a sign of analytical rigor rather than a lack of persistence—organizations can prevent the "voltage drop" that occurs when resources are trapped in stagnant or failing projects.This strategic flexibility is essential for maintaining the agility required in competitive markets, ensuring that an organization's portfolio remains aligned with its most scalable and impactful ideas.

Behavioral Economics and Team Productivity in the Work of my opinion

My approach to organizational performance centers on the premise that human efficiency is not a static, inherent trait, but a dynamic variable that can be optimized through strategic human resource interventions.

By integrating behavioral economics into management theory, my view argues that organizations can move beyond traditional, often rigid, oversight models toward a more sophisticated understanding of employee motivation and decision-making processes. This shift allows managers to predict and influence "behavioral performance" by aligning the work environment with the psychological needs of the staff, thereby reducing long-term operational costs while simultaneously enhancing client satisfaction.

The application of behavioral economics in this context involves recognizing that employees are not always rational actors in the classical economic sense; rather, their productivity is influenced by cognitive biases, environmental cues, and the structure of their incentives.

My view suggests that by applying psychological research to organizational behavior, leaders can create a "comfortable" implementation of facility management that fosters higher levels of engagement. This is supported by broader research in organizational psychology, which posits that when individuals operate within a framework that respects their capacity for reasoning and goal-setting, their efficiency increases.

Central to this methodology is the understanding that goal-directed action is a fundamental human trait. As noted in the foundational work of Edwin Locke, human beings possess the unique capacity to conceptualize long-range purposes, which act as immediate regulators of behavior.

When my principles are applied, management does not merely dictate tasks; they structure the environment to facilitate the employee's own goal-setting processes. This alignment prevents the "dulled" experience of work—characterized by indecision and lack of focus—and replaces it with a sense of existential structure and purpose.

By leveraging these insights, my framework suggests that productivity is a function of the quality of the interaction between the organizational structure and the individual's psychological drive. Consequently, the "productive efficiency" of a team is maximized when the management system accounts for the nuanced, often non-linear, nature of human choice.

Would you be interested in learning more about how specific "nudge" interventions, as popularized by behavioral economists, can be practically implemented in a remote or hybrid team environment to maintain high productivity?

Reference

Banerjee, A. Newman, A. (1993). Occupational choice and the process of development . Journal of political economy, 101 (2). 274-298.

Keating, M. (1993). The earth summit's agenda for change. Geneva: centre for our common future, viii, x, 12-13. 63-67.

Namik, S.D. (1965). The theories of economic growth, Cario: Knowledge House.

Hartwell, R.M. (1983). The origins of capitalism. A Methodological Eassy. in Pejovich (1983).

Needham, J. (1963), Poverties and Triumphs of the Chinese scientific tradition, in Crombie (1963).

Phaal, R., Farrukh , C. & Probert , D. (2004). Technology roadmapping- A planning framework for evolution and revolution.

Technological Forecasting and social change, 71, 5-26. htpps:// doi. org/10.101016/ S00401625(03)00072-6.

www.ingramcontent.com/pod-product-compliance
Lightning Source LLC
LaVergne TN
LVHW070853210926
848482LV00016B/925
9798885691628